OUR UNITED STATES GEOGRAPHY:
OUR REGIONS AND PEOPLE

by
Beverly Vaillancourt

The Peoples Publishing Group, Inc.

Free to Learn, to Grow, to Change

ISBN 1-56256-119-7

© 1994
The Peoples Publishing Group, Inc.
230 West Passaic Street
Maywood, NJ 07607

Printed in the United States of America
9 8 7

Credits

Editing by *Jocelyn Chu*
Editorial Assistance by Daniel Ortiz, Jr.
Copyediting by Sal Allocco
Editorial & Electronic Design Assistance by Jocelyn Chu, BBE and Sharen J. Levine
Map Design by Steve Steiner, Cartographer
Electronic Publishing Consultant: James Fee Langendoen
Cover Design by Klaus Spitzenberger, Westchester Graphics Group
Logo Design by Wendy E. Kury
Photo Research by Daniel Ortiz, Jr. and Jocelyn Chu
Reader Reviews by Leslie Fishbein and Faith Allen, special education and multicultural educators, and Neil Steiner, middle school geography teacher

A special thanks to the many educators and administrators around the country who participated in a research survey related to the revision of this text.

Photocredits:

p.9,Phelps/Arkansas Publicity & Parks Com.;p.9,Dept. of Parks & Tourism;p.10,Lee Snider/Photo Image;p.12,Bur. of Publicity Info.;p.12,Travel Dept.;p.13,Photo Courtesy Alabama Bur. of Tourism & Travel;p.14 Jocelyn Chu;p.15,Courtesy Dept. of Economic Devel. Div. of Tourism;p.15,Courtesy Mississippi Div. of Tourism;p.16,Courtesy Mississippi Div. of Tourism;p.17,Jocelyn Chu;p.18,Georgia Dept. of Industry Trade & Tourism;p.18,Georgia Dept. of Industry Trade & Tourism;p.19,Georgia Dept. of Industry Trade & Tourism;p.21,Louisiana Off. of Tourism;p.21,Karl Holland,Dept. of Commerce;p.22,Louisiana Off. of Tourism;p.24,South Carolina Div. of Tourism;p.24,South Carolina Div. of Tourism;p.25,South Carolina Div. of Tourism;p.27,North Carolina Div. of Travel & Tourism;p.27,North Carolina Div. of Travel & Tourism;p.28,Commerce Dept.;p.30,Florida Div. of Tourism,p.30,Florida Dept. of Commerce;p.31,Florida Dept. of Commerce Div. of Tourism;p.32,Anita Temares;p.34,Travel Dept. Bur.;p.35,PPG Files;p.36,Anita Temares;p.37,Courtesy Kentucky Dept. of Travel Devel.;p.37,Courtesy Kentucky Dept. of Travel Devel.;p.38,Courtesy Kentucky Dept. of Travel Devel.;p.40,Dave Cruise/Dept. of Commerce;p.40,Gerald S. Ratliff/Governor's Off. of E.C.D.;p.41,Stephen J. Shaluta Jr./WV Dept. of Commerce;p.42,Anita Temares;p.43,Virginia Dept. of Economic Devel.;p.43,Virginia Div. of Tourism;p.44,Virginia Chamber of Commerce;p.45,Virginia Div. of Tourism;p.46,Tennessee Tourist Devel.;p.46,Tennessee Tourist Devel.;p.47,Tennessee Tourist Devel.;p.49,PPG Files;p.50,George Gardner/Image Works;p.51,Jocelyn Chu;p.54,Maryland Off. of Tourism Devel.;p.54,Maryland Dept. of Agri. Info. Off.;p.55,Courtesy the Washington D.C. Convention & Visitors Association;p.56,Ken Layman/Robert Maust Photography;p.57,Courtesy New Jersey Div. of Travel & Tourism/Jean McDougall;p.57,Courtesy New Jersey Div. of Travel & Tourism;p.58,Courtesy New Jersey Div. of Travel & Tourism;p.59,Jocelyn Chu;p.60,Maine Off. of Tourism;p.60,Maine Dept. of Economic Devel.;p.61,Maine Off. of Tourism;p.62,Jocelyn Chu;p.63,Delaware Devel. Off.;p.64,Delaware Devel. Off.;p.65,Delaware Devel. Off.;p.66,Vermont Travel Div.;p.67,Vermont Travel Div.;p.68,Dick Smith;p.69,Dick Smith/State Planning and Devel. Com.;p.69,Lee Snider/Photo Image;p70.,James M. Mejuto;p.72.,Rhode Island Tourism Div.;p.72,Rhode Island Tourism Div.;p.73,Rhode Island Tourism Div.;p.75,Fayfoto;p.75,Fayfoto;p.76,Fayfoto;p.77,Anita Temares;p.78,Lee Snider/Photo Image;p.78,Courtesy U.S. Coast Guard Academy;p.79,Jan Doyle Photography;p.81,New York Dept. of Commerce;p.81,Zecap,Guimaraes/F4-Picture Group;pp.82-.83,Jocelyn Chu;p.85,Wisconsin Dells Visitor & Convention Bur.;p.85,Wisconsin Div. of Tourism;p.86,Wisconsin Div. of Tourism;p.88,The Image Works;p.88,Courtesy Peoria Convention & Visitors Bur.;p.89,Courtesy the Museum of Science & Industry;p.91,Indiana Dept. of Commerce;p.92,Indiana Dept. of Commerce;p.93,John Stewart;p.94,Minnesota Off. of Tourism Photo;p.94,Minnesota Off. of Tourism photo;p.95,Minnesota Off. of Tourism Photo;p.96,Jocelyn Chu;p.97,Iowa Div. of Tourism;p.97,Devel. Commisssion;p.98,Iowa Div. of Tourism;p.99,Jocelyn Chu; p.100,Missouri Div. of Tourism;p.100,Missouri Div. of Tourism;p.101,Missouri Div. of Tourism;p.103,Dept. of Commerce;p.104,Edison Fishery;p.105,Courtesy Michigan Travel Bur.;p.109,North Dakota Dept. of Tourism;p.109,Jocelyn Chu;p.110,North Dakota Dept. of Tourism;p.111,North Dakota Dept. of Tourism;p.112,South Dakota Tourism;p.112,South Dakota Tourism;p.113,South Dakota Tourism;p.114,Anita Temares;p.115,Travel Promotion Div.;p.116,PPG Files;p.117,PPG Files;p.118,Kansas Dept. of Economic Devel.;p.118,PPG Files;p.119,Kansas Industrial Devel. Com.;p.121,Fred W. Marvel Oklahoma Tourism & Rec. Dept.;p.121,Fred W. Marvel Oklahoma Tourism & Rec. Dept.;p.122,Fred W. Marvel Oklahoma Tourism & Rec. Dept.;p.123,Jocelyn Chu;p.126,PPG Files;p.126,James M. Mejuto;p.127,Chamber of Commerce;p.128,Anita Temares;p.129,Travel Montana;p.129,Travel Montana;p.130,Montana Highway Com.;p.132,Wyoming Travel Com.;p.132,Wyoming Travel Com.;p.133,PPG Files;p.134,Anita Temares;p.135,Colorado Dept. of Public Relations;p.136,Colorado Dept. of Public Relations;p.137,Jocelyn Chu;p.138,Courtesy Idaho Tourism Off.;p.138,Courtesy Idaho Tourism Off.;p.139,SCS, USDA;p.140,Anita Temares;p.141,Utah Travel Council;p.142,UPI/Bettmann Newsphotos;p143.,Jocelyn Chu;p.144,Nevada Com. on Tourism;p.144,Nevada Com. on Tourism;p.145,Nevada Com. on Tourism;p.148,M. Woodbridge Williams U.S. Dept. of the Interior;p.148,Courtesy Arizona Off. of Tourism;p.149,Courtesy Arizona Off. of Tourism;p.151,Economic Devel. & Tourism Dept.;p.151,Mark Nohl NM Economic & Tourism Dept.;p.152,NM Economic & Tourism Dept.;p.153,Jocelyn Chu;p.154,Courtesy Texas Highway Dept.;p.154,PPG Files;p.155,Byron Zirkle/Bezee Photostrations;p.156,Anita Temares;p.159,Courtesy California Off. of Tourism;p.160, State of California;p.161,Courtesy California Off. of Tourism;p.162,Peter French/Hawaii Visitors Bur.;p.162,Greg Vaughn;p.163,Bruce Asate;p.165,Oregon Tourism Div.;p.166,Oregon Tourism Div./Laurel Ridge Winery;p.167,Oregon State Highway Dept.;p.168,Washington State Travel photo;p.168,Arnold J. Kaplan;p.169,Courtesy Boeing Commercial Airplane Co.;p.171,Govt. of American Samoa;p.172,Independence Picture Service;p.173,PPG Files

TABLE OF CONTENTS

TABLE OF CONTENTS

ALPHABETICAL INDEX
To States and Territories

OUR UNITED STATES

Soviet Union

U.S.

Canada

U.S.

Atlantic Ocean

Puerto Rico (U.S.)

Cuba

Mexico

Pacific Ocean

Central America

South America

THE PEOPLE'S PUBLISHING GROUP, INC. *Our United States Geography: Our Regions and People*

PASSPORT TO DISCOVERY!

To The Student

Before you begin *Our United States*, here are some helpful GeoFacts. GeoFacts are things you need to know about the geography of our regions.

Our United States — The Land

The United States of America is made up of fifty states. Forty-eight of the states have connecting borders. These states are part of the country's mainland. Two other states, Alaska and Hawaii, are miles beyond the forty-eight state mainland. Alaska and Hawaii extend the limits of the United States into the cold arctic waters of the north and into the warm waters of the southern Pacific Ocean.

The world is made up of seven great land masses called continents (CON-tih-nentz). The United States is part of the continent of North America. North of the United States is Canada. Alaska shares a border with Canada. South of the United States lie Mexico and the countries of Central America. The island of Cuba is southeast of the state of Florida. Close to Cuba lie islands that have close trading ties with the United States.

A circle of water flows around the continent of North America. The Atlantic Ocean is to the east. The Pacific Ocean is to the west. Along the southeastern coast of the United States lies the Gulf of Mexico. Within America's mainland lie five Great Lakes. The climate (KLYM-it), or weather, of the United States is affected by each of these large bodies of water.

Our United States — The People

Today, there are over 250 million people living in the United States. This is three times the number of people who were living in the United States in 1900 when only 76 million people made their home within the country's borders.

Immigration (ih-mih-GRAY-shun), or people coming to America from other countries, has increased the number of people living in the United States. Native Americans were the land's first inhabitants. Then, immigrants coming from other countries in the last three hundred years greatly increased the population.

Also affecting America's growth have been emigrants (EH-mih-grantz), or people who move from one part of the country to another part. Along their way, immigrants and emigrants brought their heritages (HAIR-ih-taj-ez), or beliefs, language, and way of life. Today, the United States shares many different heritages.

Our United States — The Land and The People

Long ago, Native Americans settled the land that today makes up the United States. About 500 years ago, explorers from Europe looked to the continent of North America as a place to find riches. Later, people from Europe and other countries looked to America's shores as a place to practice their religion freely. Today, America still is seen by many as the land of freedom.

In the search for land and riches, freedom was taken from others. Native Americans were forced off land they had settled. Africans were enslaved (en-SLAYVD), or forced to work without choice or pay on great cotton farms. The use of enslaved Africans, also called slavery, had a great impact on American land and history.

The land — and the people — form the United States of America. It is a country like no other in the world.

Across the South

When the sun come back,
Then the time is come,
Follow the drinking gourd.
The river's bank is a very good road,
The dead trees show the way,
Left foot, peg foot, going on,
Follow the drinking gourd.

The river ends a-tween two hills,
Another river on the other side,
Follow the drinking gourd.
When the little river
Meet the great big one,
The ole man waits,
Follow the drinking gourd.

Before the Civil War, enslaved Africans, working in the cotton and tobacco fields of the South, sang songs like this. The songs told enslaved Africans about the road to freedom. This road, called the Underground Railroad, was filled with danger. A slave could be caught and taken back to his owner at any point along the road.

In this song, the "drinking gourd" was the north star. The "ole man" was the Ohio River. "Left foot, peg foot" refers to Pegleg Joe. Pegleg Joe is one of the many people who helped slaves find freedom in the North.

Slavery was one of the many themes that once tied the southern states. Themes are like links in a chain. Each theme, or link, gives the region its own identity (eye-DEN-tih-tee), or feeling. The type of land, the way people live, people's values and beliefs, history and many other things are all themes.

The growing of cotton and the use of slave labor was a theme that had effects far beyond the cotton fields of the 1800s. Beginning in 1860, eleven southern states formed a union called the Confederate States of America. During the Civil War, over 164,000 southern men died for the right to decide if slavery should exist in the South.

The fight for civil rights, or equal rights for everyone, is another theme that has tied the southern states together. After the Civil War, southern states made laws that denied, or kept, civil rights from people of color. Yet, many people in the South worked for civil rights for all. In time, new civil rights laws were made.

Another theme that ties the southern states is geography (je-OG-rah-fe). Geography is the type of land in an area, or region (RE-jun). Lowland is found in all the southern states. The low land slowly rises to hills and mountains. The many rivers of the South have affected its economy (e-CON-oh-me). Economy means value in products and money.

Southern pride is another theme. Pride is holding things in high value. Many people who live in the South have pride in their food, way of life and history. Look for these and other themes as you read the chapters. Try to see how themes help to build the region into a special area.

ARKANSAS

★ ★

GEOFACTS
- capital: Little Rock
- statehood: 1836 (25th)
- rank in size: 27th
- rank in population: 33rd (urban 54%, rural 46%)
- U.S. representatives: 4
- motto: "The People Rule"

▲ A prospector hunts for diamonds.

▲ Arkansas is a leading rice grower.

Black-eyed peas, turnip greens, fried catfish, smoked hams, quilts that tell a story and **folk tales**—this is part of the heritage of Arkansas. From the lowland delta region of the southeast to the mountains of the northwest, white emigrants traveled the land later to be called Arkansas. Along the way, these French, Scottish and other emigrants came in contact with native American Indians. Each culture had its own special heritage.

Arkansas, the "land of opportunity," is formed by two major rivers. The Mississippi River on the eastern border of Arkansas was a major water barrier to emigrants traveling west. The Arkansas River runs through the center of the state. To the north of the Arkansas River are the rugged hills and deep **valleys** (VAH-leez) of the Ozark (O-zrk) plateau. To the south are the dense forests of the Quachita (KWAW-chee-tah) Mountains. Between them lies the Arkansas River Valley. From 1821 to 1860 wagon trains traveled westward along this valley.

Arkansas is a geographic treasure. Oil and diamond discoveries are a part of Arkansas's past. Today, Arkansas is home to the only active diamond mine in North America.

Arkansas is also home to over 100 hot springs. They are located in the Ozark and Quachita mountain regions. Hot springs water is rain water which fell over 3,500 years ago. One spring, Mammoth Spring in the

GeoWords
folk tales — stories told to others over many years
valley — a long, low area lying between hills or high ground, usually having a river or stream flowing along its bottom

Critical Thinking
How can people from one culture enrich the lives of people from another culture?

Places to See! People to Know!
▶ Ozark Folk Center—shows the rich heritage of the Ozark area through music, crafts and dance
▶ Parkin Archaeological State Park — previews Indian village visited by Hernando
▶ George Catlin (b. 1796)—painter of Native Americans and frontier life
▶ William (Bill) J. Clinton (b.1948) — 42nd president

Critical Thinking

Why do you think DeSoto kept traveling west even though he never discovered gold?

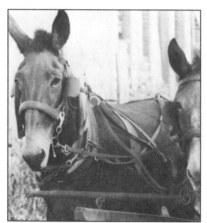

▲ Farmers sometimes use mules to work.

Did You Know?

Sourdough Pancakes

Sourdough pancakes were a favorite of Robert LaSalle. Here's how they were made.

Boil fruit peels. Remove from water. Add salt and enough flour to make a thin creamy batter. Cover the pot and let sit until sour. This will take from two to three days.

Take out two to three cups of batter from the pot the night before you are going to make pancakes. Put the batter in a bowl. Mix in one cup of flour and enough water to make a medium batter. Cover the bowl and let stand overnight.

The next day mix the following into the batter: two well beaten eggs, 1 level tablespoon of sugar, 2 tablespoons of melted butter and 1 level tablespoon of baking soda. Let dough rise for a few minutes. Drop the batter by spoon into a well-greased, hot frying pan.

The pancakes should be about four inches wide. Add more flour and salt to your starter batter until you have a thin batter. Let stand until you make sourdough pancakes again. This batter can go on for over a year.

Ozarks, sends out about 235 million gallons of water a day. This water flows into Spring River.

Which country first explored Arkansas? Spain first explored Arkansas. One explorer from Spain, Hernando DeSoto, recorded being on Arkansas land in the spring of 1541. Desoto was a powerful leader. In 1539, DeSoto traveled from Florida to Arkansas looking for gold. He began in Florida with a band of 200 horses and 600 men. His mission was to find great wealth in gold. His travels ended in Arkansas.

In all of his travels DeSoto never found gold. But DeSoto did meet up with many different tribes of Native Americans. His treatment of them was cruel. DeSoto and his men killed and **enslaved** the natives he met. He left Indian villages in ruins. In fact, the first thing DeSoto did upon crossing the Mississippi was to take over the Indian village of Quizquiz.

In 1673 two more European explorers traveled down the Mississippi River to the Arkansas River. Their names were Louis Jolliet (JO-le-eht) and Father Jacques Marquette (MAR-ket). They returned north when friendly Quapaw Indians warned them to go no further. Nine years later another Frenchman, LaSalle, claimed all of the Mississippi River Valley, including Arkansas, for France. He named the area Louisiana in honor of the French king, Louis XIV.

Which Native American tribes first lived on Arkansas land? Over 12,000 years ago Paleo-Indians lived in Arkansas. They moved from place to place hunting animals for food. As time went on, the early natives of Arkansas settled into villages. They farmed corn, beans, and squash. They built sturdy wood shelters.

One group of Native Americans, the Plum Bayou Culture, built great **mounds** between the years 750 and 900. Some of the mounds were burial mounds. Others were used as the base for houses and temples. In the mid-1800s explorer Gilbert Knapp named these mounds the Toltec Mounds. He mistakenly thought the Toltec Indians of Mexico had built them. The Toltec Mounds lie southeast of the city of Little Rock.

By 1700 three groups of Native Americans lived in Arkansas. The Quapaws (KWAW-paws) lived mostly around the Arkansas - Mississippi River area. The Caddos (KAD-oh) lived where the Red River bends. And the Osages (O-sa-jes) controlled the area north of the Arkansas River.

Battles over Arkansas land occurred between Native tribes as well as between Native Americans and white emigrants. In 1810 only about 1,060 whites were counted in Arkansas. Yet, by 1835 Arkansas had about 50,000 white emigrants. Pressure on the United States government to move the Indians off Arkansas land was strong. In the end, Native Americans were moved west of Arkansas to what today is Oklahoma.

Were Africans enslaved in Arkansas? Slavery did exist in Arkansas. By 1860 Arkansas was sixth among cotton farming states. One-fourth of the state's population were enslaved Africans. Still, Arkansas was home

THE PEOPLE'S PUBLISHING GROUP, INC. *Our United States Geography: Our Regions and People*

to fewer slaves than any other southern state. Yet, the issue of owning slaves would divide the people.

In 1861, the government of Arkansas voted to secede, or leave, the United States government. Arkansas became part of the Confederate States of America. Still, people were divided on Civil War issues. While sixty-six thousand men fought for the south, fifteen thousand men fought for the north. After the Civil War, Arkansas was **readmitted** as a state in 1868.

Civil rights remained a problem for Arkansas for many years. Jim Crow laws of the 1890s kept African Americans from having equal rights. Following the Civil War, Arkansas set up schools for African American children. Yet, it was not until 1957 that African Americans and white Americans could go to school together. This first took place at Central High School in Little Rock. Feelings against letting African Americans go to all-white schools were strong. Federal troops were needed to walk with nine African American students into Central High School.

☆ ☆ ☆ ☆ ☆ ☆ ☆ ☆ ☆

Arkansas looks forward to future growth for the state. Farmers sell such crops as rice, cotton, and soybeans. Wood, paper and plastic products also help the economy of Arkansas. Major businesses such as Walmart and Tyson Foods have their offices in Arkansas. Arkansas's focus on the future is strong. And, yet, Arkansas remains a window into America's past.

GeoWords
readmit — to admit, or allow in, again

Critical Thinking
In what ways can Arkansas be a window into America's past?

Did You Know? Jim Crow - an African American character in an 1820s song and dance routine; the dance was known as "Jump Jim Crow"; Jim Crow went on to refer to any American person given low social status

★ ★ ★ ★ ★ ★ ★ ★ **THINK ABOUT IT!** ★ ★ ★ ★ ★ ★ ★ ★

1. What three land regions are found in Arkansas?

2. What happened to Native Americans living in Arkansas in 1835?

3. What do you think Arkansas's motto means?

Workbook p. 8
Self-Check

ALABAMA

★ ★

GEOFACTS
- capital: Montgomery
- statehood: 1819 (22nd)
- rank in size: 29th
- rank in population: 22nd (urban 62%, rural 38%)
- U.S. representatives: 7
- motto: "We Dare Defend Our Rights"

▲ Machines harvest cotton today.

▲ The Civil War is part of the rich heritage of Alabama.

GeoWords

landlocked — shut in, or nearly shut in, by land

harbor — a place of deep water protected from wind and currents, making it a safe place for boats to dock

fertile — rich in things that promote growth

⚡ **Critical Thinking**

Why is Alabama's Black Belt an important farming area?

Places to See! People to Know!

▶ Horseshoe Bend national Military Park — site of the large battle between Creek Indians led by Red Eagle and Andrew Jackson's troops on March 27, 1814

▶ Russell Cave National Monument, near Bridgeport — 8,000-year-old site of cave dwelling Native Americans

▶ Booker T. Washington (b.1856) — born a slave, Washington went on to found the Tuskegee Institute in 1881. This school trained African Americans to be farmers, tradesmen, and teachers.

▶ Helen Keller (b.1880) — blind and deaf since infancy, Keller went on to become an author and lecturer

Alabama is a state filled with rolling hills, blooming wildflowers, and a variety of wildlife. About two-thirds of the state is covered with forests. Most of this woodland is made up of pine trees. Here bobcats, raccoons, deer, and other wildlife find shelter. Flowering shrubs such as dogwood and mountain laurel line Alabama's countryside. Alabama is famous for one special flowering plant called an azalea (ah-ZALE-yah).

Most of southern Alabama is lowland. This area rises to only 500 feet above sea level. Alligators thrive in the swamps of southern Alabama. Alabama's swampland gives way to the Mobile River Delta. This fifty-three mile coastline is Alabama's only area that is not **landlocked**. The Mobile River Delta opens to the Gulf of Mexico. It is an important **harbor** area for Alabama.

Between the rolling hills of the north and the low plains area of the South lies Alabama's Black Belt. This area is named for the **fertile** (FIR-tl), black clay soils found there. In the past, cotton plantations (plan-TA-shuns) were found across Alabama's Black Belt. Today, livestock farms make use of the good grassland of the Black Belt.

Are there many lakes in Alabama? There are no natural lakes in Alabama. But many rivers wind their way through the hills and lowlands. Dams built along several of these rivers form man-made lakes.

GeoWords
textiles — different types of cloth
movement — action of large group of people
for a belief or cause

Alabama's rivers have always been important to the economy of Alabama. They provide food as well as a way to transport goods to market. In 1985 a new waterway was opened. This waterway, called the Tennessee-Tombighee Waterway, connects the Tennessee River with the Tombighee River. The Tennessee- Tombighee Waterway took twelve years to build.

The Tennessee-Tombighee Waterway became a help to the economy of Alabama. By using this new waterway boats could travel directly to the Gulf of Mexico. Before, they had to first travel west to the Mississippi River; then the boats traveled south to the Gulf of Mexico. Boats using the Tennessee-Tombighee Waterway now have 800 miles less to travel to get to the Gulf of Mexico.

Critical Thinking

How have Alabama's waterways affected its economy?

How did one crop, cotton, affect life in Alabama? Alabama's mild climate is ideal for growing cotton. By the mid 1800s cotton plantations spread across Alabama's Black Belt. Several plantation owners grew rich on the sale of this one crop.

It took many people to grow cotton. enslaved Africans filled this labor force. They worked the cotton fields. Cotton had to be planted by hand. The cotton also was picked by hand. Then the seeds had to be taken out of the cotton. This was a long, slow job. Slave labor, fertile soil, and rivers used for transporting the cotton turned Alabama's Black Belt into a wealthy farm area.

Alabama's cotton economy was a major factor in its Civil War fight. The cotton plantations depended on slave labor. The people of Alabama were willing to fight to keep the right to own slaves.

On January 11, 1861, Alabama joined other southern states in seceding (sis-SE-ding), or leaving, the government of the United States. It renamed itself the Republic of Alabama. Montgomery, Alabama became the capital of the Confederate States of America.

▲ Noccalula Falls in Gadsden, Alabama

What happened in Alabama after the Civil War? The end of the Civil War, and of slavery, brought many changes to Alabama. Alabama was readmitted into the United States government in 1868. Cotton was still grown, but on smaller farms. Birmingham became an important iron and steel making center. Railroads helped in transporting goods to market. Lumber and **textiles** also became important industries for Alabama.

How did Alabama deal with the issue of civil rights following the Civil War? Though Alabama was the place where the Confederacy began, it also was the birthplace of the Civil Rights **Movement**.

For many years following the Civil War, segregation (seg-reg- A-shun), or the separation of races, created many problems in Alabama. Laws were set up to keep races apart. Whites and other races, for example, could not use the same public washroom, drinking fountain, or school.

Voting also became an issue. A new state constitution adopted in 1901 set difficult rules for voting. A man could vote if he could read and had a job, or owned at least three hundred dollars worth of property. A person

Did You Know? Cotton had other uses besides cloth. It was chewed as a toothache remedy. It was also applied to the head to cure headaches. It was believed that physically-challenged children would be born to anyone using a cotton tablecloth on their wedding day. Cotton seeds were laid along the bank of a river to insure a fisherman a bite.

GeoWords

poll tax — money charged to a person for voting

integrate — to bring together, to end racial segregation

Critical Thinking

Why do you think Montgomery, Alabama is often referred to as the cradle of the Civil Rights Movement?

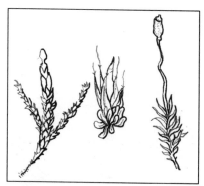

▲ Alabama's moist climate is allows many kinds of delicate mosses to grow.

also had to pay a **poll tax** to vote. These voting rules kept many African Americans from voting.

What led to greater civil rights for all people? In 1955 and 1956 civil rights leader Martin Luther King, Jr. led a boycott of public buses in Montgomery. African Americans refused to ride the buses unless they were allowed to sit anywhere they wanted. Before, people who were not white had to sit in the back of the bus. A federal order in 1956 forced Alabama to **integrate** (IN- teh-grate) public busing.

Civil rights also focused on the public schools of Alabama. In 1963 Governor George C. Wallace tried to stop the integration of public schools. President Kennedy sent National Guard troops to Alabama. African American students were then admitted to the all-white schools.

Civil rights leaders turned their attention to voting rights for African Americans. In 1965 Martin Luther King, Jr. led a five day march from Selma to Montgomery, Alabama. The people marching were protesting laws which kept African Americans from voting. The march help lead to the passing of the 1965 Voting Rights Act. This federal law opened the door to voting for 100,000 African Americans in Alabama.

What other changes have taken place in Alabama? Today, Alabama is a leader in science. Huntsville has been, and still is, a center for rocket development. In fact, Huntsville calls itself Rocket City, USA. Clothing, rubber, plastics and paper industries have replaced Alabama's steel and iron industries. And cotton is no longer the major crop of Alabama. Today, soybeans, corn, hay, peanuts, as well as cotton grow in Alabama's fertile soils.

Alabama is a growing state which links the past with the future. From folk music, crafts, and southern cooking to future space travel, Alabama reflects the South. It is often called the Heart of Dixie. Today, Alabama is certainly at the heart of growth and change in the South.

Did You Know? Alabama was once home to the Civilized Tribes. These Native American tribes included the Cherokee, Creek, Choctaw, and Chickasaw Indians. these Native Americans were called the Civilized Tribes because they had adopted European ways of living. yet, by 1840, almost all Native Americans were forced to give up their land and property. They were made to move west of the Mississippi River.

Workbook p. 9
Self-Check

★ ★ ★ ★ ★ ★ ★ ★ **THINK ABOUT IT!** ★ ★ ★ ★ ★ ★ ★ ★

1. How is Alabama's Black Belt different from the land north and south of it?

2. How did Alabama's 1901 constitution keep African Americans from voting?

3. Why was the passing of the 1965 Voting Rights Act important to African Americans in Arkansas?

MISSISSIPPI

★ ★ ★ ★ ★ ★ ★ ★ ★ ★ ★ ★ ★ ★ ★ ★ ★ ★ ★ ★

GEOFACTS
- capital: Jackson
- statehood: 1817 (20th)
- rank in size: 32nd
- rank in population: 31th (urban 47%, rural 53%)
- U.S. representatives: 5
- motto: "By Valor and Arms"

▲ A young Choctaw girl

▲ A barge at Vicksburg on the Mississippi River

Steamboats slowing gliding on the Mississippi River. Alligators, lying among lush cypress trees, basking in the warm sun. Fishermen reeling in great **trawls** filled with shrimp. The sweet smell of magnolia trees swaying in the breeze. These are just some of the sights, sound, and smells of Mississippi. With its mild climate and plentiful waterways, it is, indeed, a state of much change and beauty.

The name, Mississippi, comes from the Choctaw Indian language. It means "Great Water" or "Father of Waters." The state of Mississippi takes its name from the Mississippi River. This "great water" marks the state's western border.

The Mississippi River is the third longest river in the world. This mighty river has been both friend and foe to the people of Mississippi. Flooding along the banks of the Mississippi River produces rich farm soil. Flooding also can cause great damage.

In 1927 flooding left the town of Greenville, Mississippi under water for seventy days. The flooding made two hundred thousand people leave their homes. Today, **dikes** built along the Mississippi River help to control flooding.

How does the Gulf of Mexico affect the climate of Mississippi? Mississippi's forty-four mile southern border lies on the Gulf of Mexico. Closeness to this large body of water, along with warm temperatures, at times leaves Mississippi in a **hurricane's** (HUR-rih-kane) path.

GeoWords
trawl — a large, strong net dragged along the water's bottom to catch fish and other seafood
dikes — a bank or earth or dam built to prevent flooding
hurricane — a warm climate, violent rain storm with winds of 75 m.p.h. or greater in warm climates

Critical Thinking
How has the Mississippi River affected the economy of Mississippi?

Places to See! People to Know!
▶ Vicksburg National Military Park, Vicksburg — site of 1863 Civil War battle

▶ Delta Blues Museum, Clarksdale — holds rare recordings and exhibits about the birth of Blues music in Mississippi

▶ William Faulkner (b.1897)—author, received the 1949 Nobel prize in literature, and the 1949 and 1963 Pulitzer prize in fiction

▶ Ida B. Wells (b.1862) — co-founder of the National Association for the Advancement of Colored People (NAACP)

Critical Thinking

Why do you think cotton was called "king" in Mississippi?

▲ There are 27 state parks in Mississippi.

Did You Know? Enslaved labor was used in towns (carpenters, blacksmiths) as well as in homes and fields. Slave owners had the power to work a slave from sunrise to sunset. Slaves had no rights. Not obeying a slave owner could mean cruel punishment or death. Slave families were often split apart and sold to different slave owners. Slaves were not allowed to learn how to read or write

In 1971 Hurricane Camille roared down on Mississippi. It packed winds reaching speeds of 172 miles per hour. Hurricane Camille destroyed many homes and business. Yet, such strong hurricanes, do not happen often.

How have Mississippi's rich soils and mild climate have affected its economy and people? Mississippi's rich soils and mild climate made it a perfect area for growing cotton. By 1830 Mississippi was the country's leading cotton-growing state. Steamboats filled high with cotton bales sailed the Mississippi River. Little interest was shown for building roads at this time. The great river was the state's highway.

The demand for cotton also created a demand for cheap labor. Slavery filled this need. In the early 1800s there were almost as many enslaved Africans living in Mississippi as whites. Most people in Mississippi did not own slaves. Yet, **plantation** owners and smaller farms did depend on enslaved Africans as the plantation's labor force.

Mississippi's belief in slavery resulted in its seceding from the U.S. government on January 9, 1861. Mississippi sent 80,000 men to fight in the Civil War. Over 60,000 lost their lives. Civil War fighting destroyed many of Mississippi's grand plantation homes.

Mississippi was readmitted as a state in 1870. Enslaved Africans could no longer be forced to work the cotton fields. The end of slavery meant freedom for four hundred thousand enslaved Africans. Yet, farmers still grew cotton. They still needed a large labor force. Some plantation owners began using Chinese immigrants to work the fields.

What is the Natchez Trace? The Natchez Trace began as a set of trails traveled by Native Americans. In later years, shippers would float down the Mississippi River in flatbed boats. Then they would use the trails to return to northern Mississippi. These trails were easier to travel on than trying to row against the strong current of the Mississippi River. White emigrants traveling southward braved the wild animals and bandits that also used the trails.

In 1801 the Choctaw (CHAWK-taw) and Chickasaw (CHIK-ah-saw) Indians allowed the United States government to build a road from Nashville, Tennessee to Natchez, Mississippi. This road was named the Natchez Trace. Natchez is the name of an Indian tribe that once lived along the Mississippi River.

For many years the Natchez Trace was a very busy highway. Yet, with increased use of steamboats, people used the Natchez Trace less and less. Still, the trail was not forgotten.

Today, the Natchez Trace is a 444 mile highway. It is now called the Natchez Trace Parkway. Important events in Mississippi's history are marked along the parkway. Thick forests, lush swamps, and flowering shrubs line the parkway. People can enjoy the many state parks and camp grounds along the Natchez Trace Parkway.

What does the economy of Mississippi depend on today? About half of all Mississippi land is still farmed. Cotton remains a very important crop.

Farmers also grow soybeans, rice, sweet potatoes and other warm climate crops. Shipbuilding and electronic devices are major industries of Mississippi. The sale of shrimp, oysters and fish is important for Mississippi's economy.

How are music and the economy of Mississippi linked? Many songs of today come from the years when cotton was king in Mississippi. Songs sung by enslaved Africans working in the cotton fields told of the hardships of slavery. They also became a way in which slaves could pass on information about runaway routes. Enslaved Africans used these routes to flee from slavery. The Blues music of today has it roots in the cotton fields of yesterday.

Railroad workers also had their own special songs. The story of Casey Jones is one special railroad work song. It tells the story of how Casey Jones tried to brake his train to keep from hitting another train. Though Casey Jones lost his life, his quick action saved the lives of everyone else. Wallace Saunders, an African American railroad worker, first wrote the **ballad** (BAL-ad) of Casey Jones.

Mississippi is also home to country music. Country music also tells a story. It had its beginning among the white **sharecroppers** (SHAIR-krop-ers) of the rural South. Religion is often a strong theme in country music. Religion is an important part of southern life. It is a part of much of the music of Mississippi.

How is Mississippi a state of contrasts? Mississippi is a state filled with beautiful land and plants. Its culture is rich in song, art, and literature (LIT-ur-ah-shur). Yet, Mississippi has a history filled with tough times. As a state, it has had to overcome great economic and civil rights problems.

☆ ☆ ☆ ☆ ☆ ☆ ☆ ☆ ☆

Today, Mississippi links its past with a focus on a bright economic future. Steamboats still travel the Mississippi River. They give people from other places a feeling for Mississippi's slow-paced, scenic past. Tourist areas built around beautiful, large plantation homes attract people to Mississippi's historic sites. Seafood cooking opens the way for a strong fishing and resort industry in Mississippi. Mississippi is a growing state looking to the lessons of the past to improve and better the lives of people living in Mississippi today.

Critical Thinking

How does song link Mississippi's past with its present?

▲ William Faulkner wrote about the real people and the nature of the land of Mississippi.

Did You Know? Dancing Rabbit Creek, a place where in 1830 the Choctaw Indians signed a treaty which traded their Mississippi land for land in Oklahoma. The Choctaw signed this treaty following pressure from the U.S. government to remove all Native Americans from Mississippi land.

★ ★ ★ ★ ★ ★ ★ ★ **THINK ABOUT IT!** ★ ★ ★ ★ ★ ★ ★ ★

1. How has the Mississippi River both helped and harmed the people of Mississippi?

2. How did the Natchez Trail Parkway get its start?

3. List five things that are important to Mississippi's economy.

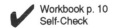

Workbook p. 10
Self-Check

GEORGIA

★ ★

GEOFACTS
- capital: Atlanta
- statehood: 1788 (4th)
- rank in size: 21st
- rank in population: 11th (urban 63%, rural 37%)
- U.S. representatives: 11
- motto: "Wisdom, Justice and Moderation"

▲ A wildlife tour at Callaway Gardens

▲ A country road in northwest Georgia

All I want in this creation,
Is a pretty little wife and a big plantation,
Way down yonder in the Cherokee Nation.

1830s folk song
sung in both Georgia and Oklahoma

GeoWords

plain — a flat treeless or almost treeless area

⚡ **Critical Thinking**

What does the poem at the beginning of the chapter say about white settlement of Cherokee land?

Places to See! People to Know!

▶ Martin Luther King, Jr. National Historic Site, Atlanta

▶ Anderson National Historic Site, Americus —site of Confederate prison where 13,000 Union soldiers died

▶ James Earl (Jimmy) Carter, Jr. (b.1924) — 39th president of the United States, governor of Georgia (1971-1975)

▶ Sequoya (b.1760) — set up a Cherokee alphabet of eighty-eight letters. By using the alphabet, the Cherokee could read and write.

The sweet smell of peach blossoms filling the air on warm spring Georgia days. Hot peach cobbler (KOB-ler) topped with ice cream, or perhaps just sliced peaches and cream, served for dessert. These are just some of the many treats the state of Georgia has to offer.

Georgia is a state where old stories tell of pirate treasures (TREH-shurs) being hidden deep in the forests of Georgia's Blackbeard Island. The treasures, if ever found, would be part of things stolen by the famous pirate Blackbeard. During the early 1700s, Blackbeard and his band of pirates attacked ships up and down the southeast coastline of the United States.

Georgia is the largest state east of the Mississippi River. Georgia is home to the largest granite rock in the world. It is called Stone Mountain. Stone Mountain rises 1,683 feet above the **plain** around it. It formed over 200,000 years ago when forces below the Earth's surface pushed a white-hot stone mass upwards. The heated rock cooled to form a huge mountain of granite.

Over the years the soil around the stone washed away. A **relief** (re-LEEF) of Robert E. Lee, Stonewall Jackson and Jefferson Davis has been carved on the side of Stone Mountain. The relief expresses the pride Georgians have for these three Civil War heroes.

Why is Georgia called "the Peach State?" Beyond Stone Mountain lies Georgia's fertile soil. The soil is ideal for growing soybeans, tobacco and pecans. Georgia is famous for its sweet, juicy peaches. For this reason, Georgia is often called "the Peach State."

More peanuts are grown in Georgia than in any other state in the country. The peanut plant looks like a small bush. The peanuts grow under the soil. Peanuts need at least four months of warm temperatures to grow. They also grow best in sandy soil. Georgia's soil, warm climate and plentiful rains are perfect for growing peanuts.

Georgia's land is also good for growing cotton. Cotton growing has been an important part of Georgia's past. It affected its history, settlement and economy.

Port towns that shipped cotton down Georgia's rivers quickly grew during the 1800s. Flat-bottom boats gave way to steamships as a better and quicker way to transport cotton. Between 1820 and 1965 seventy steamboats filled with cotton glided along the Savannah River.

Where did Georgia's white settlers come from? Georgia's early white settlers were from Spain, France and England. In 1732 a group of Englishmen, led by James Oglethorpe, set sail for Georgia. A story in the London newspaper about the people getting ready to sail to Georgia read like this:

"The Ann **Galley**, above 200 tons, is on the point of sailing . . . for the new Colony of Georgia, with thirty-five families consisting of carpenters, bricklayers, farmers . . . who take all proper instruments (such as hatchets, hammers, saws, shovels, spades, hoes, grindstones, and others . . .)"

Other white settlers of Georgia came from Italy, Germany, Switzerland and other regions of Europe. In 1734 a group of people from Austria landed in Georgia. They planted mulberry trees. They hoped to sell the silk they got from the silkworms that fed on the mulberry trees.

How did white settlement affect the Native Americans living in the area that became Georgia? Years of peace and war between Native Americans and white settlers are a part of Georgia's history. Yet, it was white settlers' greed for cotton-growing land that forced Native Americans from Georgia and other areas of the southeast.

In 1838 federal troops went from home to home forcing the Cherokee Indians to leave their homes. They could only take with them what they could carry. Many Cherokee lived like the whites who wanted their land. They owned large plantations. They enslaved people. Yet, without telling Native Americans before taking action, and without any laws to back up its action, the government took away land belonging to Native Americans.

GeoWords
relief—a design which stands out from the surface from which it was made
galley—a large boat often rowed by slaves, criminals or prisoners of war

Critical Thinking
Native Americans were Georgia's first settlers. Yet, Native Americans lost their land. Why did this not bother more people in the early 1800s?

▲ Georgia is well-known for its peach crop.

Did You Know? The Cherokee Phoenix was a bilingual newspaper. The first Cherokee Phoenix was written in 1828.

The government promised to pay the Cherokee for their homes and land. Yet, most never were paid. 16,000 Native Americans were force to move from the Georgia area to Oklahoma. Along the way about 4,000 Native Americans died. The Cherokee call this sad time the "trail where they cried."

Is the land that makes up Georgia the same across the state? Georgia is made up of three major land areas. They are the northern mountain region, the **piedmont plateau** and the coastal area.

The Blue Ridge Mountains and Cohutta Mountains are part of Georgia's mountain region. The Cohutta Mountains are part of the Great Smoky Mountains. Georgia's 1828 gold rush town of Dahlogega is located in the mountain area of Georgia. Northern Georgia has other historic areas. There also are many state parks in Georgia's northern mountain region.

Critical Thinking
Why do you think the Cherokee were not paid for their land?

Stone Mountain is located in Georgia's piedmont plateau region. The piedmont plateau covers about one-third of the state. Fertile ground covers its rolling hills. Pine trees cover much of the piedmont plateau. Turpentine (TIR-pen-tine), tar and pine oil are some products taken from pine trees.

Fascinating (FAS-cin-a-ting) swampland forms much of Georgia's coastal area. The Okefenokee Swamp, is the nation's largest wildlife refuge (REF-uge). Coral, copperhead, and other poisonous (POI-son-us) snakes warm themselves along the rivers of the swamp.

☆ ☆ ☆ ☆ ☆ ☆ ☆ ☆ ☆

Georgia is a state of growth and beauty. It has become a major transportation (trans-por-TA-shun) center of the southeast. Atlanta's airport is one of the busiest in the world. Savannah remains Georgia's main shipping port. Georgia blends its rich history with a focus on the future. It is fast becoming a leading state in southeastern United States.

Did You Know? Blackbeard the pirate, got his name from braiding his long black beard and then tying the braids with ribbon. He would make himself look fierce during battle by lighting matches under his hat. This would frame his face in fire.

★ ★ ★ ★ ★ ★ ★ ★ **THINK ABOUT IT!** ★ ★ ★ ★ ★ ★ ★ ★

1. Which region of Georgia would be best for growing peanuts and cotton?

2. Why did plantation owners begin using steamboats instead of still using flat-bottom boats to transport cotton?

3. List two things about each land region found in Georgia.

Workbook p.11
Self-Check

LOUISIANA

★ ★

GEOFACTS
- capital: Baton Rouge
- statehood: 1812 (18th)
- rank in size: 31st
- rank in population: 21st (urban 68%, rural 32%)
- U.S. representatives: 7
- motto: "Union, Justice, Confidence"

▲ Huge nets catch fish in the Gulf

▲ Toledo Bend Reservoir — a large, man-made lake

Louisiana is a state filled with exciting moments. The sound of New Orleans jazz sizzles through the air. People dressed in wild, colorful costumes pack the streets during Mardi Gras time.

The state of Louisiana is shaped much like a boot. The top of the boot spreads out to meet with Arkansas, Texas, and Mississippi. The Gulf of Mexico flows along its curved heel. The toe of Louisiana's boot looks torn and shredded. This is the state's **delta** area. And, just like the tear on a real boot, the shape of Louisiana's torn delta is always changing.

How does the shape of Louisiana's delta change? Louisiana's southern delta grows by about 1,000 acres each year. The mighty Mississippi River causes this land growth. Soil carried by the river drops off as the muddied water flows into the Gulf of Mexico. Over the years the soil builds up to form new land.

The Mississippi River also takes land from Louisiana. This great river forms Louisiana's eastern border. It then cuts through the toe of Louisiana's boot-shaped land. The river bend sand winds as it travels south. This **meandering** (mee-AN-der-ing) causes erosion along the river's **banks**. Each moment Louisiana's eastern border changes. It grows a little in some areas. It gets smaller in other areas.

GeoWords

delta — a three-sided area at a river's mouth built by the dropping off of soil and sand carried by the river

meandering — following a winding course through an area

banks — the sides of the river where the water meets the ground

⚡ **Critical Thinking**

What causes Louisiana's delta to get larger each year?

Places to See! People to Know!

▶ French Quarter, New Orleans — features eighty-five blocks of Spanish and French buildings

▶ Marksville State Commemorative Area, Marksville — site of Native American village from two thousand years ago

▶ Jean Baptiste Le Moyne (b.1680) — French-Canadian explorer and founder of New Orleans

▶ Bernardo de Galvez (b.1746) — governor of Spanish Louisiana (1777), helped Americans in their fight against British troops

GeoWords
ethnic — ways and beliefs which are common to one group of people
humid — moist, damp, feel of water vapor
bayou — slow-moving river area entering or leaving a lake
levee — a bank built up to keep a river from overflowing

Critical Thinking
How did plantations affect the lives of enslaved Africans in Louisiana?

▲ People in Louisiana are used to a watery environment.

Did You Know? An 1852 law in Louisiana made it against the law to grant an enslaved African his or her freedom.

The Mississippi River flows through ten states. Soil from Louisiana mixes with the soil captured from the banks of nine other states. The soils **blend** and flow to finally settle in Louisiana's delta.

Louisiana has been built in part from soils from many other places in America. Louisiana also has been built by people from many other places. Native Americans, African Americans, people from Europe, and the French from Canada are all part of Louisiana's rich heritage. Louisiana's people, just like its soil, are a blend. Yet, each **ethnic** (ETH-nik) group holds on with pride to its special ways.

Where did the people who settled in Louisiana come from? Native Americans first settled in Louisiana. This happened about three thousand years ago. These early settlers were mound builders.

By the time white emigrants arrived in Louisiana, several tribes of Native Americans lived in Louisiana. Slowly, white settlement drove the Native Americans from their land. Illness brought by the white emigrants also killed many Native Americans.

From 1682 to 1803, Spain and France ruled Louisiana. In 1803 France sold all of the land around the Mississippi River to the United States. This was called the Louisiana Purchase (PUR-chus). By this time, many people from Europe and the eastern United States had settled in Louisiana.

By 1800 Louisiana already had a strong economy. The growing of sugar cane and cotton helped to keep the Louisiana economy strong. Louisiana's hot, **humid** climate is good for growing sugar cane. The state's many rivers made it easy to transport cotton from the northern part of the state.

It took many people to work the sugar cane and cotton fields. Enslaved Africans filled this labor need. Most farmers at this time had only a few acres. Yet, large plantation farmers controlled much of Louisiana's fertile soils.

The blend of Louisiana's people created a special ethnic mix called Creole (CREE-ole). Today, Creole heritage lives on in fine Creole food. Louisiana's Creole cooks mix oysters (OI-sters), fish, and other seafood with vegetables (VEG-ta-bles) to make a tasty meal.

Acadians (AH-ka-de-ans) are another culture special to Louisiana. The first Acadians were French people from the northeast coast of Canada. British troops sent the Acadians from Canada. Their boats, carrying about four thousand people, came to rest in the Louisiana **bayous** (BI-yous).

Acadians are also called Cajuns. Spicy Cajun food, Cajun music, and the Cajun language give Louisiana many of its special moments.

What is a Louisiana bayou? The bayou is a wetland area special to Louisiana. Bayous are slow-moving rivers that flow into and out of lakes. The branching of Louisiana's bayous forms large swamp areas. Oil and natural gas are pumped from this area.

There are more than 3,400 square miles of rivers and lakes in Louisiana. **Levees** (lehv-EEZ) along many river banks keep the rivers from flooding.

Some river and lake water holds salt. This is caused by water flowing from the Gulf of Mexico back into the rivers and lakes. Lake and river water that holds salt is called "**brackish** (BRAK-ish) water."

Other rivers and lakes in Louisiana hold fresh water. Freshwater does not have salt in it. Certain kinds of seafood live in brackish water. Other kinds live only in freshwater. This makes Louisiana home to many kinds of fish including catfish, shrimp, and crawfish.

What is the Mardi Gras (MAR-de Graw)? Mardi Gras is from the French language. It means fat Tuesday. It began in 1857 as a special day to eat as much as possible before fasting began on Ash Wednesday. Ash Wednesday is a special day in the Catholic religion.

Today, the Mardi Gras is a special two month festival. It is held each spring in New Orleans. The Mardi Gras is a time of color and fun-filled moments. Many people from across America come to New Orleans during Mardi Gras time.

New Orleans is Louisiana's largest city. It is built five feet below sea level. Levees keep the water around New Orleans from flooding the city. Homes are built on land that once was swampland. Still, water lies just a few feet below the ground's surface. Today, just like in Louisiana's past, New Orleans is an important port city.

Do the bayous cover all of Louisiana? Louisiana's northern and central areas are higher than its delta region. Traveling north, the low southern delta area slowly gives way to rolling hills. Pine trees in Louisiana's uplands replace the Spanish Moss plant of the bayous. Deer replace alligators.

☆ ☆ ☆ ☆ ☆ ☆ ☆ ☆ ☆

Louisiana is a place of wonder. From its land to its food to its music, Louisiana has a special moment for everyone.

GeoWords
brackish — salty water or marsh water that is near the sea

Critical Thinking
Why do you think so many people enjoy the Mardi Gras?

Did You Know? How to Make Creole French Toast (Pain Perdu)

1/2 cups milk

3 eggs, beaten

1/3 cup sugar

1 teaspoon vanilla extract

grated rind of one lemon

8 slices of day old french bread, with crusts

6 tablespoons butter

powdered sugar

grated nutmeg

cane syrup

Mix milk, eggs, sugar, vanilla, and lemon rind. Let bread soak about 5 minutes in mixture. Melt butter in skillet. Fry bread over medium heat until brown. Serve with sprinkled sugar, nutmeg and cane syrup

★ ★ ★ ★ ★ ★ ★ ★ **THINK ABOUT IT!** ★ ★ ★ ★ ★ ★ ★ ★

1. How is delta land formed?

2. What makes New Orleans a good port city?

3. What is the Mardi Gras?

Workbook p. 12
Self-Check

SOUTH CAROLINA

★ ★

GEOFACTS
- capital: Columbia
- statehood: 1788 (8th)
- rank in size: 40th
- rank in population: 25th (urban 55%, rural 45%)
- U.S. representatives: 6
- motto: "While I Breath, I Hope"

▲ Camping in the South Carolina mountains

▲ Myrtle Beach, South Carolina, is a favorite vacation spot for many people from around the country.

⚡ **Critical Thinking**
How did life change for women in South Carolina during the war?

Places to See! People to Know!

▶ Fort Sumter National Monument, Charleston Harbor — site of the first shot of the Civil War

▶ Memorial Park, Columbia — the largest Vietnam War memorial outside of Washington D.C.

▶ Sara Ayers (b.1919) — Native American artist

▶ Angelina Grimke (b.1805) and Sara Grimke (b.1792) — sisters who worked to end slavery and later for women rights

South Carolina is a state filled with charm and beauty. At sunset streaks of color dance across the South Carolina coastline. At the same time, graceful ballet (BAL-leh) dancers leap and spin across a South Carolina stage. Meanwhile, on a quiet lake in South Carolina, a peaceful fisherman sits in a boat watching the waves lift and roll in their own special dance.

South Carolina is the smallest state in the south. Yet, South Carolina has had a big part in America's past. South Carolina was among the thirteen states that first joined to become the United States. This was in 1788. The people of South Carolina fought bravely against the British. They fought so the new United States could be free of British rule.

South Carolina fought against the North in the Civil War. The Union Army marched through the South burning cities and farms. Yet, the people of South Carolina held strong. Thousands of South Carolina men joined the Confederate Army. Left behind, South Carolina women tended the farm fields and worked as nurses in hospitals that were put together quickly.

Did all the people of South Carolina agree with the fight to keep slavery? On December 20, 1860, South Carolina seceded (seh-CEE-ded), or left, the government of the United States. It was the first state to secede. Yet, not all people in South Carolina agreed with fighting to keep slavery.

THE PEOPLE'S PUBLISHING GROUP, INC. *Our United States Geography: Our Regions and People*

How did the state's geography affect the history of South Carolina? The people in the northwest part of South Carolina did not live like the people in the southwestern part of the state. Small farms, with families of ten people or more living in a small log cabin, dotted northwest South Carolina. Yet, great plantations, owned by rich farmers, covered the southeastern section. Living differently caused people to think differently about issues (IH-shoos) or things that affected their lives.

As early as 1670, slaves worked the fields of southeastern South Carolina. Large rice plantations depended on slavery. Later, slaves worked long, hot days in the cotton fields. Rich plantation owners argued for slavery. Small farmers in South Carolina's northwest area felt little need for slavery. Yet, most people in South Carolina defended slavery and were willing to fight for it.

Before white settlement, South Carolina was home to at least thirty different Native American tribes. The Yamassee lived along the coastal areas. The Catawba lived along the northeastern part of the state. The powerful Cherokee lived in the mountains.

There were many times of peace and war between white settlers and Native Americans. Members of the Catawba tribe fought against the British during America's fight for freedom. Catawba also fought with the Confederate Army during the Civil War. Yet, slowly white settlers and large farms took away land from the Native Americans. Slavery, illness, war, and later the forced selling of land, drove most Native Americans from South Carolina.

What is the geography of South Carolina like? South Carolina is divided into three major regions. The Atlantic coastline is the state's lowest area. Rising above the coastline area is the piedmont. Traveling northwest, the piedmont gives rise to the Blue Ridge Mountains.

The coastal area of the state is called the "lowland." The piedmont and mountain areas of the state are called the "upland." People usually say they are from the "upland," or from the "lowland."

What is the geography of South Carolina's upland? The piedmont covers most of northwestern South Carolina. The gently rolling hills of this area rise 400 to 1,200 feet above sea level. The many rivers of the piedmont flow southeast. This is because the piedmont region slopes from northwest to southeast. Forests of maple, pine, white oak and tulip trees cover much of South Carolina's piedmont.

The Fall Line marks the eastern edge of South Carolina's piedmont. Here rivers tumble from the upland region before traveling on to South Carolina's coastal lowland. The tumbling water creates beautiful, rushing waterfalls. The waterfalls slowly wear away the soil leaving **channels** (CHAN-nels) in the rock. Ships traveling **inland** can go only as far as the Fall Line.

The Blue Ridge Mountains cover the northeastern corner of South Carolina. Sassafras Mountain marks the highest point in South Carolina.

GeoWords

channels — grooves or deep areas where water flows
inland — away from the coast and toward the land

Critical Thinking
How did geography affect the settlement of South Carolina?

▲ 18th century homes in Charleston, South Carolina

Did You Know? The Venus's Flytrap, a rare insect eating plant, grows wild in South Carolina. The Venus's Flytrap snaps closed on insects, digests the soft parts, and then opens up to throw out the insect's shell.

GeoWords

bay — an area of a lake, sea, or ocean extending into the land

It rises 3,560 feet above sea level. About seventy inches of rain falls each year in the mountains. Snow rarely falls in South Carolina. Yet, about seven inches of sparkling snow falls in the northern mountains of South Carolina.

What is the geography of South Carolina's lowland? The Atlantic Coastal Plain covers the southeastern part of South Carolina. This is the state's lowland area. Here the land is flat, broken only by many rivers and **bays**. Swamps filled with cypress trees cover much of the coastal area. From there the swamps move inland along the river's edge.

The South Carolina coast is dotted with many islands. Sandy beaches stretch along parts of South Carolina's long coastline. South Carolina's coast runs 187 miles long. Yet, South Carolina has almost 3000 miles of coastline when all bays, peninsulas and island lands are counted.

What areas are important to South Carolina's economy? Farming is still important in South Carolina. Today soybeans, tobacco and corn are leading crops for the state. Cotton remains an important crop.

⚡ **Critical Thinking**

Why were children, but not African Americans, hired to work in the textile factories?

South Carolina's is a leader in textiles. Following the Civil War, textile factories sprung up where cotton was grown. Fast-moving rivers were the factories' power source. These early factories would not hire African Americans. Instead, poor white families became a cheap labor source. Children as young as eight would work ten hours a day, six days a week for 25 cents a day.

Child labor was no longer allowed after 1917. Slowly, laws that did not allow the hiring of African Americans changed. Today, modern textile factories hire many people. Money earned working in the factories and money made selling the textiles are important parts of South Carolina's economy.

Did You Know? South Carolina has more nuclear power plants than any other state in the country.

☆ ☆ ☆ ☆ ☆ ☆ ☆ ☆ ☆

South Carolina is a growing state. New businesses, new people and new ideas are coming together with respected ways of the past. South Carolina looks toward the twenty-first century with a sense of purpose and pride.

★ ★ ★ ★ ★ ★ ★ ★ **THINK ABOUT IT!** ★ ★ ★ ★ ★ ★ ★ ★ ★

1. How does the geography of the "upland" differ from the geography of the "lowland?"

2. What three major land regions are found in Georgia?

3. How does South Carolina's textile factories affect the state's economy?

Workbook p.13
Self-Check

THE PEOPLE'S PUBLISHING GROUP, INC. *Our United States Geography: Our Regions and People*

NORTH CAROLINA

★ ★ ★ ★ ★ ★ ★ ★ ★ ★ ★ ★ ★ ★ ★ ★ ★ ★ ★ ★

GEOFACTS
- capital: Raleigh
- statehood: 1789 (12th)
- rank in size: 28th
- rank in population: 10th (urban 50%, rural 50%)
- U.S. representatives: 12
- motto: "To Be Rather Than to Seem"

▲ Fort Fisher, North Carolina

▲ A huge cliff overhangs the Johns River Gorge.

North Carolina, the Tar Heel State, has many stories to explain how it got such a second name. Tar is a sticky liquid made of coal or other minerals. One story tells of tar being thrown into a stream to stop the advancing British soldiers (SOLD-jers). This was to have taken place during the year of 1781 when America was fighting to be free of British rule. As the story goes, it was said anyone trying to cross North Carolina's streams would get tar on their heels.

Another story explaining the meaning of "Tar Heel" comes from the time of the Civil War. More than ten Civil War battles took place on North Carolina soil. It is said that in one very hard battle most Confederate soldiers left the fight. Only North Carolina men stayed to finish the battle. As this story goes, North Carolina soldiers said they would put tar on the heels of other troops. This would make them "stick better in the next fight."

A third reason for North Carolina being called the Tar Heel State is much more simple. North Carolina has forests of pine trees. At one time great amounts of tar were made from the pine trees. So, Civil War soldiers from North Carolina were called "Tarheels."

North Carolina is an amazing state. From great mountains to great **sand dunes** to great capes, North Carolina is a treasure chest of geography.

GeoWords
sand dunes — a large area covered with hills of sand

⚡ **Critical Thinking**
What is meant by a geographic treasure chest?

Places to See! People to Know!

▶ The Boyette Slave House, Kenly — only one-room cabin with the only stick and mud chimney left in the state

▶ Charlotte Hawkins Memorial, Sedalia — memorial site honoring Charlotte Hawkins, an African American educator, as well as other African Americans of North Carolina

▶ Elizabeth Dole (b. 1936) — U.S. secretary of labor, first woman to serve as U.S. secretary of transportation

▶ Tsali (b. 1790?) — Cherokee leader who led about 1000 Cherokee into the mountains of North Carolina to escape the "Trail of Tears."

GeoWords

shoreline — the area along the shore of an island, bay or other coastal area

sandbars — a sandy area which rises above the water's surface

tornadoes — inland storms packing strong winds that can cause much damage

peak - the top of the mountain

Critical Thinking

What are some health concerns about tobacco?

▲ A worker weaves a beautiful chair seat.

Did You Know? Almost one hundred years ago, the world's first powered airplane flight took place at Kill Devil Hills in North Carolina. The Wright Brothers chose Kill Devil Hills because they had been told that it was one of the places with the most wind in North America.

What kinds of land does North Carolina's treasure chest hold? North Carolina's coast runs about 300 miles. Including all the bends in North Carolina's coast, the Tar Heel State has over 3,300 miles of **shoreline**.

Many islands lie just off the coast of North Carolina. These are called the Outer Banks. Pirates such as Blackbeard, Anne Booney and Mary Read used to hide out among the islands of the Outer Bank.

Capes also grace the North Carolina shoreline. A cape is a long, narrow peninsula. Capes are often sandy. They extend into the sea. Three major capes along the North Carolina shoreline are Hatteras, Lookout and Fear.

Shifting sand often causes harm to boats making their way past a cape. **Sandbars** rise and fall with the flow of water. This is why the capes carry names such as Lookout and Fear. Many ships have been wrecked while passing Cape Hatteras. Another name for Cape Hatteras is "Graveyard of the Atlantic."

Storms come often to the North Carolina coast. About fifty inches of rain fall along the coastal region every year. At times strong storms attack the state's coast. **Tornadoes** (tor-NA- doz) and hurricanes are a concern when storm clouds form.

What other kinds of land does North Carolina have? The piedmont area forms North Carolina's center. It is about 200 miles wide. The red clay soil of the piedmont rises to about 1,500 feet. Wildflowers and woodland cover much of the piedmont. Yet, this same area is where most people in North Carolina live.

The Blue Ridge Mountains rise high above the North Carolina piedmont. Rounded at their top, the Blue Ridge Mountains are thick with forests of cedar, pine, maple and oak trees. It is here that Mount Mitchell rises 6,684 feet above sea level. Mount Mitchell is the highest mountain **peak** east of the Mississippi River.

Tucked in North Carolina's southwest corner are the Great Smoky Mountains. These mountains are named for the smoky-looking fog that often covers the mountain peaks. The Smoky Mountains are a scenic delight. Grand colors fill the mountains during the fall. Mountain streams bubble through the region. Black bears live among the trees of the mountain region.

What kinds of crops are grown in North Carolina? Farmland covers less than half of North Carolina. Sweet potatoes, fruit, corn soybeans and peanuts are grown in North Carolina. Turkey, dairy, and hog farms also are important to the economy of North Carolina. The growing of tobacco has had a great affect on North Carolina's farm economy.

How did tobacco affect North Carolina's farm economy? North Carolina did not have many grand cotton plantations. Instead, much of North Carolina land in the early 1800s was planted in tobacco. Following the Civil War, sharecroppers tended the tobacco fields.

By 1890, one man, Buck Duke, controlled 75 percent of the country's tobacco products. The American Tobacco Company, owned by Buck Duke, made 90% of all cigarettes (SIG-ah-retts) sold in the United States.

Tobacco sales still bring great wealth to North Carolina tobacco companies. With Americans smoking less, tobacco companies have expanded their markets to foreign (FOR-in) countries. Foreign countries are countries other than the United States.

Critical Thinking
How would you define regional pride? Do only rural people have regional pride?

What other kinds of factories are important to the economy of North Carolina? Textile factories have been a part of North Carolina's history. During the early 1900s women and children made up more than half of work force of textile factories.

Today children no longer work in the textile factories of North Carolina. However, women still make up much of the workforce. Today's textile mills make beautiful cloth that is sold in stores all through the country. Textiles lead tobacco as North Carolina's most important industry.

Furniture making is also an important business in North Carolina. The thick forests of North Carolina are a ready source of beautiful wood. Carefully made North Carolina dining room chairs and living room sofas can be found in stores across the country. Many cities in the piedmont area have furniture factories. One city, Highpoint, calls itself the "Furniture Capital of the United States."

What is North Carolina regionalism (REE-jen-uhl-iz-um)? Regionalism is the special way people live and think in a certain area. At one time regionalism was strong in North Carolina. People in the mountain areas had their own way of speaking, their own kinds of foods and their own way of living. The mountain ways were different from the ways of people living along the coast.

☆ ☆ ☆ ☆ ☆ ☆ ☆ ☆ ☆

Today regionalism is not as strong as it was in the past. People's lives are not as separate as they once were. Yet regional pride is kept alive in song, folktales, crafts and festivals. North Carolina was, and still is, a state of special people.

Did You Know? The Qualla Cherokee Indian Boundary is home to many native Americans in North Carolina. It is found in the western mountains. The Qualla Cherokee Indian Boundary is land once claimed by the 1,000 followers of Tsali.

★ ★ ★ ★ ★ ★ ★ ★ **THINK ABOUT IT!** ★ ★ ★ ★ ★ ★ ★ ★ ★

1. Give two reasons why North Carolina's islands have been feared by people traveling on ships.

2. Give two reasons why so many people visit the Smoky Mountains.

3. What is regionalism? List 4 ways an area's regionalism can be shared.

✔ Workbook p. 14
Self-Check

FLORIDA

★ ★

GEOFACTS
- capital: Tallahassee
- statehood: 1845 (27th)
- rank in size: 26th
- rank in population: 4th (urban 85%, rural 15%)
- U.S. representatives: 23
- motto: "In God We Trust"

▲ Palm trees swaying in sunny Florida

▲ Miami Beach, Florida

GeoWords
endangered — to put into danger

⚡ **Critical Thinking**
Why is the question of how to use Everglades land not an easy problem to solve?

Places to See! People to Know!

▶ Kennedy Space Center, Cape Canaveral — National Aeronautics and Space Administration (NASA) center for space exploration

▶ Dade Battlefield State Historic Site, Bushnell — site of battle between Seminole Indians and U.S. government troops

▶ Walter Elias (Walt) Disney (b. 1901) — artist, creator of Mickey Mouse and Donald Duck characters, created Walt Disney World in Lake Buena Vista, Florida

▶ Pedro Menendez de Aviles (b.1519) — Spanish explorer and founder of St. Augustine, Florida

Florida is a state of warm, sun-filled days. Florida is Disneyland and alligators. Florida is where many people go to escape the snow and cold winds of the north. Florida blends people of all ages with land shaped by time. The result is an exciting, and changing, Sunshine State.

Florida is made up of a long peninsula and panhandle. At its highest point, Florida is only 300 feet above sea level. Florida's sandy, southern coastline gives way to a huge swamp area called the Everglades (EV-er-glayds). This coastal plain covers most of Florida south of Lake Okeechobee.

What is the Everglades like? The Everglades is a wetland area. Water from the Everglades drains very slowly to the south. Many kinds of animals, insects and birds live in the Everglades. The Everglades is home to some **endangered** (en-DAYN-jerd) animals, such as the manatee (MAN-ah-tee) and the Florida panther.

The Everglades is home to many types of plants. The custard apple tree, mangrove and strangler fig tree are among the many interesting trees that grow in this area. In some parts of the Everglades, groups of trees break up long stretches of sawgrass. Sawgrass can grow up to fourteen feet tall!

There is an ongoing battle over the Everglades. Some people want to drain and build on parts of this vast, or large, wetland area. Other people wish to leave the land just as it is for wildlife.

What is Florida's land like beyond the Everglades? Along Florida's southern coastline runs a string of islands. These are called the Florida Keys. A one-hundred mile road ties thirty-two of the Keys together.

North of the Everglades the land gently slopes upward. This northern area of Florida is called the Florida Uplands. The area has rolling hills and valleys.

At times, **sinkholes** form in Florida's northern land. A sinkhole forms when underground water cuts through limestone. The limestone falls apart and a sinkhole is left. Everything on the surface falls into the sinkhole. Sinkholes are a big problem for people in some areas of Florida.

Many kinds of crops grow in the fertile soil of Florida's Upland. Citrus (SIT-rus) fruit, such as oranges and grapefruit, is Florida's largest **cash crop**. The sale of citrus fruit is very important to the economy of Florida. Sugar cane, cotton, corn and tomatoes, along with other crops, also are grown in Florida.

How does Florida's climate affect its economy? The warm, humid climate of Florida is perfect for the growing of citrus fruits. Florida's climate also brings in many visitors to the state. The visitors are very important to Florida's economy.

Storms, some very strong, are a part of Florida's climate. Tornadoes and hurricanes are a threat to Florida's people, homes and businesses. In 1992, for example, Hurricane Andrew caused $20 billion worth of damage in just one area of Florida.

How did early settlement affect Florida? The settlement of Florida is marked by times of peace and times of war. Ponce de Leon, an explorer from Spain, sailed to Florida in 1514. During the next 200 years, Spain and England fought over Florida land. In 1783, England claimed Florida.

For almost the next hundred years, battle lines formed on Florida land. Wars between America and England mark the late 1700s and early 1800s. Another major conflict, or battle, was the war between the United States **government** (GOV-ern-ment) and the Seminole (SEH-min-ohl) Indians.

What started the war between the U.S. government and the Seminole? In the early 1800s, several thousand white emigrants arrived in Florida. Many of them wanted to settle on the fertile farmland where the Seminole lived. In 1832, the United States government offered the Seminole land in Oklahoma.

Some Seminole agreed to move. Other Seminole Indians did not want to move west. One Seminole leader who was against moving west was Osceola. Osceola led his people in a war against the United States government.

The war between the Seminole Indians and the United States government lasted for more than ten years. In the end, Osceola and his people lost their war.

GeoWords
sinkholes — an area of ground that falls, or sinks
cash crop — crop grown to be sold
government — the group of people who pass laws for all to follow

Critical Thinking
Why do you think many Seminole Indians did not want to move west to Oklahoma?

▲ The Hispanic Festival in Miami, Florida

Did You Know? Cotton became Florida's chief cash crop before the Civil War. A person's wealth was decided by the number of enslaved Africans he kept. By 1845, it was against the law in Florida for a slave owner to free any slaves unless he helped them leave the state. In 1858, Florida law allowed a free African American to pick a slave owner and become enslaved. Only two people are on record as having asked to become enslaved.

GeoWords
population — the number of people in an area

Critical Thinking
How can people whose heritage is different add to the beauty of a state? What problems can it cause?

▲ Pelicans and manatees are native to Florida.

Did You Know? Of the people living in Miami, Florida, 63 percent are of Hispanic heritage. Miami is the 46th largest city in the United States.

By 1843, the United States government sent over 3,800 Seminole to Oklahoma. About three hundred Seminole stayed in Florida. Today, the Seminole Indians have settlement areas in both Florida and Oklahoma.

Did the people of Florida fight in the Civil War? Florida joined the Confederate States of America. Men from Florida fought with men from other southern states during the Civil War.

Florida saw great change after the Civil War. Thousands of settlers moved to Florida. They found work in laying railroad track, draining wetland and working in cigar factories. Between 1880 and 1900, almost 150,000 people settled in Florida.

Is Florida's **population** (pop-u-LA-shun) still growing? Between 1980 and 1990, Florida's population grew by three million people. Today, nine cities in Florida are among the fastest growing cities in the United States.

Almost thirteen percent of the people living in Florida were born in another country. People from Canada, Cuba, Haiti, Greece and many other countries now call Florida their home. Almost 190,000 people in Florida speak the French Creole language. Also, about 12% of the people living in Florida have Hispanic heritage.

☆ ☆ ☆ ☆ ☆ ☆ ☆ ☆

Florida's people, climate and history have shaped a state marked by change and beauty. Florida's fast growing cities must deal with the problems of crime, drugs, housing and jobs. Yet, Florida, with its amazing land and warm, sunny days, is still seen by many people as the perfect state in which to live.

★ ★ ★ ★ ★ ★ ★ ★ **THINK ABOUT IT!** ★ ★ ★ ★ ★ ★ ★ ★ ★

1. How are the Everglades different from the Florida Uplands?

2. List three ways settlement has affected the people and land of Florida.

3. List three affects of Florida's climate.

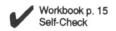 Workbook p. 15
Self-Check

The Appalachian Chain ★ ★ ★ ★ ★ ★ ★

The Appalachian Chain is a chain of mountains. Several groups of mountains make up the chain. One of the mountain groups is called the Blue Ridge Mountains. Another mountain group is called the Smoky Mountains. There are other mountain groups, too. The name given to all the mountains in the chain is Appalachian (ah-puh-LAY-shuhn). The name Appalachian comes the Appalachee Indians.

The Appalachian Mountains are the oldest mountains in North America. They were formed almost 230 million years ago by earth forces that folded the Earth's crust. Glaciers (GLAY-sherz), or great sheets of slowly moving ice, rounded the tops of the Appalachian Mountains. They are the second longest mountain chain in North America. The mountains stretch for 1,500 miles. They begin in eastern Canada and extend down the eastern part of the United States to Alabama.

The longest hiking trail in the United States crosses the Appalachian Mountains. The trail begins in Maine and runs about 1,995 miles south to Georgia. Along the trail, hikers can enjoy rivers, lakes, and national parks.

Many people living in the Appalachian Mountains farm or work in mines. About 50,000 square miles of coal lie under the surface of the Appalachian Mountains. This coal area extends through Alabama, Kentucky, Pennsylvania, Virginia, and West Virginia. Miners also dig for copper and limestone.

As in all regions, themes tie the states of the Appalachian Mountains. For example, the hardships and dangers of mining coal are told in the music and folk tales of the region. Coal mining bonded people together to work toward forming labor unions. Much unrest between the miners and mine owners happened before unions were finally formed.

Settlers traveling west were struck by the beauty of the Appalachian Mountains. That same beauty caused sadness among Native Americans as, tribe by tribe, they were forced to give up the lands they had lived on for hundreds of years.

Just as themes tie together the states of the Appalachian chain, people in different parts of the chain have a rich heritage all their own. People across the Appalachian Mountains take pride in their history, music, and way of life. As you read the chapters of this region, look for themes that tie the region. Look, also, for things that make each state a special place within the Appalachian Chain.

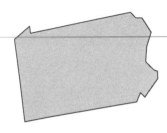

PENNSYLVANIA

★ ★

GEOFACTS
- capital: Harrisburg
- statehood: 1787 (2nd)
- rank in size: 33rd
- rank in population: 5th (urban - 69%, rural - 31%)
- U.S. representatives: 21
- motto: "Virtue, Liberty and Independence"

▲ The South's Confederate Army once fired its cannons on the Gettysburg, Pennsylvania, battlefield.

GeoWords
resource — something that is a natural part of the earth
fossil — the remains of something that lived long ago
scenic — an area filled with the beauty of nature

⚡ Critical Thinking _____

Why do you think people, such as the Amish, would choose follow the ways of the past?

Places to See! People to Know!
▶ Gettysburg National Battlefield, Gettysburg

▶ Valley Forge, King of Prussia — honors George Washington's army and its efforts during the American Revolution

▶ Guion S. Bluford, Jr. (b.1942) — first African American astronaut

▶ Rachel Carson (b.1907) — author and marine biologist who wrote *The Silent Spring*, a book that led to the banning of the pesticide DDT

Pennsylvania is a land of grand mountains bursting with color. The land is rich in coal. The coal is the result of a sea that spread across Pennsylvania millions of years ago. As the sea drained, a huge swamp claimed the land.

The packing of dead plants over millions of years left Pennsylvania with its large **resource** (RE-sors) of coal. For this reason, coal is called a **fossil** (FOS-sil) fuel. Today, coal mined in Pennsylvania is used to make electricity in many parts of the United States.

The pulling back of the great inland sea over Pennsylvania was just one land change in Pennsylvania. Next came a slow, but powerful, movement of the land. Beginning in the northwest, the Earth's crust began to fold. This folding formed the Appalachian Mountains. In Pennsylvania, the Appalachians run from the northeast to the southwest.

Did any other changes occur to form the land of Pennsylvania? After the mountains formed, great glaciers slowly edged their way southward from the Arctic. The glaciers cut across the mountains of Pennsylvania. The peaks of the mountains were rounded. Valleys were formed.

Today, about 45,000 miles of rivers and streams wind their way through the **scenic** (SEE-nik) mountains and valleys of Pennsylvania. They cut across thick forests of pine and hemlock.

The rivers are home to sunfish, yellow perch, and brook trout. They offer a place to drink to the many white-tailed deer, red fox, and bobcats that live in Pennsylvania's heavily forested land.

Heavy rains can cause the rivers to flood. Sometimes, the flooding of Pennsylvania's valleys can be very harmful. Great floods happened in 1889, 1936, and 1972. People died and property was lost.

Today, dams have been built in areas of Pennsylvania where floods are most likely to happen. The dams help to hold back flood waters. Yet, flooding is always a concern when a lot of rain falls at one time.

What are the main land regions in Pennsylvania? The mountain chains of the Appalachian Mountains cover a large area of Pennsylvania. Three other main land regions also cover Pennsylvania. One of these regions is the Allegheny (ah-lih-GAY-nee) Plateau. It covers most of northern and western Pennsylvania.

The Allegheny Plateau is part of the Appalachian Plateau that runs from New York to Alabama. This area is covered with deep, narrow valleys. Some rivers starting in this area flow east. Other rivers flow west.

Another region is the Erie lowland. This region is found in the northwest corner of the state. This flat land was once part of a lake **bed**. Grapes grow well in the sandy soil of this region.

One other region of Pennsylvania is the Piedmont. Many Pennsylvania Dutch farmers settled in this region. Apple and peach trees grow well in the fertile soil of the Piedmont region.

Other crops, such as potatoes and corn, are grown in this area. The growing of one other crop, mushrooms, also is important to Pennsylvania's farm economy.

Who are the Pennsylvania Dutch? In the early 1700s, immigrants from Germany began to settle on Pennsylvania land. The immigrants were farmers. They wanted to keep their German language. They wanted to raise their children to respect their German heritage. This group of immigrants became known as the Pennsylvania Dutch. The word "Dutch" came from the German word, "Deutsch." Deutsch means German.

Today the culture of those early German immigrants is carried on by way of fine quilt-making and furniture-carving, crafts, food, and lifestyle. One of the best known Pennsylvania Dutch groups is the Amish.

The Amish believe strongly in the ways of the past. They believe in a very simple life. Amish men wear wide-brimmed hats and long beards. Amish women and girls wear long dresses and wear bonnets. Amish children learn the German language. They go to Amish schools that stress reading and math.

The Amish will not fight in a war. They do not hold government offices. They do not use electricity or telephones. They do not drive cars. Instead, the Amish ride in horse-drawn black buggies. They farm with horse-drawn

Critical Thinking
Why do you think Philadelphia is called "the birthplace of the United States?"

▲ Philadelphia's Independence Hall

Did You Know? Many people in Pennsylvania speak Dutch. Dutch is the 24th most commonly spoken language in the United States.

plows. For the Amish, family life and support of other Amish families is most important.

Critical Thinking

How can words written more than 100 years ago still reach out to the people of today?

Were the Pennsylvania Dutch the first whites to settle Pennsylvania? Pennsylvania was first settled in the 1600s by people from the Netherlands, Sweden, and England. They were met by Algonquin and Iroquois people.

In 1682, William Penn founded the city of Philadelphia. Penn's idea was to start a colony for people who wanted to freely practice the Christian (KRIS-chin) religion.

By 1700, the city of Philadelphia had grown to a population of 20,000 people. Philadelphia became the center of America's fight for freedom from English rule. It is where Thomas Jefferson and Benjamin Franklin met in the late 1700s with other great leaders to form the laws the still govern the United States. Both the Declaration of Independence and the United States Constitution were signed in Philadelphia.

Pennsylvania became a battleground during the Civil War. About 250,000 people from Pennsylvania fought in the Union army. The largest battle was fought at Gettysburg. More than 50,000 people from the Union and Confederate armies lost their lives in the Gettysburg battle. No other battle in North America had cost so many lives.

☆ ☆ ☆ ☆ ☆ ☆ ☆ ☆ ☆

Four months later, on November 19, 1863, President Lincoln came to Gettysburg to remember the people who had died. His famous speech was called the Gettysburg Address. Even today, the words of the Gettysburg Address reach out to the people of Pennsylvania, as well as to the rest of the county.

❝... that we here highly resolve that these dead shall not have died in vain — that this nation, under God, shall have a new birth of freedom — and that government of the people, by the people, for the people, shall not perish from the earth.❞

▲ The Amish depend only on themselves for their needs for everyday living.

Did You Know? America's symbol of freedom, the Liberty Bell, hangs in Liberty Pavilion in Philadelphia. It was first rung on July 8th, 1776 in honor of the Declaration of Independence.

 ★ ★ ★ ★ ★ ★ ★ ★ **THINK ABOUT IT!** ★ ★ ★ ★ ★ ★ ★ ★

1. How are the four main land regions of Pennsylvania different?

2. List five Amish customs.

3. Why do you think people from across the United States like to visit Pennsylvania?

 Workbook p. 18 Self-Check

KENTUCKY

★ ★

GEOFACTS
- capital: Frankfort
- statehood: 1792 (15th state)
- rank in size: 37th
- rank in population: 23rd (52% urban, 48% rural)
- U.S. representatives: 6
- motto: "United We Stand, Divided We Fall"

▲ Lincoln's boyhood home, Hodgenville, Ky

▲ A Kentucky horse farm

In 1775 a frontier woodsman named Daniel Boone led thirty men into the Kentucky **wilderness** (WIL-der-nes). They began their journey in Kingsport, Tennessee. Their job was to follow a series of Indian trails to a **tract** (trakt) of land in Kentucky. This land, bought from the Cherokee Indians, was to be the site of Kentucky's first white settlement.

For three weeks Boone and his men traveled the rocky trail that would become known as "the Wilderness Road." They cut a 208-mile path through dense forests. The Wilderness Road was the only usable road through the Kentucky mountains. It ended in two places. One place south of the Kentucky River was called Harrodsburg. The other trail end was at a settlement just north of the Kentucky River. This settlement was called Boonesborough, in honor of the man who blazed the Wilderness Road.

An important part of the Wilderness Road was the Cumberland Gap. This is a narrow pass through the Appalachian Mountains. The Cumberland Gap is a point where the states of Kentucky, Tennessee, and Virginia meet.

Between 1775 and 1800, up to 300,000 settlers passed through the Cumberland Gap on their journey west. These first white settlers were, for the most part, British. Fifty years later, German and Irish **immigrants** (IH-mih-grantz) would brave the trip through the Cumberland Gap.

GeoWords
wilderness — a region with no people living in it
tract — a stretch of land or water
immigrant — a person who settles in a country other than where he or she was born

Critical Thinking
What do you think life was like for Daniel Boone and the other men while cutting the Wilderness Road?

Places to See! People to Know!
▶ Cumberland Gap National Historical Park —32 square mile park featuring a museum, hiking trails and campgrounds

▶ Mammoth Cave National Park, Bowling Green—largest cave system in the world

▶ John James Audubon (b. 1785) — noted bird artist who lived and painted in Kentucky from 1807 to 1820. The Audubon Society, an environmental group, is named for John Audubon.

▶ Kit Carson (b. 1809)—frontiersman, Indian agent

GeoWords

pasture — a grassland area used by horses, cattle and other grazing animals
environment — the area around you
strike — to stop working until certain conditions are met

Critical Thinking

What do you think it is like working in an underground coal mine? Explain your ideas.

▲ Mammoth Cave National Park

Did You Know? A religious group called the Shakers had its roots in Kentucky. Shakers led a simple life and were not allowed to marry. In the 1830s, there were 500 shakers. Today there are none. Shakers are credited for having invented clothespins, the circular saw, and the flat broom.

How was the landscape of Kentucky formed? Millions of years ago the Mississippian Sea covered the land that today is called Kentucky. Earth forces slowly pushed the land up. The sea moved south toward the Gulf of Mexico. Left behind was a land of scenic mountains and valleys. Amazing limestone caves tell the story of the time when the sea ruled Kentucky.

Why is Kentucky called the "Bluegrass State?" Bluegrass is the name given to the north central region of Kentucky. Here, bluegrass grows well in limestone-rich soils. Bluegrass is not really blue in color. However, every May, bluegrass grows tiny blue flowers. These flowers make the grass seem blue.

Once the bluegrass region was covered with forest. Settlers slowly cleared areas of this wide forest region. Today horses graze on large **pastures** (PAS-churz) of thick bluegrass. One breed of horse special to Kentucky is the thoroughbred. Thoroughbreds are strong, swift horses. Because of this, they are used in horse racing.

Horseracing is important to the economy of Kentucky. One special horse race is the Kentucky Derby. The first Kentucky Derby was held in 1875. Since then, it has been held every year on the first Saturday in May. More than 120,000 people come to see this mile and a quarter race.

How has the mining of coal affected life in Kentucky? Coal is a dark-brown rock that can be burned. Burning coal produces heat. Coal formed from plants that died one million to 440 million years ago. Kentucky produces about 20 percent of the coal used in the United States. Today, as in the past, several people from one family may work in coal mining. It is very hard work that is often filled with danger.

In the 1800s, most miners worked underground. Men, women, and even children worked in the mines. The work days were long — usually ten or more hours a day. Picks were used to break the coal. Miners using shovels then loaded the coal into horse-drawn wagons. Over the years, thousands of people died in coal-mining accidents. Many others died from breathing coal dust.

Today, most coal is mined by strip mining the land. In this method large earthmoving machines strip away top layers of earth. The coal is then dug out of the ground. With strip mining, miners no longer have to work in deep underground tunnels. Yet, strip mining destroys the surface of the land.

Kentucky is coal rich. Coal mining is important to its economy. Today coal mining companies must reclaim, or fix, the land that is strip mined. Yet, strip mining has left its scars on the mountains of Kentucky. Forests and farms have been destroyed. Wildlife has lost its **environment** (en-VYR-un-ment).

At times, coal miners have gone on **strike** (STRYK) for safer working conditions. They have also wanted better pay. Coal mining has brought both good and bad to the people of Kentucky.

In what ways has Kentucky blended its past with its present? Kentucky has a strong heritage. Folk art is a reminder of Kentucky's pioneer days. Baskets, musical instruments, furniture, wood toys, and pottery were just some of the items pioneer families made for work and fun times. Of special interest are quilt designs of African Americans as well as of rural whites. Today, many of these items are made in ways similar to what was done 200 years ago. People sell their folkcrafts.

Critical Thinking
How can folk art tell about a people's heritage?

Music is important to the people of Kentucky. Folk songs tell the story of Kentucky's settlement days. Another type of music, mountain music, is a special type of music. This music began with ballads the English and other immigrants had brought to the southern highlands of Kentucky. Instruments such as the fiddle, the banjo, and the dulcimer (DUL-sih-mer) help to give mountain music its own sound. Bagpipe tunes are another type of music. Today, bagpipe and dance groups remind Kentucky of its early immigrants.

Folk stories tell tales of the people who lived on Kentucky's mountains. One famous folk story, the feud between the Hatfield and the McCoy families, has its roots in the Civil War. Kentucky was a member of the Confederate states. Yet, not everyone agreed with the beliefs of the South. The Hatfields supported the confederate beliefs. The McCoys, on the other hand, sided with the Union army. The Hatfield-McCoy feud lasted for thirty years after the Civil War ended. Members of each family were killed in the fighting between the two families.

☆ ☆ ☆ ☆ ☆ ☆ ☆ ☆ ☆

Kentucky shows pride in its past. Yet, it looks forward to a strong economic future for its people. From its eastern coalfields to its rugged mountains to its beautiful lakes and rivers, Kentucky is a scenic wonder. Its plentiful rains and warm temperatures make Kentucky a perfect area for growing tobacco and breeding horses. And its people, holding hands with the past, look toward new ways to focus their skills and talents. Kentucky truly has a special feeling all its own.

Did You Know? Jefferson Davis, president of the Confederate States of America, and Abraham Lincoln, president of the United States during the Civil War, were both born in Kentucky.

★ ★ ★ ★ ★ ★ ★ ★ **THINK ABOUT IT!** ★ ★ ★ ★ ★ ★ ★ ★

1. How has coal mining affected the people of Kentucky?

2. Why are folk art and songs important to the people of Kentucky?

3. How did the Wilderness Road affect settlement west of the Appalachian Mountains?

Workbook p. 19
Self-Check

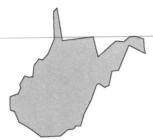

WEST VIRGINIA

★ ★

GEOFACTS
- capital: Charleston
- statehood: 1863 (35th)
- rank in size: 41st
- rank in population: 34th (urban 36%, rural 64%)
- U.S. representatives: 3
- motto: "Mountaineers Are Always Free"

▲ Mountain music in West Virginia

▲ The Potomac River winds its way through the mountains. People have settled in the valley along the river.

GeoWords
horizon — the line where the sky seems to meet the earth
erosion — a slow wearing away of the surface by natural forces such as wind or water

⚡ **Critical Thinking**_____
In what way can mountains look like ocean waves?

Places to See! People to Know!
▶ Grave Creek Mound, Moundsville — site of the tallest prehistoric mound in the U.S.
▶ Harpers Ferry National Historic Park — place where John Brown staged an antislavery raid
▶ Thomas "Stonewall" Jackson (b. 1823) — Confederate general who won many battles against Union troops
▶ Cyrus Vance (b. 1917) — U.S. secretary of state from 1977 to 1981

❝...one of the most stupendous scenes in nature❞
1783, Thomas Jefferson upon viewing West Virginia land

West Virginia, the Mountain State, truly is a land of wonder. All across the **horizon** lie rugged hills and majestic (muh-JES-tik) mountains bursting with color. Cutting through the landscape are deep river valleys. It is as if the state were a great sea, with mighty mountains rolling like huge waves across a vast and beautiful land.

Forests cover most of West Virginia. Tall white pine, red spruce, and hemlock trees rise above the forest floor. Wildflowers line nature trails traveled by hikers. Throughout the forest, deer, black bears, and foxes find shelter and food. West Virginia is home to more than 300 different kinds of birds. A lucky mountain hiker might see wild turkeys, hawks, or a great horned owl.

Where are the mountains located in West Virginia? Three land regions form West Virginia. One of these regions is the Allegheny Mountains. They run along its eastern border. These are West Virginia's tallest mountains. They rise more than 4,000 feet above sea level. The Allegheny Mountains are part of the Appalachian Mountains. **Erosion** (ee-ROH-zhun) has worn down the softer layers of the Allegheny Mountains. Today, valleys run between long, high mountain ridges of hard rock.

Another mountain range, called the Blue Ridge Mountains forms the eastern **panhandle** (PAN-han-dul) of West Virginia. These mountains also are part of the Appalachian Mountains. The fertile valley of the Shenandoah River runs through the Blue Ridge Mountains. Peach and apple orchards (OR-churds) line the valley.

Special rock, called igneous (IHG-nee-us) rock, makes up much of the Blue Ridge Mountains. Igneous rock forms when hot, melted rock cools. Metamorphic (meh-tah-MOR-fik) rock also forms the Blue Ridge Mountains. It is very hard rock. Heat and pressure from inside the Earth turns igneous rock into metamorphic rock.

The third region of West Virginia is the Appalachian Plateau. A plateau is a somewhat flat area that has been pushed up by forces below the surface of the Earth. The Appalachian Plateau lies west of the Allegheny Mountains. It has a rugged surface from streams carving valleys through the area. This has left flat-top **uplands** and steep **slopes.**

How have the mountains of West Virginia affected the state's economy? West Virginia's mountains are rich in coal. For many years, coal mining was the backbone of West Virginia's economy. However, West Virginia's coal economy depended on the demand for coal. At one time, coal was a major heating fuel.

Today, the demand for coal is less. There are fewer coal-mining jobs. Between 1980 and 1983, West Virginia had the highest rate of people out of work for all fifty states. From 1980 to 1990, West Virginia lost 8 percent of its population. Many people moved out of the state because of the lack of jobs.

How did coal mining affect the people who settled in the state? During the early 1900s, mining families from eastern and southern Europe settled in coal-mining areas. Mining companies built housing for the mining families. They were called "company towns."

Coal-mining companies often paid miners low wages for their work. Yet, the miners worked for long hours in dark mine shafts. Some of these shafts were knee-deep in water. Often, a miner was paid by the amount of coal dug out each day. For example, in 1900, a miner might get 15 cents for a ton of coal. A miner felt lucky if $1.15 was earned for a day's work.

Mining families depended on the company towns for the supplies. Company store prices often were high. Some mining companies did not pay their miners with U.S. money. Instead mining companies paid the miners with "special money" or copper tokens. This "money" could only be used in company stores. Mining families also had to pay rent for their housing. Such rent often cost too much money.

Many miners wanted to form **unions** (YOO-nyuns). They felt unions would help them get better working conditions and pay. The coal miners went on strike. Many difficult and violent years followed for mine workers. Over the years, people struggled, and many were killed before working and pay conditions for miners improved.

GeoWords
panhandle — a narrow strip of land shaped like the handle of a pan
uplands — high or hilly ground
slope — a surface area that goes up and down on an angle
unions — a group of workers united together to protect their interests

Critical Thinking
Do you think miners and their families liked living in "company towns?" Why or why not?

▲ A coal miner drives a machine deep underground. The job can be a dangerous one.

Did You Know? Sisterville was named for two sisters, Sarah and Delilah, by their father who happened to be the town founder. It was a quiet town until 1890. Then oil was discovered under the main street of the town. Quickly, the town's population grew from 300 to 1,500 people. Sisterville returned to a quiet town when the oil wells ran dry.

What other kinds of jobs are open to the people of West Virginia? West Virginia has a growing chemical (KEM-ih-kal) industry. One special chemical made in West Virginia is bromide. Bromide is added to gasoline to make car engines run better.

West Virginia also has a strong glass-making industry. Silica (SIH-lih-kah) is a mineral used for making glass. The mountains of West Virginia are rich in silica. Natural gas, also plentiful in the West Virginia mountains, is used to heat the glass-making ovens. Workers in towns like Weston and Milton form special glass items such as blown glass and stained glass.

▲ A typical Native American burial mound that has survived, along with some writing on stone.

How did West Virginia become a state? At first, West Virginia was part of Virginia. But the people in western Virginia lived a life different from those in eastern Virginia. The mountain areas of West Virginia makes farming difficult. Large slave-owning plantations, such as those in the eastern part of Virginia, did not exist in western Virginia.

When the Civil War began, many people of the western part of Virginia did not want to fight to keep Africans enslaved. They chose not to join the Confederate States. Instead, the people of western Virginia formed a new state. They called their state West Virginia. In 1863, President Lincoln signed a bill making West Virginia a state. West Virginia fought along with the North.

Following the Civil War, the government of Virginia asked West Virginia to rejoin the two states to form one state. West Virginia rejected Virginia's offer to reunite. Many people held bitter feelings against the Southern states. For example, after the Civil War, West Virginia passed a law that said any West Virginian who had fought with the South could not vote. The government of West Virginia later changed this law.

What is West Virginia like today? Today, West Virginia struggles with its economy. It is concerned about the number of people leaving the state to work elsewhere. West Virginia is looking to new businesses to help the state's economy. Tourism, for example, is a growing industry for West Virginia. The state's unbounded beauty draws many visitors each year.

☆ ☆ ☆ ☆ ☆ ☆ ☆ ☆ ☆

West Virginia has a rich heritage. Its past has given it a mixture of many cultures. West Virginia folk art, craft, and music are at the heart of this mountain state. Today, just as in the past, West Virginia carries a regional flavor all its own.

Did You Know? John Denver, a folk singer and environmentalist, sings about West Virginia and other parts of the country in a special way that makes people think about the importance of preserving the environment.

★ ★ ★ ★ ★ ★ ★ ★ **THINK ABOUT IT!** ★ ★ ★ ★ ★ ★ ★ ★

1. Why do you think large cotton plantations were not found on what was to become West Virginia?

2. Why would the government of West Virginia be concerned about a loss of population in the state?

3. List two facts about each land region in West Virginia.

Workbook p. 20
Self-Check

VIRGINIA

★ ★

GEOFACTS •
- capital: Richmond
- statehood: 1788 (10th)
- rank in size: 36th
- rank in population: 12th (urban 6%, rural 94%)
- U.S. representatives: 11
- motto: "Thus Always to Tyrants"

▲ A celebration in Alexandria, Virginia

▲ These three ships are copies of the ones that carried 104 white emigrants to Virginia in 1607. The ships are in Jamestown and are named the *Godspeed,* the *Susan Constant,* and the *Discovery.*

On an **island** on the James River stands the tower of a church built almost 400 years ago. This church was part of the first permanent (PER-mah-nent) English settlement on America's shores. The settlement was called Jamestown. Jamestown was named for James I, the King of England at that time.

Jamestown began when three small sailing boats, carrying about 100 men, landed on the shores of Virginia. The date was May 24, 1607. The men reported seeing thick forests of tall trees.

The settlers decided to build their first homes on a **peninsula**. The peninsula stuck out into the river. Water currents have washed part of the peninsula away. Today, the building stones and church tower left from that first settlement stand on an island.

The peninsula on the James River seemed to be a good choice for a settlement. The boats could easily be tied to the shore. To the English, Virginia looked like a land of plenty. Raspberries and large strawberries grew wild on the edge of the forest. Raccoon, deer, muskrat, and beaver were plentiful. Shellfish filled the shores.

What problems did the settlers find with their choice of land? The settlers soon found that the land they settled on did not have some important things needed for living. The sandy soil was not good for growing crops. Salt water from the Atlantic Ocean flowed into the river.

GeoWords

island — an area of land with water on all sides
peninsula — an area of land with water on three sides

⚡ **Critical Thinking**

How do you think the Jamestown settlers felt as they landed on the shore of the James River? Explain your ideas.

Places to See! People to Know!

▶ Chrysler Museum, Norfolk — collection of crafts representing over 5,000 years of history

▶ Museum of American Frontier Culture, Staunton — three farms show the homelife of early settlers from Great Britain, Northern Ireland, and Germany. A fourth farm shows pioneer life in the Shenandoah Valley.

▶ Lewis H. Latimer (b.1848) — son of African American Virginia slaves who escaped to freedom. Latimer worked with Thomas Edison. Held a patent for an a part in one of the first electric light bulbs.

▶ Pocahontas (b.1595) — Powhatan Indian princess credited with saving the life of John Smith, leader of the Jamestown settlement. She became a peacemaker between the Powhatan Indians and the Jamestown settlers.

Critical Thinking

Why do you think mountain areas are cooler than lowland areas?

▲ This natural bridge is one of many found in the mountains of Virginia.

Did You Know? In all, eight United States presidents were born in Virginia. They are George Washington, Thomas Jefferson, James Madison, James Monroe, William Henry Harrison, John Tyler, Zachary Taylor, and Woodrow Wilson.

There were no brooks or small streams to supply them with fresh water. The settlers were therefore forced to drink the poor river water. Almost half the settlers became sick and died.

About 8,000 Powhatan (pow-HAH-tan) Indians lived in the area of the Jamestown settlement. The Native Americans fought against white settlement of their land. Over the years, the people of Jamestown had times of peace with the Powhatan. There were also times of war. Many settlers and Native Americans died while fighting each other.

What was the climate like for the Jamestown settlers? The Jamestown settlers found a mild, humid (HYOO-mid) climate, perfect for growing tobacco. Today, tobacco still is one of Virginia's most important crops.

The climate is not the same everywhere in Virginia. It changes as the state's land changes. The east coast of Virginia is a coastal area. This area is known as the "Tidewater." Here **tides** from the Atlantic Ocean enter the Chesapeake Bay. Tidal water also enters the rivers that empty into the Chesapeake Bay. This is why the Jamestown settlers found their water salty and unfit to drink.

West of the Tidewater is the Piedmont (PEED-mont) region. The word "piedmont" comes from the French language. It means "foot of the mountain." Rolling hills, streams, and fertile valleys fill the region. It is cooler in the Piedmont than along the coast of Virginia. Farmers in this area plant tobacco, peanuts, and cotton. Cattle graze on the grassy hillsides.

West of the Piedmont, the land rises to become part of the Appalachian Mountains. The land of western Virginia is part of the Blue Ridge Mountains. Limestone caves lie under the mountains. Beautiful, rushing clear water waterfalls flow over the cliffs. Hot springs, such as those in Arkansas, bubble up to the surface from places deep inside the ground.

How do the mountains affect Virginia's climate? It is cooler in the mountains than in the lowland areas of Virginia. The growing season also is shorter. Along the coast, crops can be grown for about 240 days. Yet, in the mountain areas, the growing season usually lasts only about 150 days. This means that farmers along the coastal areas can grow crops for about three months longer than farmers in the mountains.

Valleys within the mountain areas have their own special climate. Along the Blue Ridge Mountains lies a very important and beautiful valley. It is called the Shenandoah Valley. Shenandoah is a Native American word that means "daughter of the stars." The Shenandoah Valley is part of the Great Valley of Virginia. It is warmer in the valley than in the mountains. Apples and other fruits grow well in Virginia's valleys.

Why is Virginia called the "Mother of Presidents?" Four of the nation's first five presidents were born in Virginia. One of these men, George Washington, was the first president of the United States. He, along with other Virginia leaders such as Thomas Jefferson and James Madison, helped to form the federal government we live under today.

Why is Williamsburg an important historic town? In 1698, Williamsburg became the center of government in Virginia. Before then, Virginia's government leaders met in Jamestown. Yet, the government leaders did not like the swampy area where Jamestown stood. Williamsburg was five miles from Jamestown. Williamsburg soon became an important and busy town.

Today, people can visit Williamsburg to see what life was like in the 1700s. The homes and businesses still look like they did long ago. Visitors can see Raleigh Tavern where people met to talk about forming a new government called the United States of America. Williamsburg was at the heart of America's new government.

How does Virginia's history affect its economy? Virginia has a full history. The Powhatan Indians first farmed the region. From Virginia's Native Americans, white settlers learned the land's secrets. With good crops, a mild climate, and plenty of forest for building homes, white settlers flooded onto Virginia land. Now visitors to settlement towns, such as Jamestown and Williamsburg, bring tourist money to Virginia.

Virginia, as a plantation state, fought with the South during the Civil War. Richmond, Virginia, became the capital of the Confederate States of America on Jay 21, 1861. Robert E. Lee, head of the Confederate army, was born in Virginia. Though Lee did not support slavery, he felt he had to fight for the beliefs of his home state. Lee's home and several Civil War battlefields are open to visitors. People visiting Civil War sites also add to the state's economy.

Railroads came to Virginia in the 1830s. Railworkers laid train rails across the state. In the 1800s, railroads hauled coal, dug from Virginia's mountains in the west, to eastern cities. Coal mining brought more settlers to the west. During the 1880s, for example, Roanoke grew from 700 to 5,000 people. Today, coal mining remains one of Virginia's important industries.

☆ ☆ ☆ ☆ ☆ ☆ ☆ ☆ ☆

Today, Virginia's long coastline, dotted with major cities, makes it an important **port** state. Virginia also has a growing shipbuilding industry. Products such as cotton fabric, paper, and tobacco help Virginia to be a leading **trade** state. Its growing population, rich history, and stunning land make Virginia a popular state.

★★★★★★★★ THINK ABOUT IT! ★★★★★★★★

1. Look at the population numbers for Virginia. Do you think most of the people live in the cities or in the rural areas? Why?

2. How did the water of the James River present a problem for the Jamestown settlers?

3. How can a state's past affect its economy?

THE PEOPLE'S PUBLISHING GROUP, INC. *Our United States Geography: Our Regions and People*

GeoWords
port — a place where boats and large ships dock
trade — to take products for something else, such as money

Critical Thinking
What can be learned by visiting places from the past?

▲ The African American music program at Colonial Williamsburg shows the culture of the 18th century.

Did You Know? Chesapeake is a Native American word that means "great oyster bay." Today, for every 100 oysters that once lived in the bay, only one remains. Pollution from people and boats have killed many of the oysters. Also, in the past, too many oysters were taken from the bay. Many people are trying to clean up the bay so more shellfish can live there.

Workbook p. 21
Self-Check

TENNESSEE

★ ★

GEOFACTS
- capital: Nashville
- statehood: 1796 (16th)
- rank in size: 34st
- rank in population: 17th (urban 61%, rural 39%)
- U.S. representatives: 9
- motto: "Agriculture and Commerce"

▲ Lookout Mountain: 7 states can be seen from this spot

▲ Chickamauga-Chattanooga National Military Park — site of a famous 1863 Civil War battle

GeoWords

dam — a wall built to hold back water, also to hold back water from flowing

earthquake — shaking of the Earth's surface caused by the movement of rock below the surface

aftershocks — a smaller shock coming after the main shock of an earthquake

Critical Thinking

How can Reelfoot Lake give people a view into the Earth's past?

Places to See! People to Know!

▶ National Civil Rights Museum, Memphis - offers many exhibits on the African American struggle for civil rights

▶ Lookout Mountain, Chattanooga - has a viewpoint of five states on a clear day

▶ Dr. Dorothy Brown (b.1919) - first African American woman surgeon in the South and first African American woman elected to the Tennessee General Assembly

▶ Davy Crockett (b.1786) - frontiersman and Tennessee politician who died in the Battle of the Alamo. Davy Crockett was against moving Native Americans off their land to make way for white settlers.

"....one of the most stupendous scenes in nature"
1783, Thomas Jefferson upon viewing West Virginia land

In 1811, a new lake formed in Tennessee. The people of Tennessee named the lake Reelfoot Lake. Reelfoot Lake was not made by building a **dam** along a large river. No one planned for Reelfoot Lake to happen. Reelfoot Lake was caused by an **earthquake** (ERTH-kwayk).

Between the years 1811 and 1812, three earthquakes struck the land where Tennessee, Missouri, and Kentucky meet. The earthquakes were very strong. **Aftershocks** (AF-ter-shokz) rumbled through the area for weeks at a time. The earthquakes caused some land in the area to drop 1 foot. Other land dropped almost 4 feet.

Reelfoot Lake is in the northwest corner of Tennessee. It formed when water from the Mississippi River flowed onto land that had dropped. Reelfoot Lake covers an area where cottonwood, cypress, and walnut trees once grew. Today, the stumps, or the bottoms parts, of these old trees can still be seen through Reelfoot's shallow water. Reelfoot Lake is Tennessee's largest natural (NAH-chur-al) lake.

What is a natural lake? Natural lakes are made by the land's geography. Natural lakes form when river water fills a low area. Reelfoot Lake is this kind of a lake. Other lakes form when a river closes off part of itself. This happens when soil carried by the river drops off in one area. The soil slowly builds up to dam the river.

The People's Publishing Group, Inc. *Our United States Geography: Our Regions and People*

Not all lakes are natural lakes. Tennessee has many man-made lakes. These lakes form when dams are built to keep river water from flooding an area. The river water is held back by the dam. The river water then covers a larger area and a lake is formed. This type of lake is called an artificial (ar-tih-FIH-shal) lake.

One important river in Tennessee is the Tennessee River. This river has thirty-nine man-made dams. Some of the dams form artificial lakes. The dams control flooding along the Tennessee River.

The dams along the Tennessee River also are used to make electricity (ih-lek-TRIH-sih-tee). This is called hydroelectric (hy-droh-ih-LEK-trik) power. Water rushing over the dam turns huge wheels called turbines (TUR-binz). The turning of the turbines causes electricity to be made. Hydroelectric power is an important energy source for the people of Tennessee.

What is the land like by the Tennessee River? The Tennessee River is located in west Tennessee. Here the land is hilly. West of the hills, the land drops to the Mississippi River. **Steep bluffs** line the area between the hills and the Mississippi River coastal plain. Farmers grow cotton and soybeans in west Tennessee.

The city of Memphis is in west Tennessee. Chickasaw Indians once lived throughout this area. With white settlement, Memphis became an important cotton port. During the 1800s, people from Germany and Ireland settled in Memphis.

Today, Memphis is Tennessee's largest city. It is also one of the largest cities in the United States. More than 600,000 people live in Memphis. Steel manufacturing and furniture factories are important businesses for the city.

Memphis is famous for its blues music. African Americans such as W. C. Handy and Bessie Smith helped to make Memphis a center for blues music. Another musician, Elvis Presley, mixed blues music with country music. This kind of music became known as "rock and roll."

What is the land like east of the Tennessee River? East of the Tennessee River lies a high plain area. Cedar trees cover the limestone soil. Lumbering, or the cutting and selling of trees, is important to this area's economy.

The high plain slowly slopes eastward to form the Nashville Basin. Here tobacco, wheat, tomatoes, and other crops grow in the fertile limestone soil. Beef and dairy cattle, as well as Tennessee walking horses, also are raised in this area.

One important city in the Nashville Basin is Nashville. Nashville is Tennessee's second largest city. Music recording is an important business in Nashville. Nashville is home to country music. Garth Brooks, Loretta Lynn, and Johnny Cash are just a few of the many country music singers.

What kind of land lies east of the Nashville Basin? The Nashville Basin slowly rises to form the eastern highland plain. This area is part of the Cumberland Plateau. Most of Tennessee's coal comes from this area.

GeoWords
steep — almost straight up
bluffs — high, steep banks on the shore of a lake, sea, or river

Critical Thinking
Before the Civil War, cotton plantations dotted western Tennessee. Small farms lined the mountains of eastern Tennessee. How do you think the land of Tennessee affected people's ideas about slavery?

▲ Homeplace: a tourist attraction that features a nineteenth century working farm

Did You Know? 20,000 formerly enslaved Africans from Tennessee fought with the Union Army during the Civil War.

East of the Cumberland Plateau lie the Blue Ridge Mountains. The Great Smoky Mountains are part of this mountain chain. The Cherokee Indians once lived throughout this area. They called the Smoky Mountains the "place of the blue smoke" because of the blue fog that covers the mountain.

Critical Thinking—————

What are some of the patterns that make up Tennessee's fabric?

Settlers from England and Scotland brought their music to the Smoky Mountains. Ballads sung by the settlers told of their homes and way of life. Today, these old ballads are still a part of Tennessee mountain music.

What kind of climate does Tennessee have? Tennessee has a humid, mild climate. The mountains get about 10 inches of snow a year. West Tennessee gets only about 4 to 6 inches of snow a year. Most of the state gets about 50 inches of rain a year.

Tennessee's climate, like its people, is a bit different in different parts of the state. Today, people in the different regions of Tennessee still have their own special music and way of life. Tennessee is like a cloth made of many patterns.

Yet, the fabric of Tennessee is held together by many common beliefs. Tennessee, for example, is at the heart of the Bible Belt. The Bible Belt is a wide area spread across the South. Many people who live there believe in the exact word of the Bible. Tennessee, with its mountains, folksongs, and regional ways, is a fascinating state with a history and beauty all its own.

Did You Know? On September 25, 1780, mountaineers from Sycamore Shoals joined with more than 1,000 people from Virginia and North Carolina. They set out on a ten-day, 180-mile trip to battle the British. They found their fight at Kings Mountain, South Carolina. All of the British soldiers either lost their lives or were captured. This battle helped to break the British hold on the southern part of the United States.

★ ★ ★ ★ ★ ★ ★ ★ **THINK ABOUT IT!** ★ ★ ★ ★ ★ ★ ★ ★

1. What are the three major land areas of Tennessee?

2. How does a dam form a lake?

3. Why are dams important to Tennessee?

Workbook p. 22
Self-Check

blk

OHIO

★ ★

GEOFACTS
- capital: Columbus
- statehood: 1803 (17th)
- rank in size: 35th
- rank in population: 7th (urban 74%, rural 26%)
- U.S. representatives: 19
- motto: "With God, All Things Are Possible"

▲ Lake Erie supplies Ohio's many busy factories.

❝...An hour before sunset, she entered the village of T____, by the Ohio River. It was now early spring, and the river was swollen. Great cakes of floating ice were swinging to and fro. On the Kentucky side, the narrow channel which swept round the bend was full of ice, piled one cake over another, filling up the whole river... almost to the Kentucky shore.... Her room opened by a side door to the river. She caught her child and sprang down the steps towards it. The trader caught full glimpse of her ... and was after her like a hound after a deer. With one wild cry and flying leap she vaulted ... onto the raft of ice beyond. The huge ice creaked as her weight came on it. With wild cries, she leaped from one cake to another. She saw nothing, till, as in a dream, she saw the Ohio side, and a man helping her up the bank.❞

adapted from Uncle Tom's Cabin by Harriet Beecher Stowe, Viking Press © 1981

Written in 1852, Harriet Beecher Stowe's story of Eliza's escape from slavery across the ice-packed Ohio River caused many people to have strong feelings against slavery. Ohio had passed a law against slavery in 1803. For many slaves, crossing the Ohio River meant a chance to be free.

From Ohio, the enslaved Africans traveled along the Underground Railroad to Canada. They spent their nights in the barns or cellars of farmers who did not believe in slavery. Hidden under loads of hay or wheat, they traveled past the many chestnut and buckeye trees that still grow in the forests of Ohio. Always living in danger, the enslaved Africans slowly made their way to Canada.

What is the geography of the Ohio River? The Ohio River flows for more than 450 miles. It makes up Ohio's south and southeast borders. The river

Critical Thinking

Why was the Ohio River an important crossing in the Underground Railroad?

Places to See! People to Know!

▶ Harriet Beecher Stowe House, Cincinnati — home of the author of Uncle Tom's Cabin and the African American history center

▶ Kelley's Island, Lake Erie — rocks show glacial grooves; rock carvings by Native Americans from more than 1,000 years ago.

▶ Maya Ying Lin (b.1960) — artist; designed the Vietnam War Memorial in Washington D.C.

▶ Tecumseh (b.1768) — Shawnee chief who tried to unite Native Americans against white settlement.

GeoWords
foothills — a lower hill at the bottom of a mountain

divides Ohio from West Virginia and Kentucky. Bluffs rise from 200 to 500 feet along the river's edge.

The Ohio River cuts across the Allegheny Plateau in western Ohio. Untouched by glaciers, this area is the most rugged part of the state. Steep hills and valleys fill the region. This area forms the **foothills** of the Appalachian Mountains.

The Allegheny Plateau region is Ohio's most scenic area. Waterfalls and lush forests cover the area. Found here are Ohio's resources of coal and salt. Ohio leads the nation in the mining of salt.

⚡ **Critical Thinking**
How could steamboats help cities to grow?

How does the geography of Ohio change from east to west? As the Ohio river flows west, it cuts across Ohio's blue-grass region. This area has gently rolling hills. West of this area is Ohio's Till Plain.

The Till Plain is a fertile farming region. Row upon row of tall, green corn plants cover the farm fields in the summer. Corn grows well in the warm climate of this region. About 40 inches of rain falls in this area each year.

Ohio's Great Lakes Plains region stretches across the northern part of the state. This is Ohio's snowbelt. More than 100 inches of snow falls in this area each year. Ohio's Great Lakes Plains region borders Lake Erie. Small farms along this region grow fruits and vegetables. At the same time, this area is one of the busiest shipping and trading areas of the country.

▲ Shipping lead to Ohio's rapid growth.

How have the Ohio River and Lake Erie helped with Ohio's trade economy? The Ohio River links Ohio to the Mississippi River and the Gulf of Mexico. Lake Erie links Ohio to the other Great Lakes. It also links Ohio to the St. Lawrence Seaway and to the Atlantic Ocean.

During the 1800s, steamboats traveling up and down the Ohio River brought settlers and supplies to Ohio. The steamboats and the river opened up markets in other states to Ohio farmers. Very quickly, cities sprang up along Ohio's rivers as well as along Lake Erie.

Today, Ohio has more mid- and small-size cities than any other state in the country. Six cities in Ohio have populations of more than 100,000. Ohio's largest city, Columbus, has a population of more than 630,000 people.

Did You Know? More Amish people live in Ohio than in any other state.

How did Ohio's cities affect settlement? Factories in Ohio's cities meant work for immigrants from Russia, Italy, Poland, and other countries. African Americans traveled to Ohio from southern states to find work in Ohio's factories. During World War I and World War II, women filled the factory work force as Ohio men went off to war.

Early Ohio settlers came in contact with Native Americans from different tribes. The Iroquois, Delaware, Shawnee, and Miamis all lived on Ohio land. Over the years, some Native Americans helped white settlers, while others fought against white settlement.

One Native American leader was Pontiac. In 1763, Pontiac led Native Americans of the Great Lakes Plains region against British settlement.

Another Native American leader was Chief Little Turtle. In 1792, Chief Little Turtle led the Miami, Shawnee, and Delaware Indians against white settlements along the Maumee River. Little Turtle was defeated at the Battle of Fallen Timbers. In 1795, Native Americans gave up their Ohio lands. This land covered about two-thirds of Ohio.

☆ ☆ ☆ ☆ ☆ ☆ ☆ ☆ ☆

Today, Ohio is a state of contrasts. Small farming towns dot the state, while large steel and shipping **industries** (IN-dus-trees) lead Ohio's large cities. Deer and red fox roam over seven million acres of forest while huge ships carry **goods** to people all over the world. Concerts and ballets fill city stages while folk music and crafts fill Ohio's rural homes. Ohio offers a look to "where all things are possible."

GeoWords
industries — businesses
goods — things that are made and sold

Critical Thinking
What kinds of problems might there be when a state is made up of many contrasting things? How can contrasts make a state stronger?

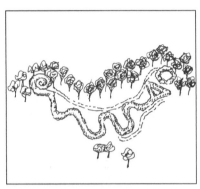

▲ The Indian Mounds near Hillsboro are several thousand years old. This one looks like a serpent with an egg in its jaws.

Did You Know? Between 1980 and 1990 Ohio gained 49,000 people. Yet, Ohio dropped in population rank from 6th in 1980 to 7th in 1990.

★ ★ ★ ★ ★ ★ ★ ★ **THINK ABOUT IT!** ★ ★ ★ ★ ★ ★ ★ ★

1. What are the four land regions of Ohio?

2. Why are the Ohio River and Lake Erie important to Ohio's trade economy?

3. Write one sentence that tells three things about Ohio.

 Workbook p. 23
Self-Check

The Land Regions of the United States

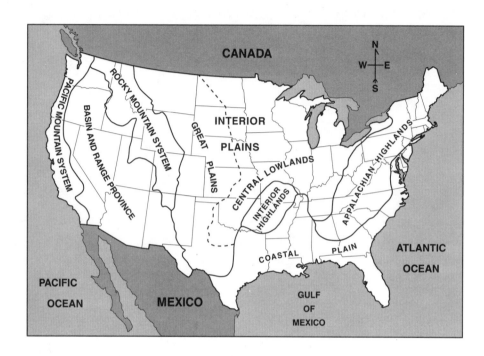

Land can be studied in two ways. First, its geology (je-OL-oh-je), or history of how it came to look the way it does, can be studied. Second, its geography, or present form, can be studied. The land that makes up the United States of America is rich in both geology and geography.

America's geology is a tale of great flows of moving ice, fire-gushing volcanoes, mighty earthquakes, and earth-carving rivers. It is a land where islands of beauty rise above the ocean's waves while great caves of wonder lie deep below the Earth's surface.

The geography of the United States is a treasure chest of land regions, or areas. Wet, lowland areas, high mountains, rocky coastlines, sandy beaches and great stretches of dry lands weave their way across the country. The land regions that make up the United States extend the limits of geography. The city of New Orleans is built below the level of the sea. Mt. McKinley in Alaska rises an amazing twenty thousand feet above sea level.

The geology and geography of the United States together form a land of vast beauty. In some areas, the flight of a large bird can be heard within the stillness of a rugged, untamed land. In other places, the land becomes a place for busy cities to grow.

At times land regions seem to change without warning. At other times, the land slowly blends from one region into another. Yet, region to region, the land that makes up the United States is filled with excitement and wonder.

The Northeast Corner

From Maryland to Maine, the Northeast Corner seems to be one busy city after another. Yet, within this region's fast-moving cities are rural areas that glow with nature's beauty. Themes across this region tie the people to the land. Themes tie the land to its history. Themes form a bridge that link the Northeast Corner with people across the country.

Six states in the Northeast Corner make up an area called New England. The six states are Connecticut, Maine, Massachusetts, New Hampshire, Rhode Island, and Vermont. But the Northeast Corner also includes Delaware, New Jersey, Maryland, and New York. New England is known for its fishing harbors and its fall colors. A group of people called the Puritans (PUR-ih-tanz) built colonies in New England in the 1600s. They came to farm the rocky land and to practice freely their religion.

Other people of other religions also came to New England to settle in America's early colonies. The idea of freedom of religion became an important part of American life and government. Today, people still come to America's shores looking for the freedom to live and think as they choose.

Early in the 1700s, people began to pull away from England. The idea of a country free of England's rule became a driving force among many colonists. This idea led to the American Revolution and the beginning of a new country, the United States of America. Today, people from all over come to the cities of the Northeast Corner. Today, just as in much of America's past, languages from all over the world can be heard in the cities of the Northeast Corner.

The Northeast Corner also is the site of America's banking and government. Our nation's capital, Washington, D.C., borders Maryland. Here, the president of the United States and the many men and women who lead our country work to make laws for all the people of the country. This region is a mix of small towns, cows grazing across rocky pastures, and crowded, busy cities. From its grand forests to its grand cities, the Northeast Corner in some way touches hands with the rest of the country.

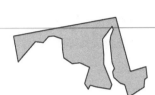

MARYLAND

★ ★

GEOFACTS
- capital: Annapolis
- statehood: 1788 (7th)
- rank in size: 42nd
- rank in population: 19th (urban 81%, rural 19%)
- U.S. representatives: 8
- motto: "Manly Deeds, Womanly Words"

▲ A Civil War monument on the rolling Maryland landscape

▲ The National Aquarium in downtown Baltimore

Critical Thinking
What feelings do you think led Francis Scott Key to write "The Star-Spangled Banner?"

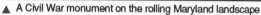

Places to See! People to Know!

▶ Antietam National Battlefield, Sharpsburg — site of the bloodiest Civil War battle

▶ Frostburg — restored buildings from when the town was an important stop along the National Road

▶ Thurgood Marshall (b.1908) — civil rights judge and first African American to serve on the Supreme Court

▶ Clara Barton (b.1821) — nurse who helped injured soldiers during the Civil War; founder of the American Red Cross

One September morning in the year 1814, British ships attacked Fort McHenry. Fort McHenry was built to protect the people of Baltimore, Maryland. The British fired rockets and bombs at the fort. The lines of fires made by the rockets lit the Baltimore sky. Bombs shot from the ships often exploded in the air. Other bombs landed on Fort McHenry.

An American, Francis Scott Key, watched the bombing of Fort McHenry. He feared great harm would come to the people of Baltimore. In the morning light, Key saw the smoke clear over Fort McHenry. To his great joy, the United States flag still flew over the fort.

Francis Scott Key expressed his joy in a poem. Later he turned his poem into a song. Many people liked the song. In 1931, Key's song about the American and British fight over Baltimore became our national anthem (AN-thum), or song. It is called "The Star-Spangled Banner."

What is the history of Baltimore? Native Americans greeted the first white settlers in the early 1500s. Later, people from Europe, seeking a place to freely practice their religion (ree-LIJ-yon), settled in Maryland. By 1790, Baltimore was an important American city. For many people, it was the starting point for the move westward. Yet, poor roads and thick forests made travel over the rough ground hard.

In 1811, the federal government began to build the first road west. It began in Baltimore. By 1850, the road reached the Indiana-Illinois border. The road was called the National Road.

Along the National Road, people who wished to settle west walked, rode horses, and drove wagons. Ranchers herded cattle eastward. The National Road was used often. At times, it looked like a busy **frontier** (fron-TEER) town street.

Baltimore grew quickly. During the 1840s and 1850s, sleek new ships called clipper ships sailed in and out of Baltimore Harbor. From 1870 to 1890, the number of people living in Baltimore doubled. People from Germany, England, Ireland, Italy, and other countries settled in Baltimore. From here, many people moved west.

What is Baltimore like today? Today, Baltimore remains one of Maryland's most important cities. It is Maryland's largest city. Yet, Baltimore suffers from many of the urban (IR-ban) problems that affect other large cities. Today, about 736,000 people live in Baltimore. Yet, in 1970, 905,000 people lived in Baltimore. The people of Baltimore are looking toward ways to improve the economy of the city. They hope to bring businesses and people back to the city.

Just as in the past, Baltimore is one of the busiest ports on the Atlantic Coast. Ships traveling from Baltimore Harbor to the Atlantic Ocean glide south through Chesapeake Bay. Ships also may pass through the Chesapeake and Delaware **Canal** (kah-NAL). This canal leads to Delaware Bay. From there, ships are able to travel to the Atlantic Ocean.

What is the area like around Baltimore? Baltimore lies on Maryland's Piedmont area. Here, beyond the stretch of Maryland's urban area, farmers plant corn and oats on gently rolling hills.

Mountain beauty graces Maryland west of the Piedmont region. The mighty Blue Ridge Mountains rise high above the Piedmont region. Crossing the northwest corner of Maryland are the Appalachian Mountains. Settlers of the past lived here in one- and two-room log cabins. Johnnycake, a kind of pancake made from corn, was a part of their daily meal.

Carving a path through the high ridges of the Appalachian and Blue Ridge mountains lies the great valley. Orchards and farms dot this fertile area.

The Atlantic coastal area spreads east of the Maryland Piedmont. The Atlantic coastal area covers more than half of Maryland. Tobacco has been grown here since the late 1600s. Before the Civil War, large tobacco plantations covered the area.

Did Maryland fight with the South or the North during the Civil War? Many people in Maryland sided with the South. Yet, President Abraham Lincoln did not want Maryland to join the Confederate States of America. He did not want Confederate states to be all around Washington, D.C.

President Lincoln sent troops to Maryland. The people of Maryland were not allowed to show that they agreed with the Confederate states. Maryland was forced to stay with the Northern states.

GeoWords
frontier — the farthest part of settled country
urban — having to do with a city
canal — a waterway dug across the land so that boats can travel from one body of water to another

Critical Thinking
How did the geography of Maryland affect how people thought about slavery?

▲ The White House is the oldest public building in the nation's capital, Washington, D.C. The White House is also a museum.

Did You Know? The word "conestoga" was first used as another way the Susquehannock Indians referred to themselves. The Susquehannock Indians greeted the first white emigrants. In 1608, John Smith wrote that the Susquehannock were "the most noble and heroic nation of Indians that dwell upon the confines of America." Conestoga later became the name for covered wagons used by families traveling west to settle.

Is Washington, D.C., part of Maryland? Washington, D.C., is not part of Maryland. Washington, D.C., is a district (DIS-trikt), or area with its own government. The letters D.C. mean "District of Columbia" (ko-LUM-bee-ya). Columbia is another name for the United States of America.

Washington, D.C., is carved out of a small part of Maryland. This is because Maryland gave the land to the United States so that our country could have a capital. Washington, D.C., covers an area of 63 square miles. The entire city of Washington, D.C., lies within those miles.

Many important government offices are in Washington, D.C. The president of the United States lives and works in the White House. Congress, where our country's laws are made, meets in the Capitol building. And our country's highest court, the Supreme Court, reviews cases heard by other courts.

Many other important buildings, museums, and places of honor are in Washington D.C. One important place of honor is the Vietnam Veterans Memorial. This V-shaped wall honors the men and women who died fighting in the Vietnam War. Another place of honor is the Holocaust (HO-lo-kost) Museum. This museum was built to remember the millions of Jews and others who died in Nazi death camps during World War II.

▲ The Vietnam War Memorial helps us remember those who lost their lives in that war.

Did You Know?

How to Make Kristen's Johnnycakes:

1 cup stone-ground cornmeal

3/4 teaspoon salt

1 cup boiling water

3/4 to 1 cup milk

Warm the meal and mix with salt in the oven before you begin. Gradually stir in the boiling water and then the milk until you have a thin batter. Heat a griddle. Grease it lightly. Pour on a large spoonful of batter to make a 3-inch cake. Brown on both sides. Serve with lots of butter. Add a dab of jam or jelly!

 ★ ★ ★ ★ ★ ★ ★ ★ **THINK ABOUT IT!** ★ ★ ★ ★ ★ ★ ★ ★

1. How did the National Road open up the West to white settlement?

2. Why didn't President Lincoln want Maryland to join the Confederate States of America?

3. Why is Washington, D.C. an important American city?

 Workbook p. 27
Self-Check

NEW JERSEY

★ ★

GEOFACTS
- capital: Trenton
- statehood: 1787 (3rd)
- rank in size: 46th
- rank in population: 9th (urban 89%, rural 11%)
- U.S. representatives: 13
- motto: "Liberty and Prosperity"

▲ Victorian homes in Cape May

▲ Princeton, New Jersey is the home of Princeton University.

In 1936, Jose Unanue started a food company in Secaucus, New Jersey. He named the company Goya Foods. Jose Unanue drew upon his Puerto Rican heritage to market ethnic foods to New Jersey's Hispanic community (com-MUN-ih-tee).

Today, Goya Foods sells more than 800 different kinds of food products. Jose Unanue's ethnic food products are enjoyed by people in many parts of the United States. The company earned $453 million in 1992. This placed Goya Foods as the number one Hispanic-owned business in the United States.

Ethnic **diversity** (di-VER-sih-tee) is a special part of the state of New Jersey. The customs, foods, and songs and dances of ethnic groups from all over the world add beauty to New Jersey cities and **rural** (ROO-ral) areas. Ethnic diversity has given New Jersey its own special heritage.

Who first settled New Jersey? Giovanni da Verrazano (vair-rah-SAH-noh), a sailor from Italy, first arrived on the shores of New Jersey in 1524. One hundred years later, an English sailor named Henry Hudson sailed into Newark Bay. Hudson told of the beauty and richness of the land.

White settlement of New Jersey came soon after Hudson's trip. In 1618, Dutch settlers from the Netherlands sailed across the Atlantic Ocean to become the first whites to settle in New Jersey. In 1630, another Dutch settlement was carved out of the New Jersey forest. Today, Jersey City stands at the site of the 1630 Dutch settlement.

GeoWords
diversity — many different kinds, variety
rural — part of the countryside, an area not part of a city

Critical Thinking
How do you think the life of the Delaware Indians was shaped by white settlement?

Places to See! People to Know!

▶ Albert Einstein House, Princeton—home of Albert Einstein, the German immigrant, who helped to create the idea of how the universe began as well as how to build the atomic bomb

▶ Abbot Farm, near Trenton—site of 2,000-year-old Native American settlement

▶ Thomas Alva Edison (b.1847)—inventor of the camera, phonograph, and electric light

▶ Jacob Lawrence (b.1917) — African American artist whose paintings are about African Americans' struggle for civil rights

▲ Sailboats are a familiar sight off the coast of New Jersey.

The Dutch were not the first to settle New Jersey land. Native Americans had lived on New Jersey soil for more than 8,000 years before white settlement. Near the Dutch settlements lived the Delaware Indians.

How did the Delaware Indians live? The Delaware, like other Native Americans, believed the land was a gift from the creator (kree-AY-tor), or the one who made the land. The land could not be owned. The land was meant to be used, respected and cared, for by everyone. Delaware men hunted and fished. Delaware women tended the tribe's crops.

Trade became an important part of life between the Dutch and Native Americans. The Dutch traded pots, blankets, guns, and other things for animal skins.

Dutch settlers carried diseases (dih-ZEEZ-ez) such as smallpox and measles. Many Delaware Indians died from the diseases brought by Dutch settlers. Life for the Delaware Indians was forever changed after white settlers came to New Jersey land.

When did other ethnic groups begin to settle in New Jersey? In the early 1800s, people from many other parts of the world began to settle in New Jersey. In the 1840s, a famine (FAM-in), or great lack of food, sent thousands of people from Ireland to the shores of New Jersey. In New Jersey, Irish people worked to help build railroads and canals.

Following the Civil War, many people from Italy, Germany, and other countries in Europe came to work in the textile factories of New Jersey. Also, many African Americans moved to New Jersey from southern states during World War I and World War II. African Americans found work in New Jersey factories that made products needed during these two wars.

How did settlement affect New Jersey? Cities grew as more people settled in New Jersey. People in rural areas began moving to the city to find work. Today, New Jersey ranks first in population density (DEN-sih-tee). This means that more people live in one square mile in New Jersey than live in one square mile anywhere else in the United States.

Large New Jersey cities, such as Newark and Atlanta, are searching for ways to solve the many urban problems facing today's cities. The need for better housing, better education, and better ways to reduce crime are just some of these many problems.

What kinds of factories are found in New Jersey? Metal products, clothing, canned food, and many other products come from New Jersey factories. New Jersey also is a leader in making the drugs needed to cure disease. Many people work in New Jersey factories. The factories are very important to the economy of New Jersey.

What is New Jersey like beyond the cities? Rural areas stretch beyond New Jersey's busy cities. New Jersey's second name is "the Garden State." Farms and forests cover two-thirds of New Jersey. Cranberries, tomatoes, blueberries, hay, and soybeans are grown in New Jersey. Dairy cattle graze on grassy hills found in the northwest part of the state.

In 1985, New Jersey farmers took a major step to make sure city growth would not take over good farmland. The State Farmland Preservation (prez-er-VAY-shun) Program preserves, or keeps, New Jersey farmland as land set aside only for farms.

Is land in northern New Jersey the same as land in southern New Jersey? The geography of New Jersey changes from north to south. Low mountain chains ripple across northern New Jersey. More than 20,000 years ago, a great glacier carved through this area. As the glacier melted, it left behind the hills, waterfalls and lakes found in northern New Jersey.

The glacier that molded northern New Jersey never reached the central (CEN-tral), or middle, part of the state. Here rolling hills give way to a southern coastal plain. New Jersey's southern lowlands are only 100 feet above sea level.

☆ ☆ ☆ ☆ ☆ ☆ ☆ ☆ ☆

New Jersey's land, just like its people, offers diversity and beauty. It is a state shaped by great forces in nature, history, and **ethnic pride**. Today, New Jersey is looking for new ways to shape and improve its cities and rural areas.

GeoWords
ethnic pride — a great belief and sense of value in the customs of an ethnic group

Critical Thinking
Why do you think farmers wanted a farmland preservation law?

▲ Albert Einstein, winner of a Nobel Prize in physics, was one of New Jersey's most famous citizens.

Did You Know? Atlantic City is well-known for its boardwalk, saltwater taffy, and tourist industry.

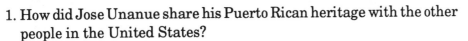

★ ★ ★ ★ ★ ★ ★ ★ **THINK ABOUT IT!** ★ ★ ★ ★ ★ ★ ★ ★

1. How did Jose Unanue share his Puerto Rican heritage with the other people in the United States?

2. How does the rank in size for New Jersey compare with the rank in population? What does this mean?

3. How does the land change from northern to southern New Jersey?

Workbook p. 28
Self-Check

MAINE

★ ★

GEOFACTS
- capital: Augusta
- statehood: 1820 (23rd)
- rank in size: 39th
- rank in population: 38th (urban 45%, rural 55%)
- U.S. representatives: 2
- motto: "I Lead"

▲ Lighthouses dot Maine's rocky coast.

▲ Maine's large, beautiful pine forests are a favorite subject for many artists.

GeoWords
dawn — the time of day when the sun rises

⚡ **Critical Thinking**
What does it feel like to watch a morning sunrise?

Places to See! People to Know!

▶ Permaquid Lighthouse, Permaquid Peninsula — one of the most painted and photographed houses in the United States

▶ Rachel Carson National Wildlife Refuge Wells — has 4,000 acres of marshland and is home to many kinds of birds

▶ George Herbert Walker Bush (b.1924) — 41st president of the United States

▶ Harriet Beecher Stowe (b.1811) — author of *Uncle Tom's Cabin*, an antislavery book that helped people's feelings to grow against slavery before the Civil War.

Digging for clams along a Maine coast can fill a quiet morning with gentle joy. Coal, wet sand, the flap of a seagull's wings, and the song of an ocean wave as it crashes along the shore are all part of the thrill in finding that one very special clam.

Wrapped in seaweed, the clams are ocean-fresh. Digging for clams, clam-bakes, and sun-colored, peaceful mornings are all part of life in Maine.

Maine is snow-covered, majestic mountains soaring high above the cold, coastal waters of the Atlantic Ocean. Maine is the sound of a lone moose thundering through the thick forest in search of its mate. Maine is the sweet scent of wildflowers as they burst into bloom on a frosty morning.

Morning in the United States begins in Maine. The east coast of Maine is graced by the first rays of sunlight. The people of Maine call this area the "Sunrise Coast." From here, **dawn** spreads across the United States.

What is the geography of Maine? The state of Maine covers more than 33,000 square miles. The Maine coastline runs 228 miles along the Atlantic Ocean. Yet, when all bays, islands, twists, and turns are added, the coastline of Maine stretches an amazing 3,500 miles!

Maine is filled with nature's (NA-churz) wonder. Forests cover almost 90 percent of Maine. Lakes cover more than 2,200 square miles of Maine land. Moosehead Lake, Maine's largest lake, is one of the largest lakes in the United States. More than 5,000 rivers and **streams** cut across Maine.

How does the geography of Maine change from north to south? To the south, Maine's coastal lowlands are lined with white sand **beaches** and salt **marshes**. Small, lively coastal towns dot the area. Maine's largest city, Portland, is found on Maine's southern coast. Portland began as a shipbuilding town. Today, it is Maine's business center.

Maine's New England upland region lies to the north and west of its coastal lowlands. The area rises from sea level in the east to 2,000 feet above sea level in the west. Fast-flowing streams cut through this mountain area. Water for the streams comes from melting snow and **springs**.

The Aroostook Plateau is located in the northeastern part of the Maine's New England upland. Fertile soil covers the Aroostook Plateau. This is Maine's potato-growing area. Potato fields cover more than 100,000 **acres** of the Aroostook Plateau. Children in this area are let out of school each fall to help with the harvesting of potatoes.

Does Maine have any other regions? Maine has one other region. It is called the White Mountains region. The White Mountains region covers the state's northwestern area. Crisp mountain air, hundreds of clear-water lakes, and towering pine forests fill this area. Here Maine's highest mountain, Mount Katahdin, rises 5,268 feet into the clouds.

Long, gravel ridges called "horsebacks" cover part of the White Mountain Region. Horsebacks also are called "eskers" or "kames." They were made by streams that flowed under the glaciers.

Was the geography of Maine formed by glaciers? Much of Maine's beautiful land was shaped by glaciers. These glaciers moved through Maine more than ten thousand years ago. Most of the state's lakes, as well as its breath-taking waterfalls, were formed when the glaciers melted.

The last glacier left Maine about 10,000 years ago. As it did, the coastal land of Maine broke away. This land sank 1,000 to 1,500 feet down into the Atlantic Ocean. The peaks, or tops, of these mountains can be seen today. They are Maine's offshore, or away from the shore, islands.

Boats sailing to Maine's rocky northern coast are warned of sharp rocks by lighthouses. Lighthouses have been used to warn sailors of the dangers along Maine's coast for more than 200 years.

What is the climate like in Maine? Summers in Maine are not often hot. On a warm summer day, the air might suddenly turn cold as it blows in from the Arctic Ocean. The growing season in northwest Maine is only a slim four months long.

Maine winters are colder than winters in places that are just as far north. This is because cold Arctic air and coastal winds keep the area from being warmed by warmer air from the south. About 70 inches of snow falls on Maine's coastal areas. Yet, 100 inches of snow each year might fall in the high mountain areas of Maine.

GeoWords
streams — a small river
beach — a flat shore of sand or small stones that is washed over by water
marshes — lowlands often covered by water, swamps
springs — water rising to the surface of Earth
acre — an area of land equal to 43,560 square feet

Critical Thinking
Why do you think so few people live in northwestern Maine?

▲ Maine is famous for shellfish. Lobster traps are a common sight on many docks.

Did You Know? Native Americans, the Algonquian, first came into contact with English and French settlers in Maine. Later settlers from Ireland and Scotland settled in the state. They brought potatoes with them to plant.

Where do most people in Maine live? Most of the people living in Maine have homes in the southern part of the state. About half of all the people living in Maine live within 20 miles of the coast. About half of the state is still wild. Few people live in Maine's northern mountain area.

Today, Maine is a leader in the sale of lumber, wood products, and paper. Many people work in Maine's shoe factories. Yet, the harvest of seafood is Maine's oldest business. Fishers in Maine harvest and sell more lobsters than in any other state.

Maine is a growing state. Whether it is clam digging, water-skiing, mountain hiking, or dogsledding, Maine offers a piece of wonderland for all who live and visit there.

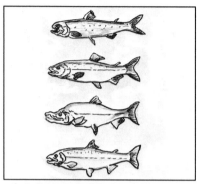

▲ In the past, the Merrimack River was filled with salmon.

Did You Know? Many Algonquin died from smallpox and other diseases brought by white settlers.

THINK ABOUT IT!

1. What is different about the three land regions of Maine?

2. In what businesses do most of the people of Maine work?

3. How did the glaciers help to form the land of present day Maine?

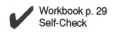
Workbook p. 29
Self-Check

DELAWARE

★ ★

GEOFACTS
- capital: Dover
- statehood: 1787 (1st)
- rank in size: 49th
- rank in population: 46th (urban 73%, rural 27%)
- U.S. representatives: 1
- motto: "Liberty and Independence"

▲ A fall harvest festival celebrates Delaware's farming.

From New Castle's rolling meadows,
Through the fair, rich fields of Kent,
To the Sussex shores, hear echoes
Of the pledge we now present:
Liberty and independence,
We will guard with loyal care,
And hold fast to freedom's presence,
In our home state Delaware.

from "Our Delaware", music by George B. Hynson, words by Will M. S. Brown

In 1802, E.I. du Pont used what he had learned while living in France to start a new business. E.I. Du Pont saw that the price of American gunpowder was high. Yet, the gunpowder was not very good. He worked out a plan to set up a gunpowder plant. The site, or place, he chose was on Brandywine Creek in Delaware.

Over the next one hundred years, the Du Pont business supplied gunpowder for many American battles. In 1902, the Du Pont Company began to make other chemical (KEM-ih-kal) products. During World War II, the Du Pont Company supplied gunpowder, nylon for World War II parachutes (PAHR-ah-shootz), and other products. Today, Du Pont is one of America's biggest companies.

Delaware is home to over half of America's richest companies. Tax laws in Delaware make it a good state for setting up a corporation (kor-por-AY-shun). A corporation is a special way of setting up a business. Today, for

Critical Thinking

Why was Caesar Rodney's ride to Philadelphia an important event?

Places to See! People to Know!

▶ Bombay Hook National Wildlife Refuge, Dover—a 15,122-acre refuge for migrating birds and home to many wildlife animals

▶ Fenwick Island — place where the first marker of the Mason and Dixon Line was placed

▶ William Julius Johnson (b. 1899) — African American baseball player who helped other African Americans enter the major leagues; entered Baseball Hall of Fame in 1975

▶ Peter Minuit (b. 1580) — a Dutchman who led a group of people from Sweden to settle on Delaware land; help build first fort by settlers from Sweden which later became Wilmington

example, many large chemical companies have their main offices in or near Wilmington.

Has Wilmington always been an important Delaware city? Wilmington began in 1731. In that year, a man named Thomas Willing decided to settle near Fort Christina. By 1775, Willington, which was now renamed Wilmington, had about 1,200 people. Even then, Wilmington was an important trade city.

Today, Wilmington is Delaware's largest city. More than 70,000 people live in Wilmington. As with other large cities, Wilmington has problems with crime. It also has the problem of making sure there is an equal chance for good jobs and housing for all people.

Critical Thinking
Which area of Delaware has the largest urban population? Why?

Wilmington offers a look into America's past. Many old buildings have been saved. Wilmington's Old Swedes Church was built in 1698. It is the oldest church in the United States that is still in use. Standing tall in the main part of the city is a large statue (STAT-choo) of Caesar Rodney.

Who was Caesar Rodney? On July 1, 1776, men from America's **colonies** (KOL-uh-nees) met to decide if the colonies should break away from England. The plan was that the colonies would become united states. The states would be free to form their own government. They would not have to live by England's laws.

▲ A stone marker on the Mason-Dixon line

Caesar Rodney was one of three men representing the colony of Delaware. Though quite ill, Rodney made an 80-mile night ride to Philadelphia. There, Rodney cast his vote for freedom. With Rodney's vote, Delaware joined the other twelve colonies in signing the Declaration (dek-lah-RAY-shun) of Independence (in-dee-PEN-dens).

On December 7, 1787, Delaware became the first state to OK America's new government. Over the years, Delaware would be the first to do many other things.

What else has Delaware been first to do? Delaware was the first state to pass a law that allowed people to practice any religion they choose. Delaware also was the first state to allow freedom of the press. Freedom of the press means that people may write to share their ideas with other people. The government may not tell people what they can write.

Did You Know? Woodburn, the home of the governor of Delaware, is reported to have been part of the Underground Railroad.

Delaware was the first state that did not allow slave owners and traders to take slaves into the state. Delaware was the only state where African Americans were free unless proven to be slaves. Yet, slavery did exist in Delaware. After the Civil War, Delaware was one of the last two states to grant freedom to all slaves.

Delaware has been a leader in helping people to rebuild old city homes. An urban **homesteading** (HOHM-sted-eng) project began in the 1970s. The project started in Wilmington. In this project, families were given old homes that needed much repair. If the repairs were made, then the families could keep the free homes. Other states have used Delaware's urban homesteading project as a model for urban projects of their own.

How is Delaware divided? Delaware is divided into three **counties** (KOWN-tees). The three counties are New Castle to the north, Kent in the center, and Sussex to the south. Each county is divided into areas called "hundreds." Each hundred has a say over how the land in the hundred is used. Delaware is the only state that divides counties into hundreds.

Is the land the same in each county? The land that makes up Delaware is on the Delmarva Peninsula. This includes Delaware, Maryland, and Virginia. The peninsula runs between the Atlantic Ocean and the Chesapeake Bay. Summers on the Delmarva Peninsula are warm and humid. Winter days bring cold winds and about 15 inches of snow.

Most of Delaware's land is a part of the Atlantic Coastal Plain. Delaware's Piedmont area lies along the state's northern region. A long sandbar lies off Delaware's southeast coast. Here, people enjoy sun-drenched, sandy beaches.

Two hundred years ago, swamp covered about 50,000 acres of land in Sussex County. Over the years, much of the land was drained to make fertile farmland. Today, about 11,000 acres of swamp is left. This wetland area is being saved. It is a **refuge** (REH-fyooj) for swamp animals and plants.

Why does Delaware call itself "the Little Wonder?" The growth of business is important to Delaware's economy. The people of Delaware also value ethnic festivals. The Nanticoke Indian Pow Wow is just one of many ethnic festivals held in Delaware.

☆ ☆ ☆ ☆ ☆ ☆ ☆ ☆ ☆

Delaware pays respect to the past while looking toward a bright future. From its **international** corporations to its thriving chicken-growing farms to its wildlife refuge areas, Delaware is packed with amazing land and people. It is, indeed, a wonder of a state.

GeoWords
counties — an area in a state
international — of or for people in various nations of the world
refuge — an area of safety

⚡ **Critical Thinking**
What value is there in saving a swamp area?

▲ A Nanticoke Indian Pow Wow in Millsboro, Delaware

Did You Know? Woodburn, the home of the governor of Delaware, is reported to have been part of the Underground Railroad

★ ★ ★ ★ ★ ★ ★ ★ ★ **THINK ABOUT IT!** ★ ★ ★ ★ ★ ★ ★ ★ ★

1. Why is Wilmington an important Delaware city?

2. Why is Delaware often called "the first state?"

3. What is urban homesteading?

Workbook p. 30
Self-Check

VERMONT

★ ★

GEOFACTS
- capital: Montpelier
- statehood: 1791 (14th)
- rank in size: 43rd
- rank in population: 48th (urban 32%, rural 68%)
- U.S. representatives: 1
- motto: "Freedom and Unity"

▲ Vermont's maple trees provide the rest of the country with delicious golden maple syrup for pancakes and waffles.

GeoWords
ranges — a chain of mountains

⚡ **Critical Thinking**
What do you think it is like to wake up in the mornings to the sweet smell of freshly baked beans and bread?

Places to See! People to Know!

▶ Rock of Ages, Barre - one of the largest granite quarries in the world

▶ Green Mountain Audubon Nature Center, Huntington - a 230 acre safe home to Vermont wildlife

▶ Madeleine May Kunin (b.1933) - first female governor in Vermont

▶ Norman Rockwell (b.1894) - artist who painted scenes of everyday life in America

The sweet smell of baked beans fills a Vermont home on a cold, snowy morning. Flavored with brown sugar and salt pork, the beans have slowly cooked all night in the oven. Placed next to the beans on the breakfast table is a basket of freshly baked bread and a pitcher of warm maple syrup.

Vermont is a state of cold, snowy winters. It is a state of color-filled forests and high mountain **ranges**. Small towns and rural areas stretch across Vermont. About two-thirds of the people of Vermont live in towns of less than 2500 people.

Does Vermont have any large cities? Only two cities in Vermont, Burlington and Rutland, have populations of more than 12,000 people. Elsewhere in the state, people make their living by dairy farming and logging. Vermont is the leading state in the making of maple syrup.

The population of Vermont is less than the population of most other states in the country. Fifteen cities in the United States have populations greater than the population of Vermont. Yet, Vermont is a growing state. Between 1980 and 1990, Vermont showed a 10 percent growth in population.

There is concern that the small towns of Vermont may change too quickly. In 1993, the National Trust for Historic Preservation listed the state of Vermont as one of the country's eleven most endangered places. The group is concerned about unplanned growth in Vermont's small towns. They want to make sure that Vermont does not become a state where large shopping malls replace the small town general (JEN-er-al) store.

Who first settled Vermont? Algonquian-speaking tribes were the early settlers of the land that makes up Vermont. Sometime in the early 1500s, the Iroquois (EAR-oh-kwoy) also settled on this northern land.

In 1609, a French explorer named Samuel de Champlain (SHOHM-playn) claimed the land of Vermont for France. French forts were built along the rivers of the region. The French traded furs with the Algonquian Indians.

Native Americans, French, English and Dutch settlements all followed the water **routes** (routs) of the region. The rivers served as a way to travel from one town to another. Rivers were a water-road for the fur trade. Rivers also were a source of power to run small **mills**. Later, water was used to power Vermont factories.

Who else settled in Vermont? Settlers from other New England states soon settled in Vermont. In the 1840s, immigrants from Ireland began moving into the state. Later, people from Sweden, Scotland, Canada and other countries settled on Vermont land. The immigrants built railroads, worked in rock **quarries** (KWAHR-rees) and farmed. Lately, Vermont has become home to immigrants from Laos, Vietnam and other Asian countries.

Today, as in the past, town meetings are an important part of Vermont government. During a town meeting the people can vote to pass new laws for the town. People elect leaders of the town government during town meetings. The town's people also can decide how the town's money is spent. These and many other issues come before the town's people during a town meeting.

What is the geography of Vermont? Vermont borders the country of Canada on the north. Lake Champlain makes up much of its western border with New York. To the east another water border, the Connecticut River, divides Vermont from New Hampshire.

There are about 430 lakes and trout **ponds** in Vermont. Many of these lakes are a gift from the glacier that carved Vermont thousands of years ago. Small streams flow into many of Vermont's clear, unspoiled lakes.

Forests cover much of Vermont. Long stretches of maple trees send forth splashes of color each fall. Bright yellows, oranges and reds are set against a dark green background of pine and spruce trees. Daisies, buttercups, violets and other wildflowers add to nature's artwork.

Why is Vermont called "The Green Mountain State?" Stand anywhere in Vermont and you will see wave after wave of mountains. There are more than 420 mountain peaks in Vermont. The Green Mountains is the largest mountain chain in Vermont. In the far past, the Green Mountains were some of the highest mountains in the world. Yet, the work of glaciers wore down the tops of this well-known mountain chain.

Granite is mined from Vermont's mountains. Granite is a very hard rock. It is used in buildings and in other places where strong rock is needed.

GeoWords
routes — a way taken to go someplace
mills — a place where grains, such as corn or oats, is ground into flour
quarries — a place where rocks are dug for other use
ponds — an area of standing water that is smaller than a lake

Critical Thinking
Why would keeping small towns from becoming urban areas be important to people in Vermont?

▲ President Calvin Coolidge took the oath of office in this house in 1923.

Did You Know? There are farms in Vermont that specialize in the making of maple syrup. Morse Farm Sugar Shack in Montpelier is such a place.

GeoWords
rustic — having to do with rural life

Rivers starting high in the Green Mountains flow either east to the Connecticut River or west to Lake Champlain. Those that flow west cross the Champlain Valley. Found here are Vermont's most fertile soils. It is also warmer in the Champlain Valley than in other parts of the state. The Champlain Valley is home to dairy farms, apple orchards and other crops. From gentle sloping hills to steep peaks, Vermont's mountains add majestic beauty to the state. Sixty to 120 inches of snow fall on the mountains of Vermont. Skiing, hiking and other mountain sports are enjoyed by many people.

☆　☆　☆　☆　☆　☆　☆　☆　☆

The people of Vermont value their state's quiet, **rustic** (RUS-tik) beauty. People from many other places come to Vermont to share in its richness. From its snow-filled winter winds to its cool summer breezes, Vermont is one of America's great treasures.

▲ A skier enjoys the beauty of Vermont's powder-topped mountains.

Did You Know? Maple syrup is made from the sap of the sugar maple tree. In early spring the sap is taken from the tree. The sap is collected in a bucket that hangs from a spout.

Another way is to run a hose from tree to tree. The collected sap then runs through the hose to a collection point.

The sap is taken to a sugarhouse. There it is cooked for many hours until it turns into syrup. It takes ten gallons of sap to make one gallon of syrup.

★ ★ ★ ★ ★ ★ ★ ★　**THINK ABOUT IT!**　★ ★ ★ ★ ★ ★ ★ ★

1. Why are Vermont's Green Mountains no longer some of the highest mountains in the world?

2. Why would rivers starting in the Green Mountains flow east or west?

3. How would you explain rustic beauty?

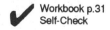

Workbook p.31
Self-Check

NEW HAMPSHIRE

★ ★

GEOFACTS
- capital: Concord
- statehood: 1788 (9th)
- rank in size: 44th
- rank in population: 40th (urban 51%, rural 49%)
- U.S. representatives: 2
- motto: "Live Free Or Die"

▲ A train climbs Mount Washington.

▲ This peaceful picture of dairy cattle grazing is a typical New Hampshire scene.

Imagine a carpet of dazzling orange, golden, and red leaves spread across the land. Imagine the sound of bells ringing in the cool, crisp air as horses glide a sled across snow-covered hills. Imagine the gurgling sound of a brook as it splashes past rocks of granite.

New Hampshire offers the beauty of the four **seasons** (SEE-sons)—their sights, smells, and sounds. New Hampshire was once covered by glaciers. Today, New Hampshire is covered by thick, colorful forests. Large rock beds of red and gray granite give New Hampshire the name "the Granite State."

The winters in New Hampshire are long. More than 100 inches of snow fall each winter. The snow turns New Hampshire's forests white. This season offers a time for winter festivals. Snow carvings, skiing, hockey, and snowball fights bring smiles to the people of New Hampshire.

New Hampshire summers are short. The growing season lasts for about 105 days in the north. The southern part of the state has a longer growing season of almost 140 days. Chicken, cattle, and hogs are raised on family farms. Summer festivals offer log-sawing contests and the showing of handmade wool cloth.

Is the land the same across the state of New Hampshire? Actually, there are three main land regions in New Hampshire. The coastal lowlands extend inland about 20 miles from the Atlantic Coast. People enjoy the

GeoWords
seasons—a time lasting about three months (fall, winter, spring, summer)

⚡ **Critical Thinking**
How do seasons affect the way of life for people in New Hampshire?

Places to See! People to Know!
▶ Shaker Village, Canterbury — site of the 1792 Shaker settlement
▶ Franconia Notch State Park, White Mountains — site of the Old Man of the Mountain and other land features
▶ Sharon Crista McAuliffe (b.1948)—Concord high school teacher chosen to be the first private citizen in space; died in the space shuttle Challenger explosion
▶ Alan Shepard, Jr. (b.1923)—first American in space (1961)

GeoWords
meadows—an area of grass and wildflowers
landmark — a point marking a special place, person, or event

white sand beaches along the 13-mile coast. Salt marshes and **meadows** (MED-ohz) dot the region.

Most of southern, eastern, and western New Hampshire is covered by the eastern New England upland. River valleys, beautiful blue lakes, and hills stretch across this region. Farmers in this area grow fruits, hay, and other crops. New Hampshire's population centers lie along this region's Merrimack Valley.

New Hampshire's White Mountain region lies north of the eastern New England upland. This area covers the northern third of the state. The White Mountains are part of the Appalachian Mountain chain. These high mountains rise above areas of flat land. The flatlands were once lake beds.

One mountain range in the White Mountains is called the Presidential (pres-ih-DEN-shal) Range. The mountain peaks in this range are named for presidents Washington, Adams, Jefferson, Adams, Monroe, and Madison.

Also found in the White Mountains is a special **landmark** called the Old Man of the Mountain. The stone coming out from the side of the mountain looks like a face. People from many places come to see the Old Man of the Mountain. Others can see it in paintings. They also can read about the Old Man of the Mountain in the many stories and poems written about him.

Does New Hampshire have any large cities? New Hampshire's largest city is Manchester. It has a population of about 99,500.

New Hampshire's second largest city is Nashua. Almost 80,000 people live in Nashua. Almost 31,000 people live in Concord.

New Hampshire is mostly a state of small towns. New Hampshire is divided into 221 towns. Laws for each town are passed by town "selectmen" and yearly town meetings. The town meetings are held each spring. At the town meetings, people living in the town have a chance to vote on many issues.

Sometimes, the issues that come up at a town meeting affect people beyond the town. An example of this happened 1974 when a group wanted to build an oil refinery (ree-FYN-er-ee) in the town of Durham. The people of Durham voted against the project. The state government agreed with the people of Durham.

Why is New Hampshire sometimes called the Primary State? Every four years, people in the United States vote for who they would like to be president of the country. Before the whole country votes, each state votes in a what is called a primary (PRY-mair-ee) election. In the primary election, the people of the state vote for one person who they think should be elected president.

New Hampshire always has the first primary election. It leads the country in thinking about who will be elected president.

Critical Thinking
What do you think is the meaning of New Hampshire's motto?

▲ A boat is docked for repairs in a Portsmouth, New Hampshire shipyard.

Did You Know? About one-fourth of the people in New Hampshire are of French Canadian heritage.

The town of Dixville in New Hampshire is the first town in the United States to say who should be president of the United States. A special voting place has been built for every person who votes in Dixville. At midnight on the day everyone votes for president of the United States, the people of Dixville cast their votes.

Critical Thinking
Why do you think New Hampshire began to pass laws protecting the state's forests?

Who first settled New Hampshire? The people who came from England and Scotland in the 1600s met with Native Americans from tribes belonging to the Abnaki Indians. Over the years, the French and English fought against each other for fur trading rights with Native Americans.

The selling of New Hampshire's trees for lumber became a growing business. The tall, white pine trees (150 to 200 feet tall) that grew in New Hampshire were sold for boat masts. The mast is the main post on a boat. It holds the boats sails. Settlements were started on land that had been cleared of trees.

In the 1870s, railroad companies set up in an area, cut all the trees and then moved on to some other area. Clean streams became choked with sawdust and dirt that was swept off the cleared hillsides by rain. Beginning in 1901, laws were passed to protect New Hampshire's forests.

The people of New Hampshire come from many ethnic backgrounds. Their ethnic pride is shown in New Hampshire's many festivals. New Hampshire truly is a state of great beauty.

Did You Know? Until 1902, only people who practiced the Protestant religion could hold office in New Hampshire.

★ ★ ★ ★ ★ ★ ★ ★ **THINK ABOUT IT!** ★ ★ ★ ★ ★ ★ ★ ★

1. What three things can be said about New Hampshire's forests?

2. What are the three regions of New Hampshire?

3. How do the people of New Hampshire have a direct say or voice in their government?

Workbook p. 32
Self-Check

RHODE ISLAND

★ ★

GEOFACTS
- capital: Providence
- statehood: 1788 (7th)
- rank in size: 50th
- rank in population: 43rd (urban 86%, rural 14%)
- U.S. representatives: 8
- motto: "Hope"

▲ Bowen's Wharf in Newport

▲ One of Rhode Island's most elegant and beautiful seaside hotels

Critical Thinking
Why do you think the leaders of the Massachusetts Bay Colony ordered Roger Williams to stop telling people what he believed?

Places to See! People to Know!
▶ First Baptist Meeting House, Providence — oldest Baptist church in the United States

▶ Great Swamp Fight Monument, South Kingstown — memorial site where Wampanoag and Narragansett Indians were killed by colonial troops in 1675

▶ George Michael Cohan (b.1878) — songwriter, dancer, playwright, and actor who wrote the words to the World War I song "Over There"

▶ Anne Hutchinson (b.1591) — believed in freedom of religion; set out from Massachusetts colony and helped found the settlement of Portsmouth, Rhode Island

In 1630, a man named Roger Williams left England to settle in the colony of Massachusetts. Williams had worked in the church of England. Yet, Williams did not always agree with what the church taught.

Roger Williams spoke out for the right of all people to practice their own religion. Williams also spoke out for the rights of Native Americans. He felt, for example, that settlers had no right to take land from Native Americans. His ideas often were in conflict with, or different from those of, the leaders of the Massachusetts Bay Colony.

Did Roger Williams stay in Massachusetts? The Massachusetts court ordered Williams to take back his teachings. Williams refused because he believed strongly in a person's right to share ideas. In January 1636, Williams left the Massachusetts Bay Colony. Helped by friends, Williams found his way across the frozen wetland.

Williams met his friend Massasoit on the eastern bank of the Seekonk River. Massasoit was the leader of the Wampanoag Indians. Massasoit gave Williams food and shelter. In the spring, Williams bought land from Massasoit and from two leaders of the Narragansett Indians.

The land Williams bought was on the bank of the Moshassuck River. Williams named his settlement Providence (PROV-ih-dens). The word providence means "by God's care." Williams opened his settlement to people of all religions.

THE PEOPLE'S PUBLISHING GROUP, INC. *Our United States Geography: Our Regions and People*

Williams asked England to let Providence, and the islands around Providence become a colony. The colony was named Rhode Island. Today, Roger Williams is known as the father of Rhode Island.

Who came to live in Rhode Island? People from many countries settled in Rhode Island. Families from France settled in East Greenwich. Jewish families from Spain and Portugal settled in Newport. The Touro Synagogue in Newport is the oldest Jewish synagogue (SIN-ah-gog), or Jewish place of worship, in North America.

Textile mills were built in Rhode Island. During the 1800s, many people from Europe and Canada came to work in the textile mills. From 1800 to 1850, Rhode Island's population doubled.

Many women and children worked in the mills. Sometimes, most of the workers were children. Children could more easily reach between small moving parts of machines to get thread. Often, children were hurt. Many people got sick from the dust and other poor working conditions in the mills.

Labor unions formed to improve the working conditions of mill workers. The textile mills gave work to many people. Yet, by the 1920s, many of the textile businesses had moved to the southern states.

For a while, many people in Rhode Island did not have work. Slowly, things changed. Today, many people work in jewelry, shipbuilding, and tourist businesses across Rhode Island.

How do people from different heritages share their past? The pride people have in their heritage is shown in the many ethnic festivals in Rhode Island. From the Santo Cristo Festival to Native American Days to Octoberfest, festivals give people a chance to share their foods, crafts, customs, and music and dance.

People's ethnic background also can be seen in many old and famous buildings. Great mansions built during the 1800s are styled after great buildings in Europe. Marble House and the Breakers in Newport are two of these great mansions. Other preserved homes in Rhode Island share the heritage of the people who built them long ago.

People from many heritages have shared their ideas and beliefs. Rhode Island was the first colony to pass a law that kept slaves from being taken into the colony. This happened in 1774, almost ninety years before the Civil War. In 1951, Rhode Island gave home rule to its cities. Home rule allows city governments to pass many laws.

What kind of land do the people who settle in Rhode Island find? Rhode Island is the smallest of all fifty states. Rhode Island is sometimes called "the Ocean State." The Atlantic Ocean washes 40 miles of Rhode Island coastline. Scattered in Narragansett Bay are several large and small islands. Narragansett Bay opens about 340 more miles of Rhode Island coastline to the Atlantic Ocean.

Rhode Island is made up of two land regions. One region is the coastal lowlands. Sandy beaches, **lagoons**, and saltwater marshes stretch across

Critical Thinking

What are some other ways people can share their heritage?

▲ Factories like this one, Slater's Mill, grew up all over New England years ago. Slater's Mill was the first.

Did You Know? More than 127,000 people in Rhode Island speak Mon-Khmer. Mon-Khmer is the twenty-sixth most commonly spoken language in the United States.

⚡ **Critical Thinking**

In what way has Rhode Island changed since the time of Roger Williams? In what way is it the same?

Did You Know?

Here's to you, belov'd Rhode Island,
With your Hills and Ocean Shore,
We are proud to hail you "Rhody"
And your Patriots of yore.
First to claim your Independence,
Rich your heritage and fame,
The smallest State, smallest State
and yet so great, so great,
We will glorify your name.

"Rhode Island," words and music
by T. Clark Brown
adopted as the state song in 1946

the coastline. The waters are filled with bluefish, butterfish, bluefin tuna, and swordfish. Lobsters, clams, crabs, and other shellfish can be found off the Rhode Island shore.

Rocky cliffs are found on the islands and along the shore of Narragansett Bay. The islands have a history of mystery (MIS-ter-ee) and danger. About 200 ships have been wrecked along the rocky island shorelines.

The Eastern New England upland covers the northwestern corner of Rhode Island. Here the land rises from 200 feet above sea level in the east to 800 feet above sea level in the northwest. Ponds and lakes dot the area.

What is the climate of Rhode Island? The climate of Rhode Islands is much like its people, the same yet very different from place to place. Warming winds from the Atlantic Ocean and Narragansett Bay give Rhode Island a mild climate.

About 44 inches of rain falls on Rhode Island each year. Its growing season lasts about 200 days. Snow falling in western Rhode Island often changes to rain in the east as the air is warmed by ocean winds. Hurricanes and coastal storms are a seasonal threat.

☆ ☆ ☆ ☆ ☆ ☆ ☆ ☆ ☆

Cattails swaying in the wind, grand resorts filled with sun-loving tourists, sailboats, busy factories, nets filled with fish, different **cultures**, beliefs and ideas. This, and much more, is Rhode Island.

★ ★ ★ ★ ★ ★ ★ ★ **THINK ABOUT IT!** ★ ★ ★ ★ ★ ★ ★ ★ ★

1. Why is Roger Williams called the "father of Rhode Island?"

2. Give three ways in which the people of Rhode Island share their heritage.

3. How do winds from the Atlantic Ocean affect the climate of Rhode Island?

Workbook p. 33
Self-Check

MASSACHUSETTS

★ ★

GEOFACTS
- capital: Boston
- statehood: 1788 (6th)
- rank in size: 45th
- rank in population: 13th (urban 84%, rural 16%)
- U.S. representatives: 10
- motto: "By the Sword We Seek Peace, But Peace Only with Liberty"

▲ Boston's narrow, cobbled streets

▲ The Boston skyline is both modern and historical.

"He said to his friend, "If the British march
By land or sea from the town to-night,
Hang a lantern aloft in the belfry arch
Of the North Church tower as a signal light, —
One, if by land, and two, if by sea . . ."

from "Paul Revere's Ride"
by Henry Wadsworth Longfellow

On April 18, 1775, Paul Revere became an American hero. On that night, Revere rode to Lexington, Massachusetts, to warn the people that the British would soon attack.

Massachusetts borders the Atlantic Ocean. Paul Revere had set up a way to be told how the British forces would be coming. He placed a person high in the bell tower of a church. From there, it could be seen if the British forces were coming across land or by the ocean. Lanterns hung in the tower and glowing in the night sky became Revere's signal.

Massachusetts was a leader in America's fight for freedom. Five years before Paul Revere's ride, an African American named Crispus Attucks along with four other colonists died when British soldiers fired on a group of Americans. This event led many Americans to think that English soldiers did not belong in America.

How else did Massachusetts lead America's freedom fight? On a cold night in December 1773, fifty colonists quietly boarded an English ship

Critical Thinking

Why do you think the people of Boston have saved buildings that were built many years ago?

Places to See! People to Know!

▶ Black Heritage Trail, Boston — walking tour that explores the history of African Americans in Boston during the 1800s

▶ Plymouth Rock, Plymouth — site of the Pilgrim's settlement

▶ Susan B. Anthony (b. 1820) — tireless fighter for women's rights

▶ Squanto (b. 1585) — Native American who saved settlers from certain death by teaching them how to plant corn and find game and fish

GeoWords
countryside — land in a rural area
cape — a piece of land that stretches out into the sea or lake
sound — a narrow area of water
surf — waves that break on a shore

Critical Thinking
Which area of Massachusetts would you like to visit? Why?

▲ Clocktowers like this one, with architectural details that reflect ancient Greek designs, are common in urban Massachusetts.

Did You Know? Three presidents named John were born in Massachusetts. They were John Adams (2nd president; 1797-1801), John Quincy Adams (6th president; 1825-1829), and John Kennedy (35th president; 1961-1963)

loaded with tea. The English had placed a tax on tea. Many people in Massachusetts drank tea. They did not like having to pay a tax to England. The colonists threw all the boxes of tea in Boston Harbor. The colonists called this the "Boston Tea Party."

The Boston Tea Party was the colonists' way to protest, or speak out against, the laws the English government made for the colonies. Two years later, on the night of Paul Revere's ride, the first shots of the American Revolution rang out across the Massachusetts **countryside** (KUN-tree-syd).

What is Boston like today? Boston is a city that blends 350 years of history with modern computer and banking businesses (BIZ-neh-sez). Red brick buildings from years past stand next to tall, new buildings made of glass and steel. Outdoor markets offer many fruits and vegetables for sale.

Boston is the largest city in Massachusetts. It has a population of more than 550,000 people. Today, Irish Americans make up Boston's largest ethnic group. Boston's festivals and foods tell about customs from all over the world. Some of the most colorful festivals are held in Boston's Chinatown. The rich ethnic heritage of Boston reaches out to all of Massachusetts. People from England, Greece, Puerto Rico, Poland, Italy, and many other countries have made their home in Massachusetts. Today, French is the state's most commonly spoken language after English. And yet, the Greek language is spoken by more than 388,000 people in Massachusetts.

Why is Massachusetts called "the Bay State?" About 1,500 miles of coastline stretch along the many bays that form the eastern edge of Massachusetts. From rocky, weather-beaten shorelines to sun-washed sandy beaches, the coastlines of Massachusetts are enjoyed by people from all over the United States.

Reaching out into the Atlantic Ocean is **Cape** Cod. Cape Cod formed over many years as the ocean piled sand upon sand against a ridge of rocks. The coastline of Cape Cod slowly shifts as the ocean molds and reshapes it. Across the beaches of Cape Cod, children build castles in the sand and enjoy the red glow of evening sunsets.

Nantucket **Sound**, Nantucket Island, and Martha's Vineyard are all found south of Cape Cod. These areas are important to the tourist economy of Massachusetts. People must take a ferry (FER-ee), or boat, to enjoy the sun and **surf** found on the two islands of Nantucket and Martha's Vineyard. People also may watch whales play in the waters of Nantucket Sound.

What is Massachusetts land like west of the Atlantic Coast? Cape Cod, Martha's Vineyard, and Nantucket Island are part of the state's coastal lowland region. Low hills, swamp areas, and small lakes and ponds spread across the coastal lowland. To the west of this area lies the eastern New England upland.

Across the eastern New England upland are reminders of the glaciers that carved the land more than 10,000 years ago. The slow-moving glaciers left behind large rocks at the bottom of low, rocky hills. Farmers have found the stony soil of this region hard to plow and plant.

West of the eastern New England upland lies the Connecticut valley. Stretching 20 miles across, this region is bordered by hills on the east, west, and north. Farmers grow tobacco, potatoes, onions, and other crops in the fertile river valley soil. Water power from the Connecticut River helped small factory towns along the river grow into important cities.

To the far west lie the Berkshire Hills. Here old, but charming, covered bridges cross clear streams. Beyond the bridges lie small towns where stone churches and village squares still can be found. Each spring people boil the sap from the sugar maple trees that stretch across this forested area to make sweet maple syrup.

☆ ☆ ☆ ☆ ☆ ☆ ☆ ☆ ☆

Massachusetts offers a special blend of history, ethnic pride, and progress with a land that holds its own special beauty. Its name is taken from the Massachusetts Indians who once called the land their home. Massachusetts means "place of the great hill." Today, just as in the past, Massachusetts is a place where great things happen.

Critical Thinking

How is the way of life in Berkshire Hills different from the way of life on Martha's Vineyard?

▲ Whale watching is a special treat in Massachusetts.

Did You Know? In 1986, workers breaking ground to build homes near Plymouth found arrow heads and spear points. The workers had come across the oldest Native American site in Massachusetts. The Native Americans had live in the area about 7,000 years ago.

★ ★ ★ ★ ★ ★ ★ **THINK ABOUT IT!** ★ ★ ★ ★ ★ ★ ★ ★

1. How was Massachusetts a leader in America's fight for freedom?

2. In which land region is Martha's Vineyard?

3. What kind of power did the factories along the Connecticut River use?

Workbook p. 34
Self-Check

CONNECTICUT

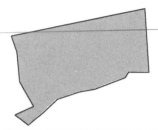

★ ★

GEOFACTS
- capital: Hartford
- statehood: 1788 (5th)
- rank in size: 48th
- rank in population: 27th (urban 79%, rural 21%)
- U.S. representatives: 6
- motto: "He Who Transplanted Still Sustains"

▲ Coast Guard training in Connecticut

▲ Mystic Seaport, Connecticut is a living example of what life was like in a Yankee seaport village in the 1800s.

GeoWords
suburbs — a city or town built near or next to a major city

⚡ **Critical Thinking**

How can small towns be a link to the past and a bridge the future?

Places to See! People to Know!

▶ Dinosaur State Park, Rocky Hill — dinosaur museum showing footprints from 185 million years ago

▶ Harriet Beecher Stowe House, Nook Farm — home of the author of Uncle Tom's Cabin

▶ Barbara McClintock (b.1902) — received the Nobel prize in medicine (1983)

▶ Thirman L. Milner (b.1933) — first African American to be elected mayor of a New England city (Hartford, 1981)

A low stony wall winds across a farmer's field in western Connecticut. In the fall, leaves of many colors dance and fall upon the wall. In the winter, mounds of snow pack the wall, turning it from stony gray to snowy white.

Long ago, a farmer used jagged rocks of granite to build the wall. It marked the limit of the farmer's land. Today, many of these stone walls can be found in the forests and fields of Connecticut. They tell of Connecticut's past and of the people who came to farm the land.

Connecticut is a state rich in history and beauty. Charming small towns dot the countryside. These small towns, with their freshly mowed lawns and tall church bell towers, are a link to America's past. At the same time, they also are a bridge to America's future.

Does Connecticut have any large cities? Connecticut's largest city is Bridgeport. It has a population of about 141,000 people. Four other cities in Connecticut have populations of more than 100,000. These cities are Hartford, New Haven, Waterbury, and Stamford.

Connecticut's **suburbs** (SUB-urbs) have problems meeting the growing need for housing and schools. At the same time, Connecticut's large cities have the problem of not being able to pay for the cost of running the cities. Connecticut's state government is working to deal with the problem of its aging cities and growing suburbs.

THE PEOPLE'S PUBLISHING GROUP, INC.   *Our United States Geography: Our Regions and People*

When did people first settle in Connecticut? People from Europe came to Connecticut in the 1600s. At that time, about 7,000 Native Americans lived across the land. The Native Americans were members of the Algonquian-speaking tribes.

At first, Native Americans greeted the people from Europe. They saw the new settlers as helpers against warring tribes. Yet, soon, warring between the tribes and the wish of some white settlers to rid the land of Native Americans led to the death of many Native Americans in Connecticut.

Who were Connecticut's first settlers from Europe? A group of people called Puritans (PYOOR-ih-tans) came to Connecticut in 1636. Only those who believed as the Puritans did could live in the colony. Puritan boys worked in the fields, chopped firewood, and took care of the horses and cows. Puritan girls helped in the home by cooking, washing, and taking care of the younger children.

School was important to the Puritans. In 1650, Connecticut passed a law that said every town with fifty or more families must hire a teacher. Both boys and girls learned to read and write. In these strict Puritan schools, children sat on wooden benches. Logs cut in half served as desks.

By 1800, some families from Connecticut looked westward for more space and better farmland. With the farmers moved a Puritan belief in hard work and a stern God. Pulled by horse and oxen, Connecticut wagons pushed into Wisconsin and Kansas and as far west as California.

What kind of land did the people moving westward leave behind? Connecticut is a small state. Fifty-three Connecticuts could fit into the state of Texas. Molded by glaciers long ago, Connecticut is a land of great beauty where the change of season brings new delights.

The Taconic Mountains are found in Connecticut's far west. Here, **ravines** cut into forests of beech, birch, maple, and oak. Deer, fox, mink, and woodchucks are sheltered by the lush forests of this region.

The mighty Connecticut River cuts across the state from north to south. Along the river is Connecticut's central valley. Corn, potatoes, tobacco, and other crops grow in the fertile soil of this valley region.

Chains of low, wooded hills lie to the west and east of the central valley. This is Connecticut's western New England upland. The soil here is thin and stony. Rivers flow across this region's **ridges** and steep hills.

The eastern New England upland covers most of eastern Connecticut. This area's forests, narrow rivers and low hills are a woodsman's dream.

Connecticut's low coastal plain stretches along the coastline of Long Island Sound. Beaches and state parks along the coast offer a time for fun for people from nearby cities. People are working to save the few salt marshes that remain in Connecticut. They would like to keep the salt marshes as a refuge for terns, gulls, sandpipers, and other shorebirds.

Critical Thinking
In what way is Connecticut a contrast between the past and the present?

▲ Yale University in New Haven, Connecticut, attracts students from across the country and across the globe.

Did You Know? Many things people use everyday were first made in Connecticut, including pins, buttons, doorbells, and tires.

Critical Thinking

What is one steady habit the people of a state might have?

Did You Know? When the *Amistad* landed on Connecticut shores in 1839, the surviving enslaved Africans aboard demanded to be returned to Africa. Many people in Connecticut could not believe the way the people from Africa were forced to live on the *Amistad*. They hired lawyers to plead the case of the Africans. The Connecticut courts ruled in favor of the Africans. Thirty-five men, women, and children were returned to their homeland.

What is the climate like in Connecticut? Connecticut's climate changes with the seasons. And yet, at times, Connecticut's climate seems to change for no reason at all.

In 1876, Mark Twain wrote that he had "counted one hundred and thirty-six different kinds of weather inside of twenty-four hours." He spoke of the wind sweeping around from place to place. He went on to joke about snow, rain, hail, and very dry weather following earthquakes, lighting, and thunder.

At times, Connecticut's climate can be full of surprises. Great snowstorms can shut down cities. Times of little rain can ruin crops and limit drinking water. Yet, most often Connecticut's climate is mild. Most days are not very hot or very cold.

Today, people from many other states and countries enjoy the climate and scenic beauty of Connecticut. From its rural charm to its exciting cities, today's Connecticut holds on to the ways of the past while looking toward a bright future. Connecticut, "the land of steady habits," holds true to its work-hard heritage.

★ ★ ★ ★ ★ ★ ★ ★ **THINK ABOUT IT!** ★ ★ ★ ★ ★ ★ ★ ★

1. Name two things from the past that still can be seen in Connecticut?

2. What five land regions make up Connecticut?

3. What joke did Mark Twain make about Connecticut's climate?

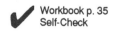

Workbook p. 35
Self-Check

THE PEOPLE'S PUBLISHING GROUP, INC.   *Our United States Geography: Our Regions and People*

NEW YORK

★ ★

GEOFACTS
- capital: Albany
- statehood: 1788 (11th)
- rank in size: 30th
- rank in population: 2nd (urban 84%, rural 16%)
- U.S. representatives: 31
- motto: "Ever Upward"

▲ The Statue of Liberty in New York Harbor

▲ The Brooklyn Bridge is a landmark in the largest, busiest city in the country, New York City.

❝Give me your tired, your poor,
Your huddled masses yearning to breathe free,❞

Emma Lazarus

These well-known words are found on the Statue of Liberty. They have called out to the millions of people who have crossed the ocean to live in America. They are meant as a welcome to people seeking a better life.

New York has been a place of welcome for people from all over the world. People passing the Statue of Liberty in New York Harbor often enter New York City. Some people leave New York to settle in other states. Others make their home in New York City. Today, one out of every two people living in New York City either is from another country or has a parent who is from another country.

New York City is the largest city in the United States. More than 7 million people live in the city. About 24,000 people live in each square mile of New York City. Only eight states have populations greater than the population of this giant and very busy city.

More than 17 million people visit New York City each year. They come to see the many museums (myoo-ZEE-ums), theaters (THEE-uh-ters), sports events, and stores of the city called "the Big Apple."

Is New York City the same everywhere? New York City is divided into five boroughs (BUR-ohs), or smaller city areas. They are Brooklyn, Queens, the Bronx, Staten Island, and Manhattan. Each borough has its own special history. Each borough has its own special ethnic heritage.

Critical Thinking
What are some problems a city the size of New York might have?

Places to See! People to Know!
▶ Ellis Island, New York City — a port of passage for more than 12 million immigrants entering the United States
▶ Jewish Burial Ground, Manhattan — oldest cemetery in New York (New York City also has many old African American, Native American, and colonial burial sites)
▶ Shirley Anita St. Hill Chisholm (b.1924) — first African American woman elected to the U.S. House of Representatives
▶ Theodore Roosevelt (b.1858) — 26th president of the United States, and a great outdoorsman

GeoWords
palisades — a line of steep rock areas
cliffs — a wall of rock

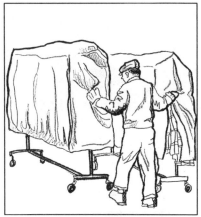

▲ New York leads the nation in the production of clothing.

Three of the tallest buildings in the world are found in Manhattan. They reach high into the New York sky. Many theaters are found on a street called Broadway. Here people enjoy some of the best music and acting in the country. People can watch graceful ballet dancers or hear a grand concert at Lincoln Center. Beyond Manhattan's center are Harlem and Chinatown.

Many Irish, Italian, and Jewish families call Brooklyn home. Bedford-Stuyvesant in Brooklyn is home to the city's largest African American population. At the southern tip of Brooklyn is Coney Island. Here, New Yorkers share the beach and boardwalk with people from everywhere.

Queens is home to many Asian Americans. Tucked in busy Queens is the Queens' Jamaica Bay Wildlife Refuge. This refuge offers a safe place for wild geese and other animals. Hiking trails offer visitors a glimpse of animals not often seen in a city.

Across New York City are places of great wealth and places of great poverty. It is a city where homeless people share the streets with people who live in grand homes. New York City is like a small window on the country. Its problems and dreams are shared by people across America.

What is the climate like in New York City? Warm ocean currents take the chill out of the cold New York air. Cities to the north of New York City have colder winters and cooler summers. The cities of Rochester and Buffalo often are buried under winter snowstorms. More than 100 inches of snow falls in northern New York each year.

The glaciers that covered New York more than 10,000 years ago left about 8,000 lakes. Resorts along many of New York's scenic lakes bring summer joy to people from New York and other states. From a small lake called Tear-of-the-Cloud flows New York's longest river, the Hudson River.

The Hudson River flows from east-central New York southward to New York City. Great **palisades** (PAL-ih-sayds) are found along the river. The Mohawk River winds its way across central New York to empty into the Hudson River. These rivers, along with their valleys, have served as trade routes and early pathways for railroads, canals, and roads. Today, ocean-going ships can sail 150 miles north on the Hudson River.

Sun rays dance across powerful waterfalls found in many of New York's rivers. Here, mighty rivers like the Hudson and quiet streams hidden in New York's forests tumble over water-worn rock **cliffs**. One of the grandest waterfalls, Niagara Falls, is found in western New York. About 15 million people visit Niagara Falls each year. Here, people can see nature's fury as rushing waters crash onto huge rocks far below.

Is New York mostly a mountain or coastal plain area? New York is a scenic mix of coastal plain, lowlands, and mountains. The Atlantic Coastal Plain covers a small area in southern New York. Both Staten Island and Long Island are part of New York's coastal plain area.

The New England upland found on New York's eastern border is an area of hills and low mountains. This region borders the Hudson-Mohawk lowland. This important river valley serves as a trade route between the Atlantic Ocean and the Great Lakes. New York is the only state that touches both the Atlantic Ocean and the Great Lakes.

To the north lies New York's Adirondack (ad-ir-ON-dak) upland. Here, mountain peaks rise more than 4,000 feet above sea level. Some of oldest rocks in North America can be found in this region. This region is well-known for its sparkling lakes, splashing waterfalls, and purple mountain peaks.

☆ ☆ ☆ ☆ ☆ ☆ ☆ ☆ ☆

The quiet forests and farmland that cover much of New York offer a sharp contrast to New York's noisy urban areas. From its busy banking centers to its small towns to its harbor stores, New York reaches out to the

Critical Thinking
In what way does New York reach out to the world?

▲ 60% of all American ducks are raised on Long Island for their meat and eggs.

Did You Know? "The land of Ganono-o, or 'Empire State,' as you love to call it, was once laced by our trails from Albany to Buffalo — trails that we had trod for centuries — trails worn so deep by the feet of the Iroquois that they became your own roads of travel."

★ ★ ★ ★ ★ ★ ★ ★ **THINK ABOUT IT!** ★ ★ ★ ★ ★ ★ ★ ★

1. What are the five main areas of New York City?

2. How did glaciers affect the land the makes up New York?

3. Tell three things about one of New York's land regions.

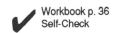 Workbook p. 36
Self-Check

The Heartland ★ ★ ★ ★ ★ ★ ★ ★ ★ ★ ★ ★ ★ ★ ★ ★

Outside the small town of Wolcott, Indiana, stands a farmhouse. It's not big, as farmhouses go. Yet, under its roof were raised many children who knew the meaning of morning chores and a hot meal served around a large table at noon everyday. The walls of the farmhouse are filled with the joy of an evening laugh, Christmas mornings and family get-togethers where cousins, aunts, uncles, and grandparents shared mounds of food and good times. Also behind the paint and wallpaper is the sound of tears when times were not so good.

There was the day when a "twister," one of those powerful Midwest tornadoes, took the barn. Those out in the field held on to trees with all their might. The house was saved, some animals too. And the time when the hay wagon caught on fire. Two boys nearly died in that one.

Over the years, more than one hundred of them, this white farmhouse has stood in honor to America's Heartland. Family, hard work, a tie to the land, and a sense of duty to the country made America's Heartland just that, the heart of the country. Today, new homes with children playing in fenced-in yards lie close to that old farmhouse.

Capping the Heartland are the Great Lakes. These five lakes, Lake Superior, Michigan, Huron, Ontario, and Erie, are the largest group of freshwater lakes in the world. They were formed by melting glaciers more than 11,000 years ago.

Around the Great Lakes great cities grew, such as Chicago, Milwaukee, and Detroit. Today, just as in the past, the Great Lakes are the Heartland's lifeline to the Atlantic. Across the Heartland lies America's cornbelt. Here, row after row of tall green corn ripples in warm summer winds. Fall harvest time brings the whir of tractors and the cutting of dried corn turned golden by time.

Early Native Americans living across the Heartland built high burial mounds. Early white emigrants built homes of sod and wood. Later, great buildings reaching many stories into the sky filled the skyline of large Heartland cities. Links to the past, and a look to the future, are just some of the themes that tie the states of America's Heartland, a very vital part of the country.

WISCONSIN

★ ★

GEOFACTS
- capital: Madison
- statehood: 1848 (30th)
- rank in size: 26th
- rank in population:16th (urban 66%, rural 34%)
- U.S. representatives: 9
- motto: "Forward"

▲ Wisconsin has many dairy farms.

▲ A boat tour along the Wisconsin Dells, sandstone formed by glaciers.

A special place, called Wildcat Mountain, is found in central Wisconsin. The road leading to its peak winds and twists as if the climb is too hard. As mountains go, Wildcat Mountain is not very high. At its highest point, it only reaches 1,238 feet above sea level. Yet, from its top, the state of Wisconsin stretches as far as the eye can see.

Below Wildcat Mountain lies the quiet town of Ontario. Beyond the town, farm fields and forests checker the land. Some of the fields are plowed by horses guided by bearded Amish men. Other fields fall to the noise of a red, green or blue tractor.

What is Wisconsin like? Farm fields and farmhouse porch swings still are found across much of Wisconsin. Wisconsin is a state where hay and cornfields bend and turn along a hillside. The fields tell the tale of glaciers that carve the state thousands of years ago. Left behind were the valleys and lakes that today burst with scenic Wisconsin beauty.

Dotting the land here and there are red barns built years ago by rough and sun-touched hands. The barns are a sign of hard work and a time-honored belief in family life. Yet, at times, the red on the barn has faded. Change and growing cities also are a part of Wisconsin.

Wisconsin is a leading state in the canning of peas, sweet corn and other vegetables. Wisconsin has been called "the Dairy State." It leads the country the sale of such dairy products as milk, cheese and butter. One city, Reedsburg, calls itself "the butter capital of the world."

⚡ **Critical Thinking**
What kinds of contrasts are found in Wisconsin?

Places to See! People to Know!
- ▶ Old World Wisconsin, Eagle — Museum site honoring Wisconsin's early ethnic heritage
- ▶ Taliesin, Spring Green — country home and school of Frank Lloyd Wright, the world-famous architect from Wisconsin.
- ▶ Shirley S. Abrahamson (b.1933) — first woman elected to the Wisconsin Supreme Court
- ▶ Josh Sanford (b.1919) — was the only Native American pilot with the World War II Flying Tigers, an ace flying team

blu

⚡ **Critical Thinking**
What is Chief Little Elk saying? Does his message still hold a meaning for us today?

▲ Celebrating Dutch heritage in Wisconsin

Did You Know? Twelve thousand Wisconsin men died fighting in America's Civil War. Wisconsin lost more men in this war than in any war since 1865. One Civil War hero from Wisconsin was Arthur McArthur, who won the Congressional Medal of Honor. His son, Douglas MacArthur (who changed the spelling of his name) became one of America's highest ranking generals.

Do farms cover most of Wisconsin? Lush forest of pine, birch and oak spread across half of Wisconsin. From central to northern Wisconsin, rolling forested hills are covered by a patchwork of color each fall. Ferns, blackberries, raspberries, and many other bird delights line the edges of the forests.

One of Wisconsin's leading industries is the making of paper. Paper mills are found in the Fox River and upper Wisconsin River Valleys. Mill workers make such paper products as tissue paper, boxes and wrapping paper. Wisconsin supplies about 12% of the country's paper needs.

Each year Wisconsin's forests, lakes and rivers draw people looking for a quiet vacation (va-KA-shun) spot. Northern Wisconsin calls out to those who love unending forest beauty. A quick look will catch the sight of deer bounding over a fallen log. Deer, beavers, foxes and coyotes all can be found in Wisconsin's forested areas.

Why is Wisconsin called "the Badger State?" A badger (BAD-jer) is a small, unfriendly animal about the size of a raccoon. Badgers are found across Wisconsin. But, this is not the reason Wisconsin is often called the Badger state. The real reason has its roots in Wisconsin's rich history.

Back in the early 1800's a **mineral** (MIN-er-al) called galena (gah-LE-nah) was found in Wisconsin. From 1825 to 1828 the number of miners living in Wisconsin's southern **prairies** (PRAIR-ees) grew from one hundred to ten thousand.

Often, miners slept inside the area they had dug. These were called dugouts. The dugouts had the same look as hollow areas dug by Wisconsin's badgers. Soon, Wisconsin came to be known as a state of badgers or "the Badger State."

How did the mining boom affect the people of Wisconsin? In 1825, the Erie Canal opened. The Erie Canal became a bridge between the Hudson River and Lake Erie. Farmers from New England states traveled across this waterway to Wisconsin. Along with the people came a belief in town government, farming, and schools for children.

For years, Native Americans living in Wisconsin watched white settlement with growing concern. At first, the Winnebago, Dakota and Menominee Indians traded furs with the French. Soon English fur traders traded bullets and other small items for beaver and otter pelts, or animal skins.

By 1800, loggers, miners and farmers had moved into Wisconsin. Also moving west were the Sauk, Fox, Kickapoo and other Native Americans forced from their eastern lands. Fights over who should live on the land sparked many battles. One such battle was the Black Hawk War, fought between Natives Americans and the United States Army.

Does Wisconsin have any large cities? Wisconsin's largest city, Milwaukee, has a population of about 628,000 people. Milwaukee began as a small settlement in 1839. Soon many people from Germany, Ireland,

Sweden and Norway settled in Milwaukee. In the 1950s and 1960s farm workers looking to find work in the city came from Mexico to Milwaukee.

Milwaukee is a city the blends the sounds of busy factories with the music of violins and the dancing of the Milwaukee Ballet. Cream-colored granite blocks and bricks grace many of its old and grand buildings. Yet, Milwaukee is having to deal with the problems that come with changing times and an aging city.

Wisconsin is a land of more than 20,000 miles of rivers and 15,000 lakes. The waters that grace Wisconsin land offer a cool drink to cattle and a day's joy to boaters.

Wisconsin's cold winters and warm summers offer their share of surprises. Great heaps of snow can fall, closing schools and taming Wisconsin's cities. Floods, rare but powerful, can wash away farmer's fields and turn calm rivers into raging waters. Yet, most of the time, Wisconsin's tall sandstone bluffs, sparkling lakes and quiet valleys offer a scenic playground for all to enjoy.

Critical Thinking
Tell what a day in January might be like in Wisconsin.

Did You Know? Chief Little Elk, after the Black Hawk War, said, "The first white man we knew was a Frenchman....He smoked his pipe with us, sang and danced with us...but he wanted to buy no land. The 'Redcoat' came next...But never asked us to sell our country to him! Next came the 'Bluecoat' and no sooner had he seen a small portion of our country, than he wished us to sell it ALL to him. Why do you wish to add our small country to yours, already so large?"

THINK ABOUT IT!

1. Name three kinds of things you might see in Wisconsin.

2. Why do you think so many people visit Wisconsin each year?

3. Why is Wisconsin sometimes known as "the Dairy State?"

Workbook p. 39
Self-Check

ILLINOIS

★ ★

GEOFACTS
- capital: Springfield
- statehood: 1818 (21st)
- rank in size: 24th
- rank in population: 6th (urban 85%, rural 15%)
- U.S. representatives: 20
- motto: "State Sovereignty, National Union"

▲ A Native American pow wow

▲ Chicago's skyline rises above Lake Michigan.

⚡ Critical Thinking

In what way could Lincoln's words about "a house divided" still have meaning for us today? (see page 89)

Places to See! People to Know!

▶ Cahokia Mounds, Collinsville — site of large Native American settlement; about sixty-five burial mounds are preserved there

▶ Lovejoy Monument, Alton — honors the antislavery actions of Elijah Lovejoy

▶ Gwendolyn Brooks (b.1917)—poet laureate of Illinois; wrote poems expressing African American concerns

▶ Carl Sandburg (b.1878) — well-known poet who received the 1940 Pulitzer prize for a book about Abraham Lincoln

In 1831, a young man walked into the quiet, small village of New Salem. He liked what he saw and decided to stay. At first he got a job as a clerk in the general store. The people of New Salem enjoyed the humor and honesty of the young man. They decided to place him in charge of the village post office.

This young man had not always lived in Illinois. He had been born in Kentucky. He moved to Illinois with his family at the age of twenty-one. People soon knew him for his easy laugh and speaking ability. It is said that he would walk 15 miles from New Salem to Springfield just to borrow a book.

As time went on, the young man studied law. People would come from miles around to hear him speak. In 1860, this tall man, who so liked to make fun of how he looked, became president of the United States. His election helped to divide a country and spark a war that would forever change the country. He would become known as one of America's greatest presidents. His name was Abraham Lincoln.

How did the election of Abraham Lincoln help to divide the country? Seven states left the United States government shortly before Lincoln became president. Soon, four more would leave. The eleven states formed a new government called the Confederate States of America. A month after Lincoln became president, the first shots of the Civil War were fired.

Before being elected, Lincoln had stated that "A house divided against itself cannot stand." In his speech, Lincoln was talking about half the country being free and half owning enslaved Africans. Yet, Lincoln could have said the same words, with perhaps a different meaning, about his home state of Illinois.

How was Illinois divided? The beliefs of the people in Illinois had their roots in where they once lived. People living in southern Illinois had moved there from America's southern states. They had traveled along the National Road. With many of the people came a belief in slavery.

Many people came to northern Illinois from Ireland, Germany, Poland, and other countries in Europe. Others came from the New England states and New York. They came looking for work in the factories of the northern cities. They also came to farm Illinois land. At first. they cleared wooded areas. When the woods were gone, they farmed the prairie.

The people of northern Illinois did not agree about slavery with the people from southern Illinois. This caused many problems. Today, more than 100 years later, there is still **regionalism** (REE-jon-al-is-um) in Illinois. Only today, the state tends to divide itself between the large city of Chicago and downstate Illinois.

How does regionalism show itself in Illinois? The city of Chicago is very different from the rolling cornfields of southern Illinois. Chicago is the city where towering steel and glass buildings called skyscrapers (SKY-skray-pers) were first built. Today, some of the world's tallest buildings are found in Chicago.

People from Chicago speak in a different way from the people in southern Illinois. The names given to things, how people are greeted, and the sound of words is not quite the same from northern to southern Illinois.

Chicago is the third-largest city in the country. Some people from southern Illinois feel the needs of Chicago often lead the state. Chicago and its suburbs have a greater population than other areas in Illinois. Yet, the needs of a large city and the needs of a rural area are not always the same.

What are the different areas in Illinois? Illinois can be divided into four regions. Chicago is in the northern region. It began as a trading post started by an Haitian named du Sable. Du Sable traded with Native Americans living in the area. Du Sable sold his trading post and left the area in 1800. Today, the land his trading post once sat on is part of Chicago's richest area.

Beyond Chicago and its suburbs, northern Illinois is a land of rolling hills. The gentle slopes of this region were a gift of the glaciers that cut across this land many thousands of years ago. Found in northwest Illinois is the small town of Galena. This town was named after the mineral mined there for many years.

Between the Illinois and Mississippi rivers lies the western region. Here the thrills of a riverboat ride blend with an area of amazing history and beauty. The Mormon settlement of Nauvoo is located in this area. This

GeoWords
regionalism — beliefs, values, and a way of life of most people in a region

Critical Thinking
In what ways is Illinois like every part of America?

▲ The future unfolds at Chicago's science museum.

Did You Know? Quincy, Illinois, was once a stop on the Underground Railroad. From Quincy, the route led to Galesburg, then to Chicago. It is believed that about 300 slaves gained their freedom by taking the Quincy route.

Critical Thinking
Why would winds from the Gulf of Mexico bring warm days and more rain to southern Illinois?

settlement lasted from 1839 to 1846. From Nauvoo, the Mormons moved 1,400 miles westward to Salt Lake City.

The Shawnee Hills stretch across southern Illinois. It is a region of valleys, river bluffs, and forest. A mild climate wraps this area. Winds from the Gulf of Mexico bring warmer days and more rain to this region than are found in northern Illinois.

Tucked between the northern, southern and western region is the central region. This is where the history of Abraham Lincoln can be found. This is where farm fields planted in soybeans and corn stretch across the flat land. Tall and flowing prairie grasses once graced the land. Today, family farms and small cities are found across this region.

☆ ☆ ☆ ☆ ☆ ☆ ☆ ☆ ☆

Illinois is in the center of America's Heartland. From the early Native American mounds in southern Illinois to Chicago's skyline of lights, Illinois holds a piece of every part of America. With it, Illinois extends its hand to a bright tomorrow.

Did You Know? Immigrants from Poland and Lithuania came to Illinois in the early 1900s. Many people in the state speak either Polish or Lithuanian as their first language.

★ ★ ★ ★ ★ ★ ★ ★   THINK ABOUT IT!   ★ ★ ★ ★ ★ ★ ★ ★ ★

1. Why is Abraham Lincoln remembered as one of America's greatest presidents?

2. Give two examples of regionalism.

3. Why is it warmer in southern Illinois than in northern Illinois?

Workbook p. 40
Self-Check

INDIANA

★ ★

GEOFACTS
- capital: Indianapolis
- statehood: 1816 (19th)
- rank in size: 38th
- rank in population: 14th (urban 65%, rural 35%)
- U.S. representatives: 10
- motto: "Crossroads of America"

▲ The Indianapolis 500 is a world famous automobile race.

It's August in Indiana. From miles around, people are traveling to Indianapolis for the state fair. Here, children will tingle with delight as they ride high on a shiny ferris wheel. Some will ride the pretty, plastic horses that go up and down to the jingle of music.

Some people will watch the hog and cattle judging contests. They will see judges walk slowly around one animal and then another. How does the animal stand? Is the color right? How has the animal been cared for? Jittery boys and girls will watch from the side. Will the blue ribbon go to their hog, or will that other child's hog win the prize?

The state fair is a part of Indiana life. It does not matter if a person lives in a busy city or on a busy farm. From its pie-making contests to its dart-throwing games, the Indiana State Fair is great fun! It also offers Indiana a time to show pride in its rural heritage.

Is Indiana mostly rural or made up mostly of cities? Most of the people in Indiana live in cities. Yet, much of Indiana is made up of small, family farms. The farmers get up at sunrise, sometimes earlier, to milk their cows. They clean their barns, farm their fields and then return to the barn each evening to milk again.

It really does not matter which day it is. It does matter what the weather is like. It could be one of Indiana's hot, humid summer days when a cold ice tea brings a sigh of relief. Or it could be one of Indiana's cold winter days when windswept snow covers the barnyard, and a sip of hot

Critical Thinking

Why do you think so many people from the city also go to Indiana's state fair?

Places to See! People to Know!

▶ Tippecanoe Battlefield and Museum, Battle Ground — site of the 1811 battle between General Harrison and the brother of Tecumseh; the battle led to the defeat of Native American claims of Indiana land.

▶ Madonna of the Trails, Richmond — statue honoring pioneer women

▶ Cole Porter (b.1891) — famed song writer

▶ Tecumseh (b.1765?) — Native American leader of the Shawnee Indians who worked to unite Native American tribes against white settlement

GeoWords
caverns — caves
shallow — not very deep

coffee makes everything seem warmer. The cows will be waiting for the farmer. The milk truck will come.

What is the land of Indiana like? Indiana has three main land regions. Part of Indiana's northern border runs along 40 miles of Lake Michigan shoreline. Here the white-capped waves of Lake Michigan can be heard splashing against tan-colored sand dunes. Wind blowing off the lake turns and reshapes the sand. The tiny tracks of birds and washed sand castles dot the water's edge.

Beyond the dunes area lies Indiana's Great Lakes Plains. Many of Indiana's lakes are found in the state's northern area. Bluegills, sunfish, and bass fill Indiana's well-loved lakes.

Flatland covers most of Indiana's Great Lakes Plains. Farmers here plow and plant the region's fertile soil in rows of corn. Much of the corn is used to feed cattle and hogs. Some of the area's farms have been worked by the same families for many years.

South of the Great Lakes Plains lies the Till Plains region. Cattle graze on the low hillsides of this region. Indiana's best farmland is found in the Tills Region. Midsized cities also are found here. Covered bridges, parks and hiking trails dot this region of forest and farmland.

What kind of land is found in southern Indiana? The Lowlands covers much of southern Indiana. This area is a marvel of limestone **caverns** (KAV-ernz), rugged bluffs, and thick forests The magic of the fall season brings many visitors to this area.

Indiana's limestone caverns were formed 300 million years ago. At this time, a **shallow** (SHAL-oh) ocean bed covered southern Indiana. Limestone is made from the bones of tiny sea animals. It is rich in the soft colors of nature.

The beauty of Indiana limestone graces many of America's cities. Limestone from southern Indiana was used to build New York's Empire State Building. It also was used to build fourteen state capitol buildings.

At one time, forests covered most of Indiana. Over the years, Indiana's forests were lost to the sound of saws. Farmers settling in Indiana cleared many of the trees for farmland. Loggers harvested many of the trees. Indiana's forests also fell to raging forest fires.

Today, only about 17 percent of Indiana land is covered by forests. Most of these forest areas are found in southern Indiana.

Are there any large industries in Indiana? Indiana's first industries were found in its northern area. By 1906, U.S. Steel owned about 9,000 acres in northwest Indiana. There, it built the world's largest steel-making factory.

U.S. Steel planned a city for 100,000 people. The city was named Gary in honor of Elbert Gary, the head of U.S. Steel. In just fifteen years, Gary became Indiana's sixth-largest city.

Critical Thinking

How do you think the coming of farmers affected Indiana's Native Americans?

▲ Indiana's steel mills produce high qualilty metals.

Did You Know? The 1930s Depression, a time of few jobs and little money, was very hard on the people of Indiana. In 1932, one out of every four factory workers in Indiana did not have a job. Many farmers lost their farms because they could not pay their bills. One out of every two miners in southern Indiana was out of work.

Today, Indiana still leads the country in the making of steel. Other factories make cars and trucks. Miners in southern Indiana dig coal, sand, and limestone. Indianapolis is a leader in the making of medicines (MEH-dih-sinz). It also is the state's meat-packing center.

Why is Indiana called "the Hoosier State?" No one really knows where the term, "hoosier," (HOO-shur) came from. Perhaps is came from early settlers called hushers. Or perhaps it came from the greeting "who's yere," meaning "who's there?" Or perhaps it simply came from an 1830s gentleman named Samuel Hoosier who was the boss of a work team..

☆ ☆ ☆ ☆ ☆ ☆ ☆ ☆ ☆

Wherever it came from, the term Hoosiers today means a firm hand-shake and a warm greeting. The people of Indiana have lived during times of little rain, tornadoes, lack of city jobs, and rock-bottom farm prices. Yet, love of the land, a belief in hard work, and a look to the future have made Indiana one the country's leading states.

⚡ Critical Thinking

How is Indiana a contrast between a farm and a factory economy?

▲ All kinds of musical instruments are crafted in Indiana.

Did You Know? These words were spoken by Chief Tecumseh:

"My heart is a stone; heavy with sadness for my people, cold with the knowledge that no treaty will keep the whites out of our lands..."

★ ★ ★ ★ ★ ★ ★ ★ ★ **THINK ABOUT IT!** ★ ★ ★ ★ ★ ★ ★ ★ ★

1. What is one way Indiana shows its pride in a rural way of life?

2. What are the three main land regions in Indiana?

3. Why was the city of Indiana started?

 Workbook p. 41
Self-Check

MINNESOTA

★ ★

GEOFACTS
- capital: St. Paul
- statehood: 1858 (32nd)
- rank in size: 12th
- rank in population: 20th (urban 70%, rural 30%)
- U.S. representatives: 8
- motto: "The Star of the North"

▲ A beautiful small town scene in Minnesota

▲ Hungry Jack Lake

The joy of a winter game of hockey can be heard across the land called Minnesota. Ten people dressed in helmets and razor-sharp ice skates hold long sticks with a just-right curve at the end. To one side of the ice stands an ever-ready goalie. Across the ice stands another ever-watchful goalie. The puck drops and flashes of color whiz by a screaming crowd. With a clash of sticks and the scrape of skates, the players begin to fire the puck past the goalie and into the net.

Minnesota is a grand mix of thrilling hockey games and quiet moments of fishing along a tree-lined lake. It is a land of Paul Bunyan stories, iron-rich hills and dairy cattle. Moose, wolves and beavers roam the forests of Minnesota. Wildflowers paint the forest edge in splashes of color.

Do forests cover most of Minnesota? At one time, forests covered over 70 percent of Minnesota. Today, thick forests of red maple, black spruce, and white cedar cover about 17 percent of Minnesota. Years of logging and the clearing of land for farms cut down Minnesota's old forests.

In 1894, a raging forest fire blazed across five counties. Several small towns burned. Ashes were left where homes and stores once stood. More than 400 people died in the fire. Rotting logs and branches left by lumber companies helped to fuel the fire. Efforts to rebuild Minnesota's forests began after the 1894 fire.

Who came to farm Minnesota land? White settlement of Minnesota began in the fur-trading days of the 1600s. As early as 1659, French

⚡ **Critical Thinking**

How does Minnesota offer a contrast of seasons?

Places to See! People to Know!

▶ Afassiz National Wildlife Refuge, Thief River Falls — wildlife refuge for 245 birds

▶ Penumbra, St. Paul — Minnesota's only African American professional theater company; started in 1976 by artistic director Lou Bellamy; Penumbra offers plays that address African American heritage

▶ Ozawindib (b. 1800) — Ojibwa Indian who guided Henry Schoolcraft in discovering the source of the Mississippi River

▶ Charles Schultz (b. 1922) — creator of the *Peanuts* cartoon strip and such characters as Snoopy, Linus, and Charlie Brown

 THE PEOPLE'S PUBLISHING GROUP, INC. *Our United States Geography: Our Regions and People*

explorers (ex-PLOR-erz) met with the Dakota Indians. They returned to Canada with a boatload of furs.

Critical Thinking
How did furtrading change the Native American's way of life?

More fur traders called voyagers (VOY-ah-jerz) came to Minnesota. They traded pots, guns and knives for furs. The voyagers changed the way of life for the area's Native Americans. For many years, the Dakota and Ojibwa Indians were hired fur trappers.

In the years that followed, people from northeast America streamed into Minnesota. Crossing the Atlantic, people came from Sweden, Norway and Germany. Minnesota immigrants cleared the land, built log homes and made plans to stay. In 1850, about 4,000 whites lives in Minnesota. By 1857, the population of whites in Minnesota rose to 150,000.

Immigrants from the east brought great changes to the Native Americans who once lived freely across Minnesota. By 1862, white settlement forced most Native Americans off Minnesota land. That same year, Congress passed the Homestead (HOHM-sted) Act.

How did the Homestead Act affect Minnesota? The Homestead Act gave the head of a family 160 acres of free land. The person getting the land had to agree to farm it for five years. Between 1862 and 1865, more than one million acres of land in Minnesota was given away for free. By 1870, the population of Minnesota had jumped to 500,000 people.

The year of 1862 also brought railroad tracks to Minnesota. With them came great factories. Charles Pillsbury started a flour company that stills bears his name. His partner began the company known as General Mills. By 1870, Minnesota's rushing rivers powered more than 500 mills. Soon, the city of Minneapolis (mihn-nee-AH-poh-lis) became known as "Mill City."

▲ Stafford Rice Park in St. Paul

What is Minneapolis like today? Minneapolis is the state's largest city with more than 368,000 people. It lies across the Mississippi River from St. Paul. Together, they are called the Twin Cities.

The Twin Cities is the sixteenth-largest city area in the country. Close by is the Mall of America. Hundreds of stores as well as a park filled with rides, popcorn, and candy are found under its roof. The Twin Cities is a fast-growing area. It is a city where friendly smiles join with greetings spoken in many languages.

What is the land like around Minneapolis? Minneapolis is found in the state's Superior (soo-PEE-ree-or) Upland. This area covers most of northern and eastern Minnesota. In the far north, rugged forests color the area. Clear lakes and bubbling rivers cut across the red-toned, iron-rich earth.

Lake Itasca is found in central Minnesota. It is here that the Mississippi River is born. From Lake Itasca, the Mississippi River flows east, then south. It becomes wider and stronger as it winds its way southeast across the Twin Cities area. It flows on to form the southeast border of Minnesota.

Minnesota's Young Drift Plains region spreads across the southern and

Did You Know? Many folk tales are told about Paul Bunyan, the great lumberjack who cleared forests in Wisconsin and Minnesota. Paul Bunyan was a "bigger than life" man who did "bigger than life" deeds. It is said that, at the age of three months, he could not sleep, so he rolled around on the ground. This destroyed trees across four square miles. Or there was the time when Paul Bunyan and his oxen, named "Babe," logged 640 acres in one cut. Was Paul Bunyan a real person? What is your guess?

GeoWords
moraines — an area of gravel and sand pushed before or along the sides of glaciers
till — soil made up of sand, gravel and clay

western part of the state. Glaciers up to one mile thick melted in this region many thousands of years ago. As they melted, they gave a gift of fertile soil called drift to Minnesota. Golden wheat fields stretch across much of this area.

Moraines (MOH-raynz) are found in the central part of the Young Drift Plains. These hilly areas are scattered with sparkling lakes.

The northern part of this region was once a great lake bed. Treeless areas mixed with marshland blend to make the northern part of the Young Drift Plains region a Minnesota surprise. A 61,000-acre wildlife refuge is found here.

Two other land regions are found in Minnesota. The Driftless Area in southwest Minnesota is an area untouched by glaciers. Here swift-flowing rivers cut across deep valleys. To the southwest lies the Till Plains. Here, glaciers left waves of **till**.

☆ ☆ ☆ ☆ ☆ ☆ ☆ ☆

Looking across the Minnesota horizon, Dakota Indians long ago called it the land of "sky-tinted waters." Minnesota is a land where up to 22,000 lakes dot the land like stars on a moonless night. From its cold, snowy winters to its warm summers of gentle breezes, Minnesota is nature's present to the Heartland!

Critical Thinking
What do you think "sky-tinted waters" means?

▲ A one-room prairie schoolhouse

Did You Know? Minnesota is a land of immigrants. In the 1980s, more than 15,000 Hmong from Laos settled in Minnesota.

  **THINK ABOUT IT!** ★ ★ ★ ★ ★ ★ ★ ★ ★

1. Why does forest no longer cover most of Minnesota?

2. Name two ways immigrants changed Minnesota land.

Workbook p. 42
Self-Check

3. What are the four land regions in Minnesota?

IOWA

★ ★

GEOFACTS
- capital: Des Moines
- statehood: 1846 (29th)
- rank in size: 25th
- rank in population: 30th (urban 61%, rural 39%)
- U.S. representatives: 5
- motto: "Our Liberties We Prize and Our Rights We Will Maintain"

▲ Corn being harvested

▲ The mighty Mississippi River is at its best in the autumn.

Quiet Iowa farm life has been the subject of songs, poems, plays and movies. One of these shows was called *The Music Man.* The songs and words of the show tell of the stubborn ways of Iowa people in a very funny story. Yet, the show also respects the strong values held by the people of Iowa. Part of one of the songs says this:

> But we'll give you our shirt
>
> And our back to go with it,
>
> If your crops should happen to die, . . .

The song goes on to welcome people to Iowa — to give it a try!

Another hit film called *State Fair* also used Iowa to tell the tale of American farm life where people help and care for each other. In it, songwriter Richard Rodgers and playwright Oscar Hammerstein let people across the country know just how important Iowa is. A part of one song goes like this:

> I am Ioway (Iowa) born and bred,
>
> And on Ioway corn I'm fed,

The song goes on to thank Iowa for its fine foods and crops — ham, beef, lamb, and barley, wheat, and rye.

⚡ **Critical Thinking**
How can respect for land be shown?

Places to See! People to Know!

▶ Effigy Mounds National Monument, Marquette — site of 191 preserved Native American Indian mounds date from more than 5,000 years ago

▶ Living History Farms, Des Moines — visitors can see farm life in Iowa from the 1800s and early 1900s

▶ Keokuk (b.1780) — Sauk Indian leader who urged peace with white settlers; the town of Keokuk, Iowa is named in his honor

▶ Dred Scott (b.1795) — Missouri-born slave taken to Iowa where he believed himself to be free; a U.S. Supreme Court ruled against Scott

GeoWords
sod — the upper layer of grassy land
drought — a long time of little or no rain

Iowa is a state of many farms. Waves of golden grasses as tall as a horse once grew across the land. Settlers during the 1800s tried and tried again to plow the Iowa prairie. They used tools that had worked in the fields of Maryland, Ohio and other eastern states. Their hard-worked efforts were met by broken plows and tired horses. Yet, the tough prairie grasses with their strong roots held firm.

What did the prairie farmers do? The people of Iowa are known for not giving up, even in the toughest of times. The farmers hired plowers with huge plows pulled by many oxen. Slowly, the wild prairie grasses gave way. To the farmers delight, fertile soil 2 feet deep was uncovered.

⚡ **Critical Thinking**
What kind of problems do you think people living in sod homes had?

The **sod** that gave farmers so much work also sheltered the farmer's family. Farmers settling on the treeless prairies had no wood for building sturdy log homes. Some homes were dug into hills. Other homes were built from blocks of sod. It was common for a cow to graze on the roof of a house! Dirt floors, sod walls, and prairie insects were part of an early settler's life.

Did early settlers meet with Native Americans? At one time, Native Americans lived across the land known today as Iowa. Yet, by 1830, the United States government forced most of the Sauk and Mesquakie Indians to move west of the Mississippi River.

Chief Black Hawk led a group of followers in a war against white settlement. They met a bitter end. Chief Black Hawk was put in chains and sent to jail. The United States government sent the Sauk and Mesquakie Indians further west. Iowa land that had been promised to them was opened up to white settlement. By 1850, almost all Native Americans had been driven out of Iowa.

▲ Des Moines, Iowa — a city of steady, rapid growth.

What is Iowa like today? Today, Iowa has a population of more than 2,776,000 people. About 90 percent of Iowa is farmed. There are about 111,000 farms in Iowa. Iowa leads the country in the sale of corn. Iowa hogs supply about one-third of the country's pork, ham, and bacon.

Food products such as corn syrup and corn oil are made in factories found in Iowa's cities. Meat-packing plants, farm tools and other farm needs are met by city factories. Quaker Oats, one of the world's largest cereal mills, is in Cedar Rapids, Iowa. Newton, where Fred Maytag invented the first washing machine in 1884, still makes many washing machines used in the United States.

How has Iowa changed? How is it the same? Over the years, some people who grew up on Iowa farms left the farm to find work in cities across the country. By 1960, more people in Iowa lived in Iowa's cities than on Iowa's farms. During the 1980s, low farm prices and **drought** affected many of Iowa's farmers. Some farmers had to sell their land to pay off large bills.

Today, Iowa's youth is being urged to stay in Iowa. At the same time, people from large cities are looking to Iowa as a place to live. Iowa's strong sense of working together for the good of all, as well as small town life, offer a sense of clear values to many people.

Did You Know? Many people who moved out of Iowa, looking for "greener pastures," return because of the good quality of life.

What is the land like across Iowa? Iowa is an artist's dream, with fields of color splashed across the state. Plains cover much of Iowa. The plains rise and fall in waves of rolling hills. Many years ago, glaciers carved the land. The glaciers filled valleys with the fertile soil enjoyed by today's farmers.

In northeast Iowa, an area of pine-covered cliffs rises above the Iowa plain. This area was untouched by most glacier action. Here, hiking trails cut across rugged hills. Pine forests offer shelter and food to rabbits, squirrels, fox, and other small animals.

Iowa's largest lakes were made by building dams across rivers. Smaller lakes, made by melting glaciers, dot the northwest region of the state. Rivers in Iowa flow either west to the Missouri River or east to the Mississippi River.

☆ ☆ ☆ ☆ ☆ ☆ ☆ ☆ ☆

In 1838, Chief Black Hawk asked white settlers to keep and honor the land as his Native American brothers had. Today, in his honor, Iowa is called "the Hawkeye State." A deep respect for the land, its beauty, and

Critical Thinking
Why do you think Iowa's early farmers didn't just quit and go back east when times got tough?

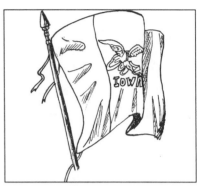

▲ The Iowa state flag

Did You Know? Mrs. Ockerman was one of Iowa's first school teachers. In 1849, Mrs. Ockerman taught in a log cabin that cost $60 to build. She was paid $12 a month and free meals for her teaching.

★ ★ ★ ★ ★ ★ ★ ★ **THINK ABOUT IT!** ★ ★ ★ ★ ★ ★ ★ ★

1. What three things do the words from *The Music Man* and *State Fair* say about Iowa?

2. What kind of problems did early white emigrants have?

3. Tell four things about the land that makes up Iowa.

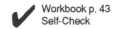

Workbook p. 43
Self-Check

MISSOURI

★ ★

GEOFACTS
- capital: Jefferson City
- statehood: 1821 (24th)
- rank in size: 19th
- rank in population: 15th (urban 69%, rural 31%)
- U.S. representatives: 9
- motto: "The Welfare of the People Shall Be the Supreme Law"

▲ Fur trader, Hannibal museum

▲ St. Louis, Missouri

"Saturday morning was come, and all the summer world was bright and fresh, and brimming with life. There was a song in every heart. . . .There was cheer in every face, and a spring in every step. The locust trees were in bloom, and the fragrance of the blossoms filled the air.

Tom appeared on the sidewalk with a bucket of white-wash and a long-handled brush. Thirty yards of broad fence nine feet high! It seemed to him that life was hollow.

. . . Sighing he dipped his brush and passed it along the topmost plank. . . . Jim came skipping out at the gate with a tin pail, and singing 'Buffalo Gals.' Bringing water from the town pump had always been hateful work in Tom's eyes, but now it did not strike him so.

. . .'Say Jim; I'll fetch the water if you'll whitewash some.'"

from *The Adventures of Tom Sawyer*
by Mark Twain

Critical Thinking

How does Mark Twain show his love of the Missouri climate?

Places to See! People to Know!

▶ Trail of Tears State Park, Cape Girardeau — honors a part of the route taken by the Cherokee Indians during their forced march from the southeast to Oklahoma

▶ Laura Ingalls Wilder-Rose Wilder Lane Home and Museum — home from which Laura Ingalls Wilder wrote *Little House on the Prairie* and six other books about prarie life during the 1800s.

▶ Susan Elizabeth Blow (b.1843) — opened the first public kindergarten in the U.S. in St. Louis (1873)

▶ Thomas Anthony Dooley (b.1927) — worked to bring medical aid to Vietnamese and Laotian villages

The story of clever Tom Sawyer and his friend Huckleberry Finn was first read and enjoyed by people in 1876. The story comes from life in Mark Twain's boyhood town of Hannibal, Missouri. Today, the times of Tom Sawyer, Huckleberry Finn, Aunt Polly, Becky, and other people brought to life in Mark Twain's books are shared with visitors who come to the Mississippi riverboat town of Hannibal.

What is the land like around Hannibal? Hannibal lies in Missouri's Till Plains. This area of gently rolling hills lies north of the Missouri River. Thick, slow-moving glaciers crossed this region many years ago. Left behind were fertile layers of till.

Some of the state's most fertile soils lie in the Till Plains region. Here, small streams slowly rise and fall as they cut across farmer's fields planted in corn and soybeans. Cattle can be found grazing on lush grasses, grown on pastures that bend and turn across the region's hillsides.

GeoWords
pioneer — an early settler

South and west of the Missouri River lies the Osage (OH-sayj) Plains. The region was left untouched by the grinding, power-packed glaciers that carved much of Missouri's land. Scenic beauty waits around every turn in this region. Sailboats, fishing boats, and speedboats are found on the many clear, fun-filled waters of the Osage Plains.

Critical Thinking
Why do you think Missouri's southeast region is called Boot Heel?

The Boot Heel region is a small area in southeast Missouri. Here, thick layers of mud and sand make up a fertile soil enjoyed by the area's cotton farmers. At one time, this area was part of a swampy arm of the Mississippi River. Over the years, it was drained and cleared for farming.

Where are the Missouri Ozarks? The Missouri Ozarks are found in the southern part of the state. This region is bordered by the Mississippi, Missouri, Sage, Neosho, and Arkansas rivers. Scattered across the region are fast-flowing streams, 10,000 gurgling springs, and many well-loved lakes.

Missouri has more than 1,400 dark caves that stir with the sound bats hanging from limestone walls. Missouri's caves at one time were shelter to the region's Native Americans. Later they were used by runaway slaves traveling the Underground Railroad.

The Ozarks are one of nature's great gifts of beauty. Its cool valleys are lined with birch, beech, oak, and other trees that most often are found in northern climates. Hiding among the branches of these trees are deer and sturdy black bears.

▲ Recreating the days of Mark Twain in an outdoor theater.

At one time, much of Missouri's forest fell to the crack of a mighty ax. At other times, the roar of a raging forest fire claimed Missouri's trees. Yet, today about 2.5 million acres of the Ozark region has been set aside as a preserved forest area.

The highest land between the Appalachian Mountains to the east and the Rocky Mountains to the west lies in the Ozarks. Here, peaks of granite reaching 1,700 feet into the sky rise above the Missouri plains. Tree-capped bluffs tower over the region's peaceful river valleys.

How did Missouri become the "Gateway to the West? Sun-touched, flowing prairie grasses still dot Missouri land. They stand as a reminder of the land seen by **pioneer** (PY-on-eer) families crossing the Missouri plain during the 1800s.

For many people, Missouri was the start to a new life. Beyond the Missouri prairie and the ever-changing Missouri River lies the open west. Great steamboats carrying people and cargo would travel from St. Louis to Independence. From there, pioneers filled with hope and dreams would load their wagons and head west.

Yet, the Santa Fe and Oregon trails were filled with danger, great sadness, and the hard work of crossing mountains, long stretches of

Did You Know? Flooding of the Mississippi River in 1993 almost swept away the boyhood home of Mark Twain (real name Samuel Clemens). The people of Hannibal worked around the clock to sandbag the levee along the river to save their city from being swept away by the raging, swollen river. About 20% of the city did flood. Yet, the hard work of many people helped to hold the levee and save the boyhood memories of Mark Twain.

GeoWords

deserts — a dry, sandy region that has few, if any, plants

prairie and **deserts**. Many men, women, and children died from overwork, little water and attacks by Native Americans.

Illness took most lives during the 1,000-mile trip to Santa Fe or the 2,000-mile trip to Oregon. Those who made it west faced the unsure job of putting their lives back together, making a home and finding work.

☆ ☆ ☆ ☆ ☆ ☆ ☆ ☆ ☆

Missouri is a land where northern winter winds cover barns and tall city buildings in soft fluffs of snow. Welcome rains cool warm, humid Missouri days. Toe-tapping folk songs, fine crafts, and the tangy taste of BBQ ribs on a bright summer day bring a touch of Missouri to the rest of the country. Missouri today, just as in the past, stands as a gateway to America's future!

Critical Thinking

How do you think the people starting out west from Independence felt about their coming travels? Give a contrast of feelings.

Did You Know? Missouri leads the country in the mining of lead, lime, and zinc and copper. Missouri red granite and marble are sold across the country.

 **THINK ABOUT IT!**

1. What Earth force helped to form Missouri land?

2. How is the Boot Heel region different from the Till Plains region?

3. Give three reasons why you think the Ozarks are important to Missouri's tourist economy.

 Workbook p. 44
Self-Check

MICHIGAN

★ ★

GEOFACTS
- capital: Lansing
- statehood: 1837 (26th)
- rank in size: 25th

- rank in population: 30th (urban 61%, rural 39%)
- U.S. representatives: 16
- motto: "If You Seek a Pleasant Peninsula, Look About You"

▲ Michigan's beautiful woods and lakes attract summertime visitors.

"Get a horse!" This saying was often told to drivers of odd-looking buggies with motors in the early 1900s. The buggies were called horseless-carriages (KAH-ruh-jes). They were first built in Michigan. Often, these horseless carriage wonders would get stuck in muddy roads meant for horse travel.

Most roads in 1900 were long stretches of dirt. Rain quickly could turn a dry road into a muddy mess. Many drivers had moments when a sturdy horse seemed like a fair trade for a mud-covered horseless carriage. Yet, the horseless carriage would prove to change the country forever.

How did the horseless carriage change the country? Horseless carriages soon became known as "cars." Cars brought the city to the rural areas. People could live in a rural area but still work in a city. Beliefs, values, and problems of "city folk" and "farm folk" slowly blended as cars brought them closer together.

Another change brought on by "horseless carriages" was the way factories worked. Gas-powered cars were first built by Henry Ford, Ransom Olds, and the Dodge brothers in the early 1900s. The use of a factory assembly (ah-SEM-blee) line began with these early car makers. Here, workers along a line kept adding parts until a finished car appeared.

Detroit, Michigan quickly became a leading center for the making of cars. Michigan's land was rich in the **natural** (NAT-chur-al) resources of iron and copper needed for building car factories and cars.

GeoWords
natural — formed by nature

Critical Thinking
In what other way do you think the "horseless carriage" changed America?

Places to See! People to Know!

▶ International Institute of Metropolitan Detroit, Detroit — holds a collection of Asian, African and Native American folk art and costumes

▶ Tulip Festival, Holland — held each May when the tulips are in bloom, this festival celebrates the area's Dutch heritage with Dutch parade, Dutch dances, and a tour of the only wooden-shoe factory in the United States

▶ Sojourner Truth (b.1797) — born a slave; became a reformer who traveled the country speaking out against the evils of slavery

▶ Minoru Yamasaki (b.1912) — designed many of Detroit's outstanding buildings

Critical Thinking

Why do you think people from city areas travel many miles to stay for a week or two in Michigan's wilderness areas?

Michigan also became the center for other factories. Today, Kalamazoo leads the state in the making of paper. Battle Creek is home to Kellogg and Post Cereals. Gerber Foods has the country's largest baby-food factory in Fremont, Michigan.

Over time, immigrants from Europe worked on many of Michigan's assembly lines. African Americans from southern states moved to Michigan's cities for work. Immigrants from Mexico worked on Michigan's farms, filling in for farmhands who went to work in the city.

Are iron and copper Michigan's most important natural resources? Today, the mining of copper and iron has slowed. Yet, Michigan is rich in water resources. Often called a "water wonderland," Michigan has more than 3,200 miles of colorful shoreline.

More than 11,000 inland lakes, along with many rivers and streams, stretch across Michigan. They offer quiet moments to summer fishermen hoping to catch one of the many muskie, trout or salmon that thrive in Michigan's cool waters. In the winter, ice fishers sit waiting for a catch of bass or perch.

Tourism is an important part of Michigan's economy. Each summer, tourists flock to Michigan to enjoy a stay in a cabin far into Michigan's northern wilderness. Here forests of oak and maple offer cover to the area's elk, moose, and deer. Fall brings a burst of color to Michigan's lush forests.

▲ Shipping on the Great Lakes is Michigan's lifeline.

Snow-centered sports such as skiing and snowmobiling are enjoyed during the winter months. Michigan gets anywhere from 30 inches of snow in the south to 160 inches of snow in the north. Hockey, ice skating, snowball fights, or just building a grand snow figure topped with a funny hat and red knit scarf are other winter joys.

Is the land in northern Michigan like the land in the southern part of the state? Michigan is made up of two great peninsulas. The Upper Peninsula is bordered by Lake Superior, Lake Huron, and Lake Michigan. The Superior Upland covers the western part of the Upper Peninsula. This rugged plateau area rises to 2,000 feet above sea level.

The eastern part of the Upper Peninsula is part of the Great Lakes Plains. This lowland area has thin soils, making farming hard. Here, Chippewa and Menominee Indians once lived in dome-shaped bark wigwams. They gathered wild rice along the shore, hunted in thick forests, and fished in cold waters.

Michigan's Lower Peninsula is bordered by Lake Michigan to the west and Lake Huron to the east. Tall, green jack-pine trees grow in the sandy soil that stretches across the northern limit of the peninsula. Soft sand dunes shaped by the wind lie below the high, wind-blocking bluffs that trim Lake Michigan's shoreline.

Did You Know? In 1909, Michigan built the first concrete highway. It was near downtown Detroit. It ran for only one mile, but drivers of America's new horseless carriages praised it as a modern marvel.

Where are most of Michigan's farms found? Low hills gently roll across much of the Michigan's Lower Peninsula. Michigan's best farmland is found here. Bright red cherries, deep purple grapes, and juicy apples are grown along the eastern coastal area. Dairy and beef cattle, tomatoes, celery, and corn are raised on small family farms.

The rise and fall of farm prices, little rain, and early frosts have all made farming in Michigan hard. Big problems came in 1973. It was then that a **toxic** (TOK-sik) chemical (KEM-ih-kal) called PBB was unknowingly mixed in animal feed.

Thousands of cattle who ate the chemical had to be killed. Within a short time, the PBB had spread into meat, eggs, milk, and cheese. Many people ate products with PBB in them before experts found out about the animal-feed mistake.

Which is Michigan's largest city? Detroit is Michigan's largest city. African Americans make up the largest population of people living in Detroit. In 1973, Coleman Young was elected Detroit's first African American mayor. Between 1973 and 1993, Young worked to bring businesses, new housing, and jobs to Detroit.

☆ ☆ ☆ ☆ ☆ ☆ ☆ ☆ ☆

Michigan is a state where busy city street sounds contrast with the soft hum of farm life and the hush of snow-covered **woods**. Within it all, Michigan holds a piece of all of America, its dreams, and its future.

GeoWords
toxic — very harmful, filled with poison
woods — a forest area

Critical Thinking
In what way does Michigan hold a piece of all of America?

▲ Mackinac Island's Huron Street

Did You Know? Three Michigan Native American tribes formed a union called "The Three Fires." The tribes were the Chippewa, the Potawatomi, and the Ottawa. All three tribes shared a common language and heritage. All three tribes believed in a supreme being and lesser spirits who took care of the winds and the waters.

★★★★★★★★ **THINK ABOUT IT!** ★★★★★★★★

1. Give two reasons why Detroit became the center of the car industry?

2. Why is water Michigan's most important natural resource?

3. In what part of Michigan is the state's best farmland found?

Workbook p. 45
Self-Check

Our United States Environment

★★★★★★★★   ★★★★★★★★

▲ The Mississippi River Valley — "Great Flood of '93"

THE AFFECTS OF NATURE

Nature has a great effect on the environment. Tornadoes, hurricanes, earthquakes, and other forces of nature all affect how the land looks and how people can use the land. They also affect the animals and plants that use the land for shelter and food. Within a very short time, nature can quickly change the look and use of an area.

The "Great Flood of '93"

The spring of 1993 brought more rain to the Mississippi River Valley than usually falls. First slowly, then very quickly, rivers began to rise beyond their normal height. Over the spring and early summer months, rivers that flow into the Mississippi River began to overflow their banks. The Mississippi River also overflowed its banks. Soon acres upon acres of land were flooded with river water.

The flood area extended along the Mississippi River from Minneapolis, Minnesota to St. Louis, Missouri. Flooding went as far west as Sioux Falls, South Dakota. To the east, flooding extended to Chicago, Illinois, taking in much of western Illinois. All along the flood area people lost their homes and farms as river water swept the buildings downstream.

Cities built along the flooding rivers tried to build up their levees. People spent long hours filling millions of sandbags to place along the banks of the rivers. In some cases the levees held. In others the river's fury was just too strong. Levees broke. Cities were flooded. In some cases, city water supplies were damaged and people had the double problem of water everywhere, but no water fit to drink.

The "Great Flood of '93" finally came to a stop in the fall of the year. By the end, there was over five billion dollars in damage. Over two million acres of land had been flooded. Altogether, farmers lost almost three billion dollars because they had no crops to harvest and sell. Countless animals and plants were lost to the flood. Even the future paths of some rivers may have been reshaped. The "Great Flood of '93" forever changed the environment of the Mississippi River Valley.

Hurricane Andrew

Hurricane Andrew tore across the states of Florida, Louisiana and Mississippi in the summer of 1992. Packing winds of up to 168 miles per hour, Hurricane Andrew slammed into the city of Homestead. Within a few short hours, the hurricane caused billions of dollars of damage to southern Florida. Over one million people had to leave their homes along the hurricane's path.

Not much within the direct path of Hurricane Andrew seemed to escape the power of this mighty storm. In the end, over 250,000 people were left homeless as the result of Hurricane Andrew's fury. The hurricane's damaging winds and rain also caused changes in the environment of the Florida Everglades. This directly affected the animals living in the Everglades.

As Hurricane Andrew crossed Louisiana, its wind speeds slowed to about 60 miles per hour. Cropland and buildings were damaged. Tornadoes, a spinoff of hurricanes, caused damage beyond the reach of Hurricane Andrew.

THE EFFECT OF PEOPLE

People also can cause great changes in the environment. Here is a list of some changes brought about on the environment by people.

1. Farm runoff into the waters of the Everglades is causing a change in the kinds of plants that grow and the number of animals that can survive in the changing waters.

2. Building around Yellowstone National Park could become a threat to the underground water supplies; planned copper mining on land just outside the park may be a threat to the animals that feed in that area as well as to the tourists that enjoy the scenic environment.

3. Concern is mounting over the loss of wetlands to housing across the United States. About 290,000 acres of wetland are lost every year. Wetlands not only control flooding, they also are a resting and feeding area for many kinds of birds.

4. The use of chemicals by farmers is a threat to the water supplies of millions of Americans. Chemicals used in the past have seeped into the ground and then flowed into underground water. The danger comes when water with chemicals is pumped out of the ground for use by people and animals.

Control of the effect on the environment by nature is very hard. Yet, more and more people are becoming concerned about the effect on the environment by people. People are looking into ways to use the land without destroying the environment. Sometimes this means very limited use of the land to protect the environment.

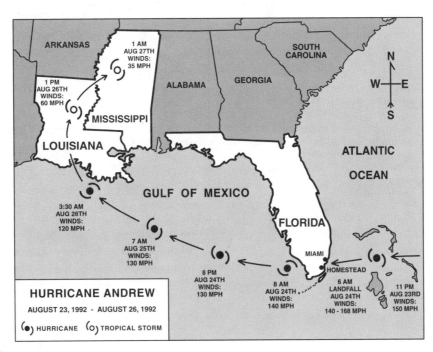

▲ Path of Hurricane Andrew

The Great Plains

There's a painting lit in golden lights at the end of a hallway in Oklahoma's capitol building. Standing to the right in the painting are Native Americans dressed in the bright colors of their tribe. Standing to the left are pioneer folk dressed to tackle the rugged prairie soil. In front, dressed in flowing white gowns, dance five famous ballerinas from Oklahoma.

This painting carries many of the themes of the Great Plains region. The life of Native Americans changed and then changed again as the United States government moved tribes across the plains region. Pioneer families came by horse, cart, and train to farm the tough prairie soil. Soon, cities and the sharing of ideas gave the people of the Great Plains a focus in new directions (dih-rek-shunz).

At one time, great herds of buffalo, sometimes more than a mile long, would freely roam the rolling hills of Kansas, Oklahoma, and the other Great Plains states. Today, longhorn and hereford cattle have taken their place in grazing the short but hardy prairie grasses. All along, farmers made the American plains their home.

"It's hard to explain the joy of walking a rough furrow behind a team of sweaty horses, ..."* Farmers wrote about the real joy and pride they felt in accomplishing their chores, however tiring.

Farming is one theme that is part of every state in the Great Plains region. Tall rows of corn plants, waving fields of wheat, and thick patches of oats ready for harvest bring a feeling of pride for a job well done to farmers across the area.

Farming has never been a easy job. Yet, farming took one of its most difficult turns during the 1930s dust-bowl years. It was then that farmers waited day after day for rains that never came. Farm fields across the Great Plains dried in the hot summer sun. Without plants for cover, top soils turned to dust and blew east to settle someplace else miles away.

The land and the climate of the Great Plains region can be trying. It can also be swept with beauty. Over the years, people have stood strong in the face of hardship to stay with the land. Respect for the land, respect for the past, and respect for the needs of the future are just some of the themes the Great Plains region shares with the rest of the country.

*from *Farm Town: A Memoir of the 1930s,*
© S. Greene Press, 1984 text by Grant Heilman; photos by J.W. McManigal

NORTH DAKOTA

★ ★

GEOFACTS
- capital: Bismark
- statehood: 1889 (39th)
- rank in size: 17th
- rank in population: 47th (urban 53%, rural 47%)
- U.S. representatives: 1
- motto: "Liberty and Union, Now and Forever, One and Inseparable"

▲ "Teddy" Roosevelt

▲ The cabin near Medora, North Dakota, where President Theodore Roosevelt was born

North Dakota is an exciting land of wonder. It is a state where roaming herds of powerful buffalo once thundered across the wind-swept plain. It is a land where proud Native Americans lived in peace and in war.

It was across this wide-open land that a Native American woman helped Meriwether Lewis and William Clark find their way to the Pacific Ocean. Without her, Lewis and Clark's bold travels up the Missouri River in 1804 could have failed. Had this happened, American history might have taken a different turn. Today, North Dakota's largest lake, a mountain peak, a river, and a mountain pass all have been named in her honor.

Who was this woman? The woman's name was Sakakawea (also spelled Sacagawea and Sacajawea). She was born a Shoshoni. Taken by an enemy tribe, Sakakawea was sold as a slave to a French Canadian fur trader named Toussaint Charbonneau.

Sakakawea married Charbonneau. Together with Charbonneau and their newborn son, Sakakawea joined Lewis and Clark. Starting from Fort Mandan, she led them across the lands she had known as a child. She spoke on their behalf to the many Native American tribes they met along the way. She showed them which berries to eat when food became scarce.

What happened after Lewis and Clark's trip? On the heels of Lewis and Clark came many fur traders. Soon, fur trading posts dotted North Dakota along the banks of the Missouri River. At first, trading posts helped Native Americans.

Critical Thinking

How might North Dakota's history been different if Lewis and Clark had not opened up western lands to fur traders?

Places to See! People to Know!

▶ Knife River Indian Villages National Historic Site, Stanton — preserved homes built by Hidatsa, Mandan, and Arikara tribes; tour includes the home of Toussaint Charbonneau and Sakakawea

▶ Theodore Roosevelt National Park, Badlands — 70,000 acres of Badlands and prairie preserved along the Little Missouri River

▶ Manuel Lisa (b. 1771) — fur trader who set up several trading posts along the Missouri River; known for his fairness in trading

▶ Sitting Bull (b.1834) — Sioux chief and warrior who led bands of Native Americans against white settlement Dakota land

Critical Thinking

In the early 1900s, settlers came to North Dakota by train. How else do you think trains affected North Dakota?

▲ The International Peace Garden — a symbol of friendship between the United States and its neighbor, Canada.

Did You Know? Along her travels west, Sakakawea was surprised to meet her brother, who had become a chief. Finding her brother meant safe travel and fresh horses for their trip across the Rocky Mountains. A statue of Sakakawea stands in Bismark, North Dakota.

Native Americans traded furs by the thousands for knives, guns, blankets, and other things. The furs were made into coats and hats for people living in the eastern states. As Native Americans changed from farmers to hired fur traders, their way of life also changed.

Steamboats, railroads, and thousands of white settlers began to pour into North Dakota in the last half of the 1800s. The Homestead Act opened up free land to settlers. Native Americans wondered how land they had lived on for years could now be given away and sold by the United States government.

What happened between the Native Americans and the United States government? The United States government treated Dakota land like any other land deal. They offered to buy the land from the Native Americans. The government wrote treaties (TREE-tees), or deals, that promised money for the land. The treaties also promised Native Americans land in some other place.

Often, whites did not live up to their part of the treaty. One such treaty, the Laramie Treaty, was signed with the Sioux Indians. Promises of money, food, farm machines, and whites not settling on **reservation** (reh-zer-VAY-shun) land all were broken.

What is the land like in North Dakota? Think of flat stretches of golden brown prairie. Now think of hills of rock rising out of the plains. The hills stand alone, as if lost in the plain.

Found in the southwest part of the state, these gently sloped hills, called **buttes** (byoots), have been molded and shaped by wind and water. Small rivers wind their way across the rugged valleys of this area. Farmers graze cattle and horses on the area's short grasses.

North Dakota's Badlands are found in the southwest corner of the state. This land is a maze of treeless buttes, rocks, and ravines. Lignite (LIG-nyt), a type of coal, fills the rocks of the area. Slow-burning, smoky lignite fires start when lightning strikes the ground. The fires turn black-toned lignite rock into a rainbow of reds, blues, and golds.

From north to south across the center of North Dakota is the Drift Prairie. Found here are the Turtle Mountains, one of the few forested areas in the state. Fertile soils lie in the eastern part of this region. Short grasses and thin soils are in its western part.

Lakes that dot the drift prairie offer fun-filled days to the people of North Dakota. Ice skating, skiing, and year-round fishing are enjoyed by the area's farmers and small-town folk. Across the area fly millions of birds who use the drift prairie as their resting and feed spot during their north-south travels.

What area lies in eastern North Dakota? To the east lies the Red River valley. Here, long-ago, glaciers left this area with the best soil in the state. A checkerboard of color stretches across this area. Golden squares of wheat, lush green fields of beans and potatoes, and bright yellow rows of sunflowers cover this important farm region.

North Dakota's natural resources find their way across the country. North Dakota supplies much of the country's meat, sunflower oil, flour, and sugar beets. Salt mined from North Dakota is used in animal feed and city water softeners. Lignite and oil are used to power machines. Road builders use North Dakota sand and gravel.

What is the climate like in North Dakota? Winter in North Dakota brings cold northern winds that sweep across the plains. Blizzards (BLIH-zards), strong snow-packed storms, are a winter threat. North Dakota's short summer season is hot and dry.

☆ ☆ ☆ ☆ ☆ ☆ ☆ ☆ ☆

Immigrants from cold northern countries in Europe settled in North Dakota during the late 1800s and early 1900s. Today, people from India, Vietnam, Korea, and China call North Dakota their home. Native Americans still make their home on reservation land. North Dakota with its land, climate, and people is a state where change and beauty come together.

Critical Thinking
What do you think are some of the changes in North Dakota that make it a place of beauty?

▲ Theodore Roosevelt Park

Did You Know? Petrified (PEH-trih-fyd) wood, or dead trees that have into stone, is found in North Dakota's Badlands.

★ ★ ★ ★ ★ ★ ★ ★ **THINK ABOUT IT!** ★ ★ ★ ★ ★ ★ ★ ★

1. Who was Sakakawea?

2. How did fur trading change life in North Dakota?

3. Contrast North Dakota's Badlands with its Red River valley.

Workbook p. 50
Self-Check

SOUTH DAKOTA

★ ★

GEOFACTS
- capital: Pierre
- statehood: 1889 (40th)
- rank in size: 16th
- rank in population: 45th (urban 50%, rural 50%)
- U.S. representatives: 1
- motto: "Under God the People Rule"

▲ A Native American dance

▲ Mount Rushmore forms the faces of presidents Washington, Jefferson, Roosevelt, and Lincoln.

⚡ **Critical Thinking**

Explain in detail what you think it was like to live in a sod home on the South Dakota prairie during the winter.

Places to See! People to Know!

▶ Rockerville Ghost Town, Rapid City — replica of an 1878 mining town

▶ Wounded Knee Battlefield, Wounded Knee — site where 350 Sioux, including women and children, who were marched to Wounded Knee, were killed by members of the U.S. army

▶ Gutzon Borglum (b.1867) — created and carved the faces of Washington, Jefferson, Lincoln, and T. Roosevelt on Mount Rushmore

▶ Crazy Horse (b.1849) — led the Sioux in an effort to keep the Black Hills as Sioux land; fought in several battles against the U.S. army, including the Battle of the Little Bighorn

Blizzards are something well known to the people of South Dakota. These powerful, snow-filled storms rip across the land, packing 70 mile-per-hour winds. The snow is so thick that an outstretched hand is soon lost in a blur of white. Animals out on the plain bow their heads to the storm and brace themselves for the worst.

Frigid (FRIH-jid), or very cold, winters are a part of life in South Dakota. Yet, so are wonderful summers when the days are mild and the sun is high. But summer, too, can have its surprises. Hot, dry days with no tree on the plain to give shade also are a part of South Dakota's climate.

South Dakota history, like its climate, is filled with an untamed spirit. Carving out a life on the open prairie, sheltered only by a sod house; gold rushes; and wild-west shoot-outs are all part of South Dakota's past.

Do buffalo still roam across the South Dakota prairie? Today, herds of buffalo freely graze across 73,000 acres in Custer State Park. Yet, at one time, great herds of buffalo fed on hardy grasses that grew across the plains of South Dakota.

THE PEOPLE'S PUBLISHING GROUP, INC. *Our United States Geography: Our Regions and People*

Buffalo hunts were an important part in the life of the Sioux Indians. From the buffalo, the Sioux got meat, clothes made from the hides, and spoons and tools made from buffalo bones. Much of the culture of the Sioux Indians centered around the mighty buffalo.

Critical Thinking

Why do you think the Sioux Indians did not want to give up their lands to the United States government?

The building of railroads across South Dakota land brought many white settlers. They came from states such as Wisconsin, Minnesota, New York, and Pennsylvania. Thousands of immigrants from Norway, Hungary, Holland, and other countries in Europe used what they knew, and what they had to learn quickly, to survive the cold Dakota winters.

White settlement and the building of railroads led to the end of the great buffalo herds. By 1870, so much hunting by whites came very close to wiping out the buffalo in South Dakota. With few buffalo to hunt, the life the Sioux had known for many years came to an end.

Is most of South Dakota covered by plains? South Dakota has two main land regions. One region lies east of the rushing Missouri River. This is South Dakota's plains region. More than 10,000 years ago, this region was scoured by glaciers. Left behind was a vast, or very large, prairie of gently rolling hills.

Melting glaciers filled low areas, dotting this region with 120 cold, sparkling lakes. The calm beauty of these clear-water lakes is seen in the golden sunset of a South Dakota day. Around the lakes and along the trout-filled rivers of this region grew South Dakota's prairie towns.

▲ Huge bison herds once roamed North Dakota.

South Dakota's second land region lies west of the Missouri River. Free from the carving work of glaciers, this area is a mix of forested mountain beauty and land untouched by tree or flower.

Found in the western region are the Black Hills. This area of striking beauty is a nature-lover's dream. From far away, the lush, deep green forests of the area take on a black tone. The crashing sound of water rushing over a high waterfalls and the cry of a mountain lion can both be heard in South Dakota's Black Hills.

Between the White and Cheyenne Rivers lie the Badlands. Over time, blowing winds and water have shaped the sandstone rock that lies across the area. Here glowing rock color replaces the green of the forests and the endless prairie browns found in other parts of the state. Fossil hunters walk this amazing land where rock meets sky and trees are forgotten.

Do most people in South Dakota farm the state's prairie areas? South Dakota is special in that half of the people live in rural areas. Many people make their living by raising large herds of cattle on the open prairie. Sheep and wool also are important to the state's economy.

Corn and wheat are the state's largest crops. Also grown are rye, oats, and sunflowers. South Dakota is a leader in the sale of honey.

Did You Know? The Sioux called themselves the Dakota, which means "allies" or "friends." Both North and South Dakota are named in honor of this proud Native American tribe.

Farming in South Dakota is affected by the state's ever-changing climate. Great blizzards in 1966 and 1975 killed many cattle that were

left stranded on the open range. In 1988, a summer drought caused the drying out of crops needed to feed animals during the cold winter months.

☆ ☆ ☆ ☆ ☆ ☆ ☆ ☆ ☆

South Dakota is a state where strong-willed people and sturdy animals must stand up to the state's harsh climate. Yet, South Dakota is a land where the word, "beauty" gets its meaning. It is here that great towers of rock blend with the colors of the forest and the stretch of the prairie. It is as Laura Ingalls Wilder told of South Dakota: "The prairie, the whole vast prairie, and the great sky and the wind were clear and free. . . ."

▲ Life on the plains was harsh for emigrants.

Did You Know? South Dakota is the site of the largest gold mine in the Western Hemisphere. South Dakota land also is rich in the natural resources of silver, oil, and red granite. South Dakota red granite has been used to build many monuments in the United States.

★ ★ ★ ★ ★ ★ ★ ★   **THINK ABOUT IT!**   ★ ★ ★ ★ ★ ★ ★ ★

1. Compare South Dakota's climate to the climate in Mississippi.

2. How did the life of the Sioux Indians depend on the buffalo?

3. Contrast South Dakota's Badlands with its land east of the Missouri River.

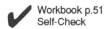 Workbook p.51
Self-Check

NEBRASKA

★ ★

GEOFACTS
- capital: Lincoln
- statehood: 1867 (37th)
- rank in size: 15th
- rank in population: 36th (urban 66%, rural 34%)
- U.S. representatives: 3
- motto: "Equality Before the Law"

▲ A typical pioneer homestead

▲ Golden wheat grows in abundance on Nebraska's flat plains

At one time, perhaps as close as 8,000 years ago, great animals with 6-inch long teeth roamed the land now called Nebraska. The animals, called mastodons (MAS-tuh-danz), looked somewhat like today's elephants. Yet, reaching out beyond their 3-inch-wide, 6-inch-long teeth were sets of long, powerful tusks.

Huge cats that look like today's tigers also roamed Nebraska land. These mighty cats had 8-inch-long fangs! They hunted mastodons and huge pigs. Fossils of turtles, camels. and crocodiles all have been found on the Nebraska plain. The fossils tell of a land that once was more like a rain forest than what it is today.

What is Nebraska like today? Nebraska is a land of gently rolling plateaus. Its lowest point is found in the southeast. Here, the land rises to 800 feet above sea level. To the west, the land is higher than 5,400 feet above sea level. The land rises from east to west at a rate of about 10 feet for each mile.

The eastern part of Nebraska is part of the Missouri River till plains. Here, great glaciers left layers of till, a mixture of sand, clay, gravel, and boulders. Winding streams cut across this perfect farming area. Swaying fields of yellow corn spread across this region.

⚡ **Critical Thinking**
What do fossils tell about Nebraska's past?

Places to See! People to Know!

▶ Mormon Pioneer Cemetery, Omaha — gravesite of 600 Mormons who died in the fierce winter of 1846 -1847

▶ Pike-Pawnee national Landmark, Guide Rock — site of a large early 1800's Pawnee village

▶ Susette LaFlesche (b.1854) — daughter of an Omaha chief; spoke out for the rights of Native Americans; helped to pass the Dawes Act which gave Native Americans the right to own land

▶ Mari Sandoz (b.1901) — author of *Pioneer Life on the Plains*

GeoWords
groundwater — water found under the surface of the ground
irrigation — spreading water over the surface of the ground by using sprinklers or a series of canals

Critical Thinking

Why is protecting Nebraska's groundwater so important?

▲ Nebraska's Boys Town was founded in Omaha in 1917 by Father Flanagan from Ireland. This statue is a symbol of the pioneering spirit — of helping one another in the face of hardship.

Did You Know? Many children in Nebraska live far from their school. Some travel as far as 50 miles one way to go to school.

West of the till plains lies the Great Plains region. Here, rolling hills of sand rise across the area. The sand hills of the Great Plains region were formed when wind picked up great loads of sand from dried river beds. The sand was dropped across the plain. Long ago, this region looked like a great desert with wave after wave of rising sand.

Today, the sand hills area is covered with short, hardy sand grasses. The grasses hold the sand in place. Cattle graze across this area.

Does Nebraska get much rain? Far more rain falls in eastern Nebraska than to its west. Along the till plains, farmers enjoy about 28 inches each year of rain. Yet, in the west, only about 14 inches of rain falls each year. The region's sand hills soak up the life-giving rains. Rains slowly filter down below the surface of the sandy soil.

Great rivers of rainwater that formed over thousands of years are found below Nebraska's sandy surface. This **groundwater** is pumped out of the ground. It is spread across much of Nebraska. At one time, Nebraska was called the "Great American Desert." Today, **irrigation** (ir-uh-GAY-shen) has turned Nebraska into an important farming state.

Is irrigation Nebraska's only water source for its western lands? Almost 2,000 lakes dot Nebraska's land of golden bluffs and rolling hills of green grasses. Most of these lakes are found in the sand hills region. Other lakes are man-made. These lakes were formed by damming the shallow Platte River.

Rivers are also an important source of water to the people of Nebraska. Ground water keeps the rivers of the sand hills running strong. The rushing waters of the Niobrara River flow across scenic northern Nebraska. This and other northern rivers follow the curve of the land to empty into the Missouri River.

More than half of Nebraska's land is drained by the Platte River. This river was the lifeline of early settlers traveling across Nebraska along the Oregon Trail. Today, irrigation and dams have slowed the Platte River. Yet, it still remains one of Nebraska's most important river system.

How did the Oregon Trail affect Nebraska's history? Between 1840 and 1860, about 500,000 people wound their way along the Oregon Trail. It was a long, dusty trip. Hunger and disease took many lives. Of the 7,500 people that traveled the road between 1842 and 1844, only 300 families made it to Oregon!

At first, few people stayed in Nebraska. The United States government had set aside Nebraska land for settlement by Native Americans. Yet, the 1862 Homestead Act soon opened land in Nebraska for white settlement. Railroads and wagons brought farmers from eastern states to Nebraska's river valleys.

Problems between settlers and Native Americans grew worse as more and more people moved onto the Nebraska plains. Native Americans had already been forced west from land settled by whites in the east. They did not want to lose their lands again.

Nebraska's early farmers faced many other problems. Times of drought brought an end to their crops. Some years brought great gray clouds of grasshoppers. The insects would land upon one field after another. Long days of hard work would be quickly undone as the grasshoppers ate every plant! The spirit of many of Nebraska's pioneer farmers was broken by the state's hard life.

What is farming like in Nebraska today? Today, Nebraska farms grow wheat, potatoes, sugar beets, and corn. Much of the country's popcorn comes from corn grown in Nebraska. Nebraska is a leading state in the raising of beef cattle, hogs, sheep, and chickens. Farm products such as butter, ice cream, flour, and sugar are made in Nebraska's cities.

At one time, most farms in Nebraska were small, family farms. Slowly, large businesses began to buy the small farms to make large, business-owned farms. In 1982, the people of Nebraska voted for the Family Farm Preservation (preh-zer-VAY-shen) Act. This law limits the amount of farmland a business can buy.

☆   ☆   ☆   ☆   ☆   ☆   ☆   ☆   ☆

Nebraska comes from the Oto Indian word "Nebrathka," which means "flat land." Today, Nebraska's flat land helps to feed the country. From its gentle waterfalls that bathe the sandy soil to its vast prairie to its moonlike rock ridges, Nebraska's land is filled with life and surprises.

Critical Thinking
Why is the farming in Nebraska important to the country?

Did You Know? The sod-covered houses used by many of the plain's early settlers were patterned after homes built by the Omaha Indians. They farmed and lived year-round in the same place. Other Native Americans, such as the Sioux, Cheyennes, and the Arapahos, moved with the buffalo herds.

 **THINK ABOUT IT!**

1. Contrast Nebraska's two land regions.

2. How does irrigation help Nebraska's farmers?

3. What was the Oregon Trail? How did it affect Nebraska?

 Workbook p. 52
Self-Check

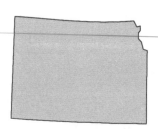

KANSAS

★ ★

GEOFACTS
- capital: Topeka
- statehood: 1861 (34th)
- rank in size: 14th
- rank in population: 32nd (urban 69%, rural 31%)
- U.S. representatives: 4
- motto: "To the Stars Through Difficulty"

▲ The Wild West lives on in Dodge City, Kansas.

▲ President Eisenhower's Kansas home

Oh give me a home where the buffalo roam,
Where the deer and the antelope play;
Where never is heard a discouraging word,
And the skies are not cloudy all day.

How often a night, when the heavens are bright,
With the light of the glittering stars —
I stood there amazed, and I asked as I gazed,
If their glory exceeds that of ours.

⚡ **Critical Thinking**
Why do you think the people chose Home On The Range for their state song?

Places to See! People to Know!
▶ Cherokee Strip Land Rush Museum, Arkansas City — has many reminders of the great land rush in southern Kansas
▶ Old Mill Museum, Lindsborg — tells of the towns Swedish American heritage as well information on the Native Americans and pioneers who lived and traveled across the area
▶ Amelia Earhart (b. 1898) — first woman to make a solo flight across the Atlantic Ocean
▶ Gale Sayers (b. 1943) — named the greatest running back in the National Football League's first half century

These words come from the song "Home on the Range." The song was written in 1873 by Kansas settlers Brewster Higley and Dan Kelley. Home on the Kansas range in 1873 could be filled with danger. Often, people lived far from each other. In fact, Higley and Kelley lived some 20 miles apart. This was quite a distance when travel meant a long, dusty ride on a horse.

"Home on the Range" was first called "My Western Home." It soon became the song of the cowboy. Men driving cattle across the vast Kansas prairie would fill a starry night with campfires and songs like "Home on the Range." Today, festivals and tourist sites bring a bit of Kansas history to people from all over.

How was Kansas first settled? Settlement of the West slowly wound its way across Kansas in the mid-1800s. Pioneers braved the Oregon and Santa Fe trails to reach unknown parts of the country. Some stopped in

Kansas. Thinking they had found just the right piece of land to farm and build a home, they placed a claim on Kansas land.

In the 1890s, the federal government opened Native American land along the southern border of Kansas for white settlement. The land was called the Cherokee Strip. In the fall of 1893, a race was planned for people to claim 160 acres of land each for their own. Soon, the populations of the border towns of Kiowa, Caldwell, and Arkansas City were bulging with hopeful landowners.

On the morning of September 16, almost 150,000 people riding horses and driving wagons lined up for the race. At noon, a shot was fired. In a flurry of dust, people rushed forward, wagon against wagon, horse against horse, to stake their claim. By sunset, 8 million acres of land had new owners. Today, that race for land is relived each September in Arkansas City.

To the west, another piece of Kansas history is retold. It was here in the cowtowns of Dodge City, Abilene, and Ellsworth that peace officers (PEES aw-FIH-serz) and bandits won Kansas fame. Such men as Wyatt Earp, Bat Masterson, Doc Holliday, and Wild Bill Hickok were hired to bring law and order to these often lively towns where the six-shooter ruled.

Why is Kansas called the "Jayhawker State?" The jayhawk is meant to be part forceful blue jay and part sharp-eyed hawk. The jayhawk is not a real bird. Yet, to the people of Kansas, the jayhawk stands for their strong-willed spirit. This spirit is often tested by the state's land and climate.

Prairie covers the state of Kansas. Great fields of golden wheat stretch like a blanket across the western plain. To the east, sparkling springs hide in the lush forest of dogwood and cottonwood. Across rolling hills and flatland prairie, chickens and prairie dogs bob and scamper to their own dance on the prairie.

Rising out of the prairie in northwest Kansas are tall chalk bluffs and **spires**. These watchtowers of rock stand like lone guards over the dry, brown prairie. They were first shaped by a great inland sea that once washed over Kansas. Later, winds that mold and shape carved look-outs in these rocks that honor the forces of nature.

South of the spires that dot northwestern Kansas lie rolling hills of limestone. This is the flint hills region. Native Americans used flint from these hills to make arrowheads (AHR-roh-hedz) and tools. Erosion by water and wind have molded much of Kansas. Yet, the flint hills stand strong against nature's erosive forces. Today, bluestem grass offers fine grazing for the cattle that wander across this region.

Another great earth force, glaciers, scraped across northeastern Kansas. Left behind were layers of fertile till. Crossing the area are winding, freshwater rivers. To their side rise scenic wooded bluffs. Rows of corn blend with the hustle of busy cities in this important region.

All rivers in Kansas flow eastward. This is because Kansas land gently tilts from west to east. One river, called White Woman Creek, flows

GeoWords
spires — a rock that, because of wind erosion, is wide at the bottom and narrows as it rises

Critical Thinking
How do you think people felt as they raced across the Cherokee Strip? Give reasons for your ideas.

▲ Kansas wheat at harvest time

Did You Know? Times of little or no rain also are a part of Kansas life. Dust storms, where the wind picks up dried soil that once held grass, form during these times of drought. Great blizzards of dust choked the air of Kansas in the 1930s. Glimpses of the Kansas dust-bowl years can be seen in farm scenes from *The Wizard of Oz*.

GeoWords
brush — small bushes and other plants

underground for a distance. Rivers in Kansas have been dammed to form lakes that offer cool relief on a hot Kansas day.

What is Kansas weather like? Rain-thirsty **brush** can be found across the Kansas western prairie. About 16 inches of rain falls in the west. To the east, about 40 inches of crop-growing rain falls in Kansas each year.

Critical Thinking
Why do you think most tornadoes happen in Kansas in late spring and early summer?

In 1939, a movie called *The Wizard of Oz* was made. In it, Dorothy and her Kansas prairie home are swept away by a powerful tornado. Tornadoes are a threat to Kansas. Tornadoes happen when hot, humid air smacks into cool air sweeping down from the north. Most of these damaging "twisters" rage across Kansas in May and June.

Kansas is the country's land center. Kansas also remains at the center of the country's business and farm interests. Across Kansas rode much of America's past. From the sound of footsteps crossing the dry Kansas prairie to the morning song of a Kansas meadowlark (MEH-doh-lark), Kansas blends its never-quit spirit of the past with a bright focus on the future.

Did You Know? If you fold a map of the forty-eight states that border each other in half from north to south, then fold the map again from east to west, Kansas will be found at the map's center.

★ ★ ★ ★ ★ ★ ★ THINK ABOUT IT! ★ ★ ★ ★ ★ ★ ★

1. Why would some people stop to settle in Kansas instead of traveling on to Santa Fe or Oregon?

2. List three forces of nature. Tell how each force can change the look of land.

Workbook p.53
Self-Check

3. How does Kansas land change from east to west?

OKLAHOMA

★ ★

GEOFACTS
- capital: Oklahoma City
- statehood: 1907 (46th)
- rank in size: 18th
- rank in population: 28th (urban 68%, rural 32%)
- U.S. representatives: 6
- motto: "Labor Conquers All Things"

▲ Native American Exposition at Anadarka

▲ Quachita National Forest

To the glory of Native Americans the dance members of Oklahoma's Indian tribes during the Red Earth festival. Grand shows of color honor the beliefs and history of American Indians.

To the roar of a thrill-loving crowd rides the calf roper in one of Oklahoma's many exciting rodeos (ROH-dee-ohs). Bold acts of skill honor the quick-thinking, fast-riding Oklahoma cowboy.

Weary hikers rest to the hush of an evening sunset and the crackle of an open campfire rest. The tired but happy walkers have spent the day honoring some of Oklahoma's land of stunning beauty.

And, to the wide grins of people across America play out the roles of the time-honored musical *Oklahoma!* It is here that the feelings of many of Oklahoma's people are heard in the show's theme song:

> Oklahoma! where the wind comes sweepin' down the plain,
>
> And the wavin' wheat can sure smell sweet
>
> When the wind comes right behind the rain.
>
> We know we belong to the land
>
> And the land we belong to is grand!

⚡ **Critical Thinking**
Why would the smell of wheat and rain be important to people?

Places to See! People to Know!

▶ Pioneer Woman Statue and Museum, Ponca City — site of bronze statue honoring pioneer women as well as a museum of pioneer clothes, tools and crafts

▶ National Cowboy Hall of Fame and Western Heritage Center, Oklahoma City — site of the Rodeo Hall of Fame; holds the world's largest collection of cowboy memories including a kachina doll collection held by the late actor John Wayne

▶ Ralph Ellison (b.1914) — wrote *The Invisible Man* in 1952 about the African American experience in America

▶ Will Rogers (b.1879) — American humorist; part Native American; began as a roper in the wild-west shows of the late 1800s; went on to Hollywood fame

GeoWords
mesa — a tabletop area of land that rises above a lower plain

⚡ **Critical Thinking**
How does climate affect Oklahoma land?

▲ Turner Falls in the Arbuckle Mountains

Did You Know? White emigrants who tried to sneak into land set aside for land rushes were called "sooners." People who placed glowing ads about Oklahoma land for sale were called "boomers" because they caused Oklahoma's population to boom. Today, Oklahoma is sometimes called the "Sooner State" and sometimes called the "Boomer State."

What makes Oklahoma land so grand? From the Red River region to the flattened hills of the state's panhandle, Oklahoma is graced with nature's paintbrush. Deep-red soil cuts across the center of the state from north to south. Deep-green forests of oak stretch across the sandstone hills. To the northeast lie the soft tans of the High Plains. A rainbow of color tops the granite rock of the Wichita Mountains in southwestern Oklahoma.

Oklahoma is a state where open land stretches for miles on end. Wild mustang horses roam wild and free in the National Wild Horse Refuge in northeastern Oklahoma. Roadrunners share the land with scissor-tailed flycatchers, blue herons, and wild turkeys.

Oklahoma tilts from northwest to southeast. The Black **Mesa** (MA-sah) in Oklahoma's Panhandle is the highest point (4,973 feet above sea level). Along the Little River in Oklahoma's southeast corner, the land only rises to 287 feet above sea level.

Clear-water lakes and gently flowing rivers add to Oklahoma's beauty. Oklahoma has over 300 lakes with a total of more than 2,000 miles of shoreline. Most of the lakes are found in the southeast part of the state. Here, about fifty inches of earth-soaking rains fall each year. In contrast, only about fifteen inches of yearly rain falls in Oklahoma's Panhandle.

Oklahoma is a leading state in the growing of wheat and the raising of beef cattle. Peanuts, corn, soybeans, and cotton also are grown.

Oklahoma is a state rich in the natural resource of oil. One of the state's first oil wells was drilled by Frank Phillips in 1897. Today, oil wells dot the state. Oklahoma's oil wealth is affected by world oil supplies and price.

How did the state of Oklahoma get its shape? Oklahoma land was first set aside for Native Americans. In the early 1800s, land west of the Mississippi River was kept as Indian Territory (TAIR-ih-toh-ree). The United States government planned to move all Native Americans living east of the Mississippi River to these western lands.

In 1818 and 1825, the government signed treaties with the Osage and Quapaw Indians living in the Indian Territory. The treaties moved these two Native American tribes off their land to lands further west. Later, treaties were signed with western tribes to make room for the Osage and Quapaw. Osage and Quapaw land was set aside for Native Americans from the east.

Slowly, members of the Five Civilized (SIH-vih-lyzd) Tribes (Choctaw, Cherokee, Chickasaw, Seminole, and Creek) were forced off their eastern lands. Under the watch of the U.S. army, the Native Americans were marched across the country and onto the lands of the Indian Territory. The Trail of Tears is remembered as one of the worst of these forced marches.

Once on Indian Territory, the Five Civilized Tribes set up new tribal governments. The United States government promised the Indians that this new land would be theirs "as long as grass shall grow and rivers run." Yet, this was not to be.

What happened to the land set aside for Native Americans? After the Civil War, there was a second Trail of Tears. Native Americans were again forced to leave their lands. Reservations were set up for Native Americans tribes. Today, more Native Americans live in Oklahoma than in any other state. Thirty-six Native American tribes are at home in Oklahoma.

The crunch of wagons wheels on prairie soil brought wave after wave of pioneer farmers to Oklahoma. Large areas of land were settled by great land rushes like the Cherokee Strip land rush. Fights sometimes started between a rancher who wanted to graze his cattle across the prairie and a farmer who wanted to fence in his land.

People from China, Japan, Canada, Mexico, France, and other countries also came to settle on Oklahoma soil. Yearly, Oklahoma festivals such as the Czech Festival, Tulsa's Scottish Games and Gatherings, Oktoberfest, and many Native American events honor the state's rich heritage.

☆ ☆ ☆ ☆ ☆ ☆ ☆ ☆ ☆

City names like Wagoner, Hog Shooter, Broken Arrow, and Oil City tell of Oklahoma's often sad and difficult past as well as its hopeful dreams. To borrow from the Sauk and Fox language, Oklahoma is a land where the "ma no ka mi" (spring), "la na wi ki" (autumn), "ta kwa ki" (summer) and "la lo li" (winter) bring changing beauty to a vast and splendid land.

Critical Thinking

Today, many Native American tribes feel that people do not know the true history of the American Indian. Why is it important to learn the true history of Native Americans?

▲ Three Oklahoma youth in Native American dress

Did You Know? Five Native American ballerinas of Native American heritage from Oklahoma have become world famous. They are Maria Tallchief, Marjorie Tallchief, Yvonne Chouteau, Rozella Hightower, and Moscelyne Larkin.

 **THINK ABOUT IT!** ★ ★ ★ ★ ★ ★ ★ ★

1. What are five things you might see in Oklahoma?

2. List two things about Oklahoma land that change from east to west.

3. What was the second Trail of Tears?

 Workbook p. 54
Self-Check

The Climate of the United States

★ ★ ★ ★ ★ ★ ★ ★   ★ ★ ★ ★ ★ ★ ★ ★

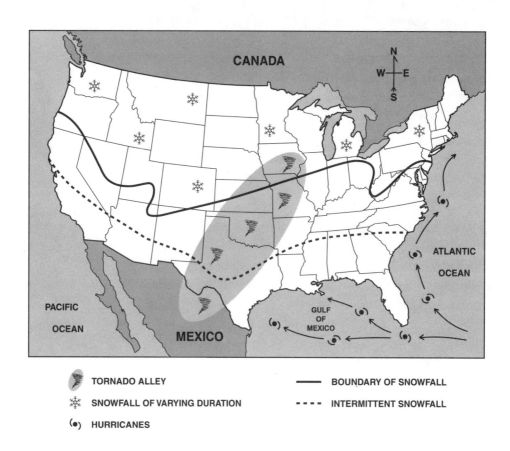

🌀 TORNADO ALLEY	—— BOUNDARY OF SNOWFALL
❄ SNOWFALL OF VARYING DURATION	- - - - INTERMITTENT SNOWFALL
(•) HURRICANES	

The United States is made up of many different climates. Climate is one of nature's forces. Climate is the weather that is expected for a region. Climate affects the country's environment, how the land is used, where people choose to live, and even how people feel from day to day.

A region's geography has an effect on a region's climate. Mountains, dryland areas, lakes, valleys, lowlands, and coastal regions all have climates that are true for each certain region. Likewise, an area's climate has a direct effect on the type of land, kind of plants, and types of animals found in a region.

Heat from the sun and the turning of the Earth cause climate. The spinning of the Earth causes a change in heat patterns along the surface of the Earth. This change in heat patterns changes wind and moisture from place to place. For the most part, these patterns are the same from year to year. Climate patterns bring expected weather to a region.

Land surfaces heat and cool far more rapidly than do water surfaces. So, the surface air over land is warmer in the summer and colder in the winter than over ocean water. Land in the center of the country tends to be drier and hotter in the summer and colder in the winter, than coastal areas.

The climates of the United States are as varied as the kinds of land that make up the many regions found in the country. Climate directs the activities of people. Climate gives meaning to the word "season." Often, based on a region's climate, people decide how and when the region's land will be used.

The Rocky Mountain States ★ ★ ★ ★ ★

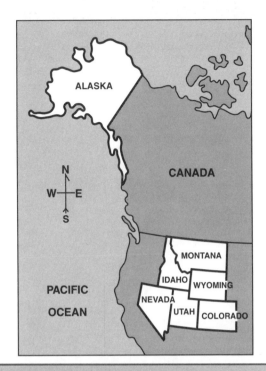

One fine day in 1893, Katharine Lee Bates stood looking out to the east from her place on Pike's Peak in the Colorado Rockies. Taken by the wonders of nature that stretched out before her, Katharine Lee Bates placed her thoughts and feelings into a poem. The poem began:

> O beautiful! for spacious skies,
> For amber waves of grain,
> For purple mountains majesty
> Above the fruited plain!

Around 1898, music was added to her poetry, and a song was born. Today, this well-loved song is known as "America the Beautiful." To the east of where Katharine Lee Bates stood on that fateful day stretches America's breadbasket, the Great Plains. To the west rises the "majesty" of the Rocky Mountains. These grand mountains form the largest mountain system in the United States.

The Rocky Mountains form the Continental (con-tih-NEN-tal) Divide. Rivers to the west of the Continential Divide flow to the Pacific Ocean. Those east flow to the Great Plains and beyond. Earth forces shaped the Rocky Mountains millions of years ago when powerful crushing and cracking of the Earth's crust forced it high into the clouds. Along the sides of the mountains are fossils from the sea, as well as rocks that formed inside the Earth. Over the years, wind and rain have worn down the Rocky Mountains. Yet, several peaks still tower over the plain at amazing heights of 13,000 and 14,000 feet above sea level.

One of the many themes that weaves its way across the Rocky Mountains is mining. Great finds of Rocky Mountain gold and silver built towns seemingly overnight. The towns became ghost towns just as quickly after the mines had given up all the riches they had to offer.

The lives of Native Americans, whose homelands stood as barriers to the fur traders, miners, pioneer farmers, and town builders of the 1800s, also quickly changed. Diseases and war brought by whites, and loss of native lands finally took their toll on the region's Native Americans. Those who survived were placed on reservations.

Flowing across this region of rugged beauty, frontier, and cities that were built on land where tears and sweat were shed are themes that join today to the past and the future. These themes, just like the riches of the Rocky Mountains, are waiting to be found.

ALASKA

★ ★

GEOFACTS
- capital: Juneau
- statehood: 1959 (49th)
- rank in size: 1st
- rank in population: 49th (urban 68%, rural 32%)
- U.S. representatives: 1
- motto: "North to the Future"

▲ Polar bears in Alaska's arctic region

▲ Foggy mountain peaks and icebergs in Glacier Bay

GeoWords
glacier — a huge mass of ice which can range in thickness from 300 feet to 10,000 feet

permafrost — a layer of soil that is always frozen

igloos — a rounded shelter; Alaskan Eskimos built igloos with sod, whalebone and driftwood

Critical Thinking
What is meant by the "the last frontier?"

Places to See! People to Know!

▶ Sitka National Historical Park — sight of the Sitka Indians last battle of resistance against Russians

▶ Totem Bight State Historical Park — nineteenth century Indian totem poles

▶ Libby Riddles (b.1956) — first woman to win the Iditarod Sled Dog Race (1985)

▶ John Muir (b.1838) — worked with President Theodore Roosevelt to set aside forest land in Alaska as national forests

Alaska has the highest mountain in North America, the largest **glacier** and the longest chain of volcanos. Alaska is home to the polar bear, grizzly bear, moose, elk, fifteen different kinds of whales, musk ox, and puffins. While **permafrost** covers the ground to the north, great forests of pine spread across the southern part of the state. And above it all, beautiful shows of color, called the northern lights, burst across the Alaskan night sky.

Alaska is often called the "land of the midnight sun." This is because one-fourth of the state is above the Arctic Circle. Here, there are days of daylight and days of night.

Alaska also is often called "the last frontier." More than two-thirds of all Alaskans settled there from other areas. Yet, the spirit of Alaska comes from its native peoples. In fact, the word Alaska comes from the native word "al-ay-es-ka," which means "great land."

Who were the first Alaskans? More than 15,000 years ago, a land bridge connected Siberia and Alaska. It is believed that the early people crossed from Siberia to Alaska on this land bridge. Today, the bridge lies below the Bering Sea.

The early Alaskans moved to different areas. Eskimos settled along the Bering Sea and up to the Arctic Ocean. Being great hunters, the Eskimos

THE PEOPLE'S PUBLISHING GROUP, INC. *Our United States Geography: Our Regions and People*

survived on caribou, waterfowl, seals, and whales. They lived in **igloos**. Mask-making became a very important part of the Eskimo culture. Often, dancers wore the masks during **festivals**. Another group, the Aleuts, settled along the Aleutian Islands. Today, there are only a few Aleut settlements. But long ago, there were many Aleut settlements. The Aleuts lived off the sea. From the sea animals, they got meat for food, skin for clothing and shelter, and bones for tools. Masks also were important in the culture of the early Aleuts.

A third group of early Alaskans, the Indians, settled in the interior of Alaska. Also great hunters, the Indians lived on caribou and moose. Rivers were fished for salmon. The Indians developed snowshoes for walking on the top of snow. **Totem** poles were an important part of Native American culture.

How did the Alaska Native Claims Settlement Act affect Native Alaskans? In 1971, the United States Congress passed the Alaska Native Claims Settlement Act. It gave 44 million acres of land to the Aleuts, Eskimos, and Indians. This act was passed to make up for land wrongly taken from Native Alaskans. As the result of this law, Native Alaskans formed many businesses. Yet, the **customs** of each culture have not been forgotten.

Do most people in Alaska live in cities? Most of Alaska is untamed frontier area. On the average, there are 68 people within each 100 square miles. Yet, most of the people of Alaska live in cities. In fact, more than 40 percent of the state's population lives in the city of Anchorage.

Anchorage was first settled in 1915. It began as a camp of tents and log cabins. The settlers of Anchorage came to help build the railroad across Alaska's rugged land. Today, Anchorage is a major city with a population of more than 226,000 people. Still, Anchorage keeps close ties with its history.

Every year, the Iditarod Trail Sled Dog Race is held on the first Saturday of March. The race begins in downtown Anchorage. This 1,049-mile race honors the **mushers** who raced from Anchorage to Nome in 1925. These mushers raced through the cold and snow to bring medicine to save the people of Nome. The people of Nome were very sick. The medicine brought by the mushers saved many lives.

Another special festival is Quiana Alaska. This festival is held each October. It is a special time when Native Alaskans celebrate their customs. At this time, Eskimos and Indians perform their native dances. They tell stories about the past. It is a time for the native people of Alaska to share their **heritage**.

How did Alaska become a state? The United States bought the land that was to become Alaska from Russia in 1867. William H. Seward was **secretary of state** at that time. He worked out an agreement between the two countries to buy the land. The United States paid $7.2 million for the land which became Alaska. This was about two cents per acre.

GeoWords
festivals — special celebrations
totem — an object that is a symbol of a family, clan, or tribe
customs — the special way of doing things among different cultures
mushers — people who drive dogsleds
heritage — the past culture of a group of people

Critical Thinking
Why do you think William Seward pushed for buying Alaskan land?

▲ The oil pipeline in the frozen tundra

Did You Know? "Eskimo ice cream" is made of snow, whale blubber or fat, and blueberries.

Critical Thinking

The first oil tanker to leave Prudhoe Bay carried 7.2 million gallons of oil. This is the same as the amount paid for the Alaskan land. If feelings were high against the pipeline, why do you think Alaska and the federal government ended up building it?

▲ Alaska's Eskimos have adapted to both land and sea.

Did You Know? The Alaska malamute is a working dog that was first used by the Malamute tribe to pull sleds across the snows of the northwestern part of the state.

Workbook p. 58
Self-Check

People called the purchase of Alaskan land "Seward's Folly." Many people did not agree with paying millions of dollars for what they thought was a land of ice and snow. But that was before gold and oil were discovered in Alaska.

How did the discovery of gold and oil change Alaska? The discovery of gold in 1896 brought a rush of people to Alaska searching for their fortune. Small towns swelled with **gold rushers**. Between 1890 and 1900, the population of Alaska almost doubled.

The discovery of oil in Prudhoe Bay in 1968 brought many changes to Alaska. A north to south 800- mile pipeline was built across Alaska to transport the oil from Prudhoe Bay to Valdez. Oil was to bring wealth to Alaska. Still, many people did not want the pipeline. They felt an oil leak would be very harmful to the environment.

For several years, oil was piped across Alaska with few problems. Then in 1989, disaster struck. An oil tanker called the *Exxon Valdez* spilled 10 million gallons of oil into Prince William Sound. Hundreds of miles of coastline became covered with oil. Birds, fish, seals, and many other water animals died. Many people tried to stop the spread of oil. Yet, much damage was done to the environment. The *Exxon Valdez* spill was the worst oil spill in the history of the United States.

☆ ☆ ☆ ☆ ☆ ☆ ☆ ☆ ☆

Today, Alaska remains a land of contrasts. Oil, tourism, and fishing are its major industries. The vast wilderness holds great beauty for some. They would like to see Alaska remain wild. For others, Alaska is a land of **natural resources** which could bring riches to the people of the state. The balance between preserving (or holding on to) wilderness, and taming (or settling and using the natural resources of) the Alaskan frontier remains a great **challenge** (CHAH-lenj) for the people of Alaska.

THINK ABOUT IT!

1. What are two festivals that help preserve the different heritages found in Alaska?

2. The discovery of which two natural resources changed the use of Alaska's land?

3. What is meant by the term "nature's ruling hand?"

MONTANA

★ ★

GEOFACTS
- capital: Helena
- statehood: 1889 (41st)
- rank in size: 4th

- rank in population: 44th (urban 52%, rural 48%)
- U.S. representatives: 1
- motto: "Gold and Silver"

▲ Rocky Mountain Bighorn Sheep

▲ Glacier National Park on Swift Current Lake

Montana is a state of unbounded beauty where nature's wonders spread out to the north, south, east, and west. It is where wildflowers in shades of purple, yellow, and pink stretch above the green prairie grasses to catch the morning sun. It is where great gray mountain peaks rise into the clouds. It is where autumn golds and oranges grace the banks beyond cool, bubbling streams.

Tucked away in northwestern Montana is Glacier National Park. Here, people can walk the length of a vast glacier. Warm summer winds seem to have no effect on these great mountains of ice. Visitors in rolled-up shirtsleeves can peer down deep cracks in the glacier. Very quickly, the earth-carving power of these great mounds of packed ice can be felt.

What is the land in Montana like? Montana is made up of two land regions. To the east lie the Great Plains. This area covers move than half of Montana.

Endless stretches of grassland carpet the Great Plains region. Here, cattle freely roam across rolling hills and wide river valleys. Here, fields of golden wheat ripple in the Montana wind. Other crops grown in this region are potatoes, sugar beets, and barley.

The Rocky Mountains cover western Montana. The mountains of this area are covered with forests of fir, pine, and spruce. Flat, grassy river valleys crisscross the region. In southwestern Montana, the valleys

Critical Thinking

What do you think it feels like to look down into the depths of a glacial crack?

Places to See! People to Know!

► Custer Battlefield National Monument, Little Bighorn River Valley — site of Sioux and Cheyenne victory over Lieutenant Colonel George Custer in 1876.

► Fossil Beds, Hell Creek — site of discovery of nearly complete skeleton of Tyrannosaurus Rex

► Pierre-Jean De Smet (b.1801) — called "Black Robe" by the Native Americans; did missionary work among Salish and Blackfeet Indians; kept knowledge of gold and silver in mountains quiet for fear of changing the lifestyle of Montana's Native Americans

► Plenty Coups (b.1848) — Crow Indian leader; represented American Indians at the dedication ceremony for the Tomb of the Unknown Soldier

Critical Thinking

What does the flow of the Missouri River tell you about the tilt of land from America's north to south?

stretch 30 to 40 miles wide. Yet, to the north, river valleys cut a more narrow trail of 1 to 5 miles in width.

More than fifty mountain ranges stretch across Montana. Some of their names are Big Belt, Swan, Madison, Little Belt, Crazy and Flathead. Montana mountains rise to more than 12,000 feet above sea level. Logging is an important industry in this region.

The mighty Missouri River gets its start in Montana. It is here that the Madison, Jefferson and Gallatin rivers come together to form this all-important river system. Fort Peck Dam was built along its eastern course. From the damming of the Missouri River comes the outstretched clearwater beauty of Fork Peck Lake.

Is it always cold in Montana? It is not always cold in Montana. Yet, the state does have mild summers and cold winters. Montana's coldest temperature was a -70° below zero. Montana also has reached a scorching 117°(F).

Montana's climate is affected by the Rocky Mountains. Weather to the west of the Rocky Mountains has cooler winters and warmer summers than the area east of the mountain range. The mountains protect western Montana from cold northern winds that blast their way across the Great Plains.

More rain falls in western Montana. Here warm moist air swoops up the western mountain ridges. Rain falls when the warm air meets cooler air along the mountainsides.

▲ An open copper mine in Butte, Montana

Snow falling from above and faults in the Earth's crust far below make Montana a state filled with surprises. More than 30 inches of snow may fall each year on the great mountain ridges of northwestern Montana. Much of the snow stays on the ground for six months of the year.

Earthquakes have happened in Montana. The state's worst earthquake time was in 1935. It was then that no less than 1,200 shocks were felt for eighty days in the Helena area.

What kind of animals are found in Montana? The great cry of a sleek mountain lion or the roar of an awesome moose can be heard in the stillness of a Montana morning sunrise. Agile mountain goats catch the afternoon sun high in Montana's mountains. Bald eagles, grizzly bears, and gray wolf are all protected by laws.

Montana is home to about 300 birds. Magpies looking for a tasty insect can be seen carelessly walking along the backs of roaming animals. Trumpeter swans, rare and stunning in their size and beauty, spend winter along Montana's lakes.

Did You Know? At one time, swamps and tropical rain forests covered the area that is now Montana. Great dinosaurs such as *Tyrannosaurus Rex, Triceratops* and *Stegosaurus* roamed the land.

How was Montana settled? Early Native Americans that lived across the Montana plain hunted buffalo and gathered wild roots and berries. Soon, fur traders and trappers entered Montana. Trading posts opened along Montana rivers. Life quickly changed for Native Americans living on land that was to become Montana.

Real change came to Montana when gold, silver, and then copper were found in its mineral rich mountains. Montana's gold rush began in 1862. Overnight, towns such as Bannuck, Virginia City, and Nevada City grew.

Among such **gulches** (GUL-ches) as Alder Gulch, Grizzly Gulch, and Last Chance Gulch rushed thousands of people wanting to file claims to land. The mining of gold and silver made some men vastly rich. Such quick wealth brought a band of stagecoach robbers to Montana, looking to stake their own lawless claim to Montana riches.

Yet, it was copper that brought greatest wealth to Montana. Marcus Daly and William Clark were two "copper kings" who fought for control of Montana's copper wealth. Copper mining brought immigrants from northern Europe and China to Montana. African Americans moved north to Montana from southern states.

Copper interests had a big impact on Montana. Laws were passed around the copper interests. Copper strip mining scarred Montana land. Mining was hard and often filled with danger. Copper mining in Montana came to a close in the 1970s. Today, coal and oil have replaced Montana's copper-mining efforts.

☆ ☆ ☆ ☆ ☆ ☆ ☆ ☆ ☆

Montana is sometimes called "the Last Best Place. "Other names given to Montana are "the Treasure State" and "Big Sky Country. "All names fit Montana well. From its quiet glacial lakes to its rugged western mountains to its rolling grasslands, Montana is one of America's treasures.

GeoWords
gulch — a ravine, or deep valley

Critical Thinking
Why do you think people in Montana put forth great effort to stop copper strip mining?

Did You Know? "I am tired of fighting. Our chiefs are killed. It is cold and we have no blankets. The little children are freezing to death. I want to have time to look for my children and see how many of them I can find. Maybe I shall find them among the dead. Hear me, my chiefs. I am tired. My heart is sick and sad. From where the sun now stands, I will fight no more forever."

Chief Joseph upon surrendering, 1877

 **THINK ABOUT IT!**

1. Write a sentence that tells four things about Montana.

2. Why does more rain fall in western Montana than along the Great Plains?

3. How did the finding of gold and copper affect Montana?

 Workbook p. 59
Self-Check

WYOMING

★ ★

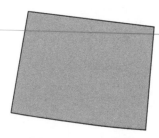

GEOFACTS • capital: Cheyenne
• statehood: 1890 (44th)
• rank in size: 9th

• rank in population: 50th (urban 65%, rural 35%)
• U.S. representatives: 1
• motto: "Equal Rights"

▲ The Grand Teton Mountains

▲ Horses graze in Wyoming's open pasture lands.

Critical Thinking
What do you think it would feel like to stand next to one of Yellowstone's geysers when it erupted? Explain your answer.

Places to See! People to Know!
▶ Fossil Butte National Monument, Kemmerer — rock formation that carries the world's largest remains of prehistoric fish
▶ Grand Tetons National Park, Yellowstone — scenic area
▶ Esther Hobart Morris (b.1814) — first woman judge in the United States
▶ Peggy Curry (b.1911) — author of such Wyoming books as *Fire in the Water*, *Red Wind of Wyoming* and *The Oil Patch*.

Once every sixty-five minutes, in the northwest corner of Wyoming, a great rush of steam shoots out of the earth. For about four minutes, the steam reaches almost 160 feet into the air. And then the steam seems to vanish, not be seen again until sixty-five minutes later.

This well-timed burst of steam comes from a **geyser** (GY-ser) named Old Faithful. It is found in Yellowstone National Park. There are about 200 active geysers in Yellowstone. Some, like Old Faithful, explode in great gusts of steam in steady time. Others, like the Beehive Geyser, burst forth without notice.

How are geysers formed? Geysers form near rivers or lakes where water drains into the depths of the Earth. A channel from the surface reaches straight down, deep into the Earth. Cold water seeps into this channel until it reaches very hot rocks far below the surface. The water is heated above the boiling point.

Soon, steam forms. Slowly, the water in the channel rises and begins to spill over the top. As this happens, the power of steam takes over. Quickly, all the water in the channel turns to steam and explodes to shoot high above the Earth's surface.

After erupting, some of the water is lost to the air as steam. Some falls back to the Earth as water and refills the channel. Some Yellowstone geysers are cone shaped. These geysers shoot and refill with the same water over and over again.

GeoWords
canyon — a narrow valley with steep sides
gap — an opening in a mountain ridge

The rocks that heat Wyoming's explosive (eks-PLOH-siv) waters are from Wyoming's past. About 600,000 years ago, land that came to be known as Wyoming was rocked by massive, or very large, volcanic action. Heat from the melted rock still lies under Wyoming soil, acting like a great underground frying pan.

What else is found in Yellowstone National Park? Yellowstone's 3,472 square acres is filled with surprises. Living freely in its protected environment are more than 60 different kinds of animals, 200 kinds of birds, and many kinds of reptiles and amphibians (am-FIH-bee-ans). The park is very much like it was more than one hundred years ago, when it became the world's first national park.

Visitors to Yellowstone can be greeted by a lumbering 300-to 400-pound three-foot tall black bear. With sharp claws and teeth to match, this Yellowstone animal commands respect. Also found are grizzly bears plus mule deer, coyotes, moose, and many other wild animals. More elk are found in this area than anywhere else in the world.

Within Yellowstone National Park's striking beauty are mountains, grasslands, and forests. Steaming mineral springs wrapped in color dot the park. Jagged, snow-touched mountains rise above evergreen forests. Waters from Yellowstone River plunge 308 feet, tumbling far into the depths of the Grand **Canyon** of Yellowstone.

In 1988, a raging forest fire scorched much of Yellowstone's grand forests. There was a great loss of wildlife and plantlife. Slowly, Yellowstone is being reborn. First, great meadows of stunning wildflowers grew through the charred ashes of trees that once graced the land. Next, Yellowstone began to reforest.

What other great sights are found in Wyoming? Wyoming is a mix of grasslands, towering mountains, and flat-bottom basins. The Great Plains covers the eastern part of the state. Here, sheep and cattle brushed by dry winds graze under sunny skies.

The Rocky Mountains sweep across western Wyoming from north to south. Wyoming's tallest mountain peaks are found in the Wind River Range. Here, snow-capped mountains soar to higher than 13,000 feet. At the southern end of this mountain range is found the **gap** used by settlers traveling west in their dust-covered, trail-worn wagons.

Wyoming's basin areas are scattered between the Great Plains and the Rocky Mountains. These are mostly treeless areas. Rainfall is less here than in the mountains. Ranchers graze great herds of cattle and sheep across the basins.

The Continental Divide splits and goes around Wyoming's Great Divide Basin. Water does not flow east or west. Whatever rain falls in the Great Divide Basin stays in place.

How much rain does Wyoming get each year? Places like the Great Divide Basin get very little rainfall. Sagebrush and short, brown grasses

⚡ **Critical Thinking**
What do you think would happen if a lot of rain fell at one time in the Great Divide basin?

▲ Men and women show their skills at Wyoming's rodeos.

Did You Know? Oil and natural gas are Wyoming's leading minerals. Most of Wyoming's oil and natural gas is found in the southeastern part of the state.

Critical Thinking

Why do you think the people of Wyoming decided to grant women's rights long before any other state or the country?

cover these dry areas. Some basin areas get as little as 5 inches a rain every year.

Most of Wyoming's rain falls in the state's northwestern mountains. Here, up to 50 inches may fall each year. Up to 260 inches of snow can bury Wyoming's mountains. Great swirls of wind can cause dust storms in the summer and blizzards in the winter.

Wyoming is the second highest state in the country. Graced by nature's artful hand, Wyoming land rises about 6,700 feet above sea level. Cool summer days in the mountains contrast with hot days in such places as the Red Desert of the Great Divide basin.

What are some events that make up Wyoming's history? Battles that cost many lives were fought between the United States Army and Native Americans in Wyoming. Great chiefs, such as Red Cloud and Washakie, led their people in battles against white use of Indian land.

Wars between cattle owners and sheep ranchers cause years of anger, fighting, and death between Wyoming's settlers. Through it all ran the thread of women's rights. In 1869, Wyoming was the first state to grant women the right to vote and to hold political office.

☆ ☆ ☆ ☆ ☆ ☆ ☆ ☆

The forces of nature carved and shaped Wyoming. Today, the rushing waters of a Wyoming waterfall or the blinding power of a Rocky Mountain snowstorm are reminders of nature's ruling hand.

▲ The life of a cowhand is hard work in Wyoming

Did You Know? The Pony Express ran along the Oregon Trail across Wyoming. People wishing to send a letter to someone across the country would send it by Pony Express. A letter could cost as much as $5 to send. Letters would pass from rider to rider who ran from robbers and Native Americans in an effort to deliver the mail. The Pony Express lasted from 1860 to 1861, when it was replaced with trains.

★ ★ ★ ★ ★ ★ ★ ★ THINK ABOUT IT! ★ ★ ★ ★ ★ ★ ★ ★

1. Explain how a geyser forms.

2. Tell three things that contrast Wyoming's mountains with its basin areas.

3. What is meant by the term "nature's ruling hand?"

 Workbook p. 60
Self-Check

COLORADO

★ ★

GEOFACTS
- capital: Denver
- statehood: 1876 (38th)
- rank in size: 8th
- rank in population: 26th (urban 82%, rural 18%)
- U.S. representatives: 6
- motto: "Nothing Without Providence"

▲ Space and military activity are part of life in Colorado.

Thomas Hornsby Ferril lived all his life in Colorado. One of the poems he wrote is called "Waltz Against The Mountains." He was born in 1896, just twenty years after Colorado became a state. Denver, the city his poem is about, grew from the gold rush that overtook Colorado in 1859. For many years, people from the east flocked westward looking for gold in the Colorado mountains.

How important was gold in people's settlement of Colorado? Gold fever hit Colorado in 1859 when a rich **lode** of gold was found west of early Denver City. Word quickly spread across the Great Plains, and eastward, of Colorado mountains teeming with gold. Soon almost 100,000 people, called "fifty-niners," headed west to strike it rich.

Many "fifty-niners" were misled by ads making claims of huge gold finds in Colorado. Some of them, caught by little water and food as they tried to cross the prairies of the Great Plains, turned back before reaching Colorado. Others who made the trip spent long days panning for gold along Colorado river banks. A few lucky ones found gold.

GeoWords

lode — a vein, or area, where a mineral can be found

Critical Thinking

Why do you think "Waltz Against The Mountains" is a good title for a poem about Denver?

Places to See! People to Know!

▶ Mesa Verde National Park, Cortez — site of ancient Native American cliff dwellers; the park covers 52,000 acres

▶ United States Mint, Denver — place where United States coins are made; makes more than five billion coins each year

▶ Clara Brown (b.1803) — enslaved woman who bought her freedom and then joined the 1859 gold rush; turned her home into a hospital and boarding house for poor miners

▶ Black Kettle (b.1820) — Cheyenne chief who saw the people of his village killed by U.S. Army troops; killed by General Custer's troops during a time when peace efforts were being made between Black Kettle and the U.S. government

Critical Thinking

Why do you think mining companies wrote ads that made the amount of gold in Colorado seem greater than it really was?

▲ Colorado's timber trees and fishing streams provide great natural beauty.

Did You Know? People moving north from Mexico settled the towns of Garcia, San Luis, and Conejos. These were Colorado's first towns not settled by Native Americans.

Denver began as a tent city filled with hopeful gold diggers. Many who decided to stay sent for their wives and children back east. Soon, more people rode across Denver's unpaved, dusty main street. Frame houses replaced tents. Stores supplied goods for the townspeople.

Today, Denver is Colorado's busiest city. About half of all people living in Colorado live in or around the city of Denver. More than 460,000 people live in Denver alone. This rapidly growing city has more hospitals, colleges, banks and business centers than any other city between the states of Missouri and California. The dome of Denver's capitol building is covered with a thin layer of gold to honor the city's start as a gold-mining town.

What happened to the Native Americans who once settled on the land that became known as Colorado? For years, Native Americans lived across the plains and within the mountain cliffs that line present-day Colorado. Experts believe that wandering tribes of Native Americans found food and shelter from Colorado land as long as 20,000 years ago.

By 1848, lands that had been claimed by France and by Mexico became part of the growing United States. Few concerned themselves with the fact that Native Americans had lived on the land for centuries.

Treaties were made with Native Americans forcing them from land they called their home. The killing of buffalo to stop the Native Americans' food supply and the use of the Army against them gave Native Americans little choice but to sign treaties.

Today, about 3,000 Native Americans (Ute) live on two reservations in southern Colorado. Native Americans make up about 1 percent of Colorado's population. Almost half of all people living in Colorado were born outside the state. People have moved to Colorado from Mexico, Europe, Asia, and every state in the United States.

Why is the land of Colorado so well liked? The word Colorado is Spanish for "colored red." Red can be seen across Colorado from the rushing red water of the Colorado River to the earthy brown reds of mountain cliffs that once sheltered cliff-dwelling Native Americans.

Colorado can be divided into four main land regions. To the east lies the Great Plains region. The land here gently slopes upward from the east to the base of the Rocky Mountains in the central part of the state. Irrigation is used to turn some of the dry plain into fertile farming area. Ranchers use other areas for grazing beef cattle.

The Comanche National Grassland and the Pawnee National Grassland are two areas where farming is no longer allowed. In these areas, grasses that grew before farmers broke the sod in the 1800s now grow again. Much of these two grassland areas have been set aside as park and wildlife refuges.

The Rocky Mountains are found west of the Great Plains. These snowcapped peaks of beauty stretch as high as 14,000 feet into the sky. Much of the lush forested land that bends and turns across the mountains is still frontier land. Great layers of winter snow cover the aspen, ash, and oak trees that turn the mountains the color of gold each fall.

The soft, powdery snow of Colorado brings ski-loving people to its many winter resort areas. Summer brings people who love to raft along the rushing, white-capped waves of Colorado's gleaming, cold-water rivers. Others enjoy a fall hike in one of Colorado's scenic Rocky Mountain valleys where the music of nature can be heard across the changing colors of the land.

What regions lie west of the Rocky Mountains? The Colorado Plateau lies to Colorado's far west. The Colorado Basin is tucked away in the state's northwest corner. Cattle and sheep graze across rolling hills of the plateau region and the sagebrush plain of the basin.

☆ ☆ ☆ ☆ ☆ ☆ ☆ ☆

Today, the mining of oil and coal has replaced the gold finds of the past. Yet today, just as in the past, for those who live and for those who visit, Colorado's towering beauty is an ever-present reminder of nature's majesty.

Critical Thinking
Why do you think much of Colorado's Rocky Mountain region is still a frontier?

▲ White emigrants crossed the Rocky Mountain region in covered wagons.

Did You Know? Spanish explorers brought horses to the Southwest. Horses became part of Native American life during the early 1600s. With the horse, Native Americans could better follow roaming buffalo herds. Horses made the packing and moving of buffalo-hide shelters easier. Whole villages would follow the seasonal wanderings of the buffalo as the animals grazed across the plain.

★ ★ ★ ★ ★ ★ ★ ★ **THINK ABOUT IT!** ★ ★ ★ ★ ★ ★ ★ ★

1. What affect did the finding of mountain gold have on Colorado?

2. What affect did the loss of buffalo have on Native Americans?

3. Why is Colorado a favorite spot for people who love to ski?

 Workbook p. 61
Self-Check

IDAHO

★ ★

GEOFACTS
- capital: Boise
- statehood: 1890 (43rd)
- rank in size: 13th
- rank in population: 42nd (urban 57%, rural 43%)
- U.S. representatives: 2
- motto: "It Is Forever"

▲ Baron Lake in Idaho's Sawtooth Mountains

▲ The Idaho landscape can look like a patchwork quilt.

⚡ **Critical Thinking**

How can the Rocky Mountains protect western Idaho from cold winds blowing down from Canada?

Places to See! People to Know!

▶ Craters of the Moon National Monument, Arco — volcanic land; site of caves and craters

▶ Shoshone Ice Cave, Shoshone — site of a lava tube three blocks long where flowing air currents form ice crystals underground

▶ Moses Alexander (b.1853) — the nation's first Jewish governor (1915-1919)

▶ Ted Trueblood (b.1913) — received state and national honors for his work to save the environment

French fries. Hot, crispy golden french fries. How best to have this wonderful Idaho treat? Perhaps the fries should be smothered with ketchup. Perhaps a dip of vinegar would be best. Or perhaps just some melted cheddar cheese on the very ends of each sizzling potato would add that just-right taste to this tempting Idaho delight.

When it comes to potatoes, Idaho farmers grow the most. About 25 percent of the country's potatoes are grown in Idaho. Most of these potatoes are grown in the Snake River valley. Along with potatoes, Idaho farmers grow sugar beets, mint, onions, barley, corn, and wheat.

Does Idaho have a warm or cold climate? Idaho's geography affects the state's climate. Idaho has a milder climate than the Great Plains states that share the same latitude. Gentle sea winds blowing from the Pacific bring warm, moist air to western Idaho. The state's towering Rocky Mountains protect much of Idaho from blasts of chilling northern winds.

Temperatures (TEM-per-ah-churs) can be forty degrees colder in the mountains than in the valleys. Winter temperatures average about 10° degrees below freezing. Summer's gentle warmth is felt across much of Idaho.

Rainfall is greater over the northern part of the state. About 60 inches of snow falls in Idaho's mountains. The Snake River in the south, on the other hand, gets only about 10 inches of rain each year.

Idaho has not been able to escape nature's weather swings. Nature can wrap Idaho in frigid winter days as well as torrid, or very hot, long summer days when it seems like the coolness of an evening breeze will never come. Trees exploding in flames after being struck by lighting have caused terrible forest fires during times of drought.

Is Idaho covered by forests? About 40 percent of Idaho is covered by forests. Here, golden aspens shimmer in the bright sunlight. The long, thin, soft green branches of willow trees lift and fall in the wind like dancers upon an endless stage. Deep green spruce, fir, and pine trees carpet Idaho's mountain ranges. And across Idaho meadows blaze the red flowers of the Indian paintbrush plant.

Idaho is home to more than 350 different kinds of birds. Birds such as the prairie falcon, red-tailed hawk, and golden eagle soar across Idaho land in search of small animals. These birds of prey call the rocky cliffs of the Snake River home.

Are there many rivers in Idaho? Thousands of small rivers and some very large ones, wind across Idaho. Many of these rushing, foaming waters demand great respect. Some of Idaho's rivers flow so rapidly that only expert rafters dare try their luck at challenging the water's **current**.

One of Idaho's many important rivers is the Snake River. This river gets its start south of Yellowstone National Park in the mountains of Wyoming. The Snake River flows for more than 1,000 miles. Along its winding path it plunges 200 feet over great towers of rock. Its powerful currents cuts across rugged canyons of amazing wild beauty.

Much of Idaho's economy depends on the Snake River and its valley. Dams on the Snake River allow cargo ships to sail about 500 miles inland from the Pacific Ocean. More than half of all people who live in Idaho live in the Snake River Valley.

River waters are used to irrigate dry soil. Great fields of wheat, touched in shades of gold, grow next to dry sagebrush **wasteland**. Irrigation has changed rain thirsty topsoil in Idaho's southern region into healthy fields. Such fields would have amazed the weary travelers who between 1830 and 1850 cut across Idaho on the Oregon Trail. To them Idaho seemed like a vast dry land where farming was not possible.

Was gold found in Idaho during the 1800s gold rush? Just as in other Rocky Mountain states, gold fever caught on in Idaho. Rough, lawless towns quickly grew as gold diggers rushed into the Clearwater River region. Men hoping to "get rich quick" flooded the reservation lands of the Nez Perce Indians.

The Nez Perce, Shoshone, and Bannock Indians were soon forced from their lands by cattle-driving white settlers and gold-seeking miners. Battles where many died often resulted as Native Americans fought to keep land they had settled years before whites arrived. Among the dead were white immigrants, members of the U.S. Army, Native American warriors, and Native Americans. In the end, the surviving members of Native American tribes were placed on reservation land.

GeoWords
current — a moving stream of water
wasteland — an area of land where little, if anything, can grow

Critical Thinking
Why do you think the early gold towns were lawless?

▲ Dams on the Snake River create power and water reserves.

Did You Know? In 1986, Idaho decided to bring caribou back to the state's mountains and forests. Caribou once roamed freely across Idaho's northern woods. Classes of school-children adopted their own caribou. They gave their caribou a name. Over the years, school children have tracked the wanderings of "their" caribou through the use of special collars place on each caribou before being set free.

Today, the rich heritage of Idaho's Native Americans is shared in colorful yearly festivals. Other festivals honor the heritage of Idaho's immigrants from Italy, Sweden, Finland, Asia, and Mexico. Idaho's seasons also are honored. Fun-packed winter carnivals (CAR-nih-vals) give winter artists the chance to build grand and funny shapes with Idaho's thick winter snows.

Toe-tapping, knee-slapping songs such as "The Girl Named Ida-Ho," "Way Out in Idaho," "Ragtime Annie," and "Wake Up Susie Reel" are played with great joy at Idaho's National Oldtime Fiddlers Contest. Fiddlers of all ages packing well-loved and sometimes well-worn violins tighten their bows to let Idaho folk music sing out across a bright summer day.

☆   ☆   ☆   ☆   ☆   ☆   ☆   ☆   ☆

From Idaho's eerie caves deep inside a dead volcano to its rocks where people long ago etched their names to its dunes of sand rising above the flat plain, Idaho is a state where people have touched and come to love a vast and untamed land.

▲ An authentic Native American dwelling using whole tree branches

Did You Know? In 1988, it was learned that the Idaho National Engineering Laboratory (INEL) was one of the most toxic sites in the country. People were concerned that toxic waste was leaking into the Snake River water system. Plans to build four new nuclear power plants drew support as well as loud protests from the people of Idaho.

★ ★ ★ ★ ★ ★ ★ ★   **THINK ABOUT IT!**   ★ ★ ★ ★ ★ ★ ★ ★ ★

1. Give three reasons why the Snake River is important to Idaho's economy.

2. How did irrigation change Idaho?

3. Would you like to live in Idaho. Why or why not?

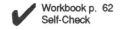
Workbook p. 62
Self-Check

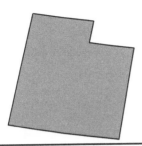

UTAH

★ ★

GEOFACTS
- capital: Salt Lake City
- statehood: 1896 (45th)
- rank in size: 11th
- rank in population: 35th (urban 87%, rural 13%)
- U.S. representatives: 3
- motto: "Industry"

▲ Bryce Canyon National Park is a place where Utah, Colorado, New Mexico, and Arizona meet.

"Warning! Rocks fall often in American Fork Canyon. Areas of greatest hazard on the trail are marked by blue stripes; avoid stopping in these places. Be alert for the sound of falling rocks. If a rock seems to be headed your way, take cover: move close to rock walls, stay low, and protect your head. Don't throw rocks yourself. Stay on the trail; shortcutting causes erosion and can start a landslide. . . ."

National Park Service, U.S. Department of the Interior Tourist Guide

One fall day in 1887, Martin Hansen was cutting trees high on the southern slopes of American Fork Canyon. Coming across the tracks of a mountain lion, Hansen wondered where the footprints led.

Climbing the steep slope, Hansen followed the tracks to a high ledge. Searching further, Hansen found an opening in the rocks. This opening led to a cave, a cave that would later be named for him.

Word soon got out about the beauty of Hansen Cave. Others climbed the canyon slope to see the cave for themselves. Many took colorful pieces of rock from inside the cave. These cave wonders were then sold. Soon, much of the beauty of Hansen Cave was gone.

In 1915, a second cave, Timpanogos Cave, was found. Then, in 1921, Hansen's son and grandson found a third cave. This cave was named Middle Cave. Quickly, efforts were taken to protect all three caves from more damage done by cave-treasure hunters. Today, visitors to Utah can enjoy all three caves.

⚡ **Critical Thinking**

How do you think Martin Hansen felt when he found the cave which later became named for him? How do you think he felt after the cave had been stripped of its treasures? Give reasons for your answers.

Places to See! People to Know!

▶ Golden Spike National Historic Site, Promontory — site of the "golden spike," the last driven spike of the Transcontinential Railroad

▶ Drive Through the Ages Geological Area, Vernal — signs along a route that crosses the Uinta Mountains tell of the land's geology dating back a billion years.

▶ Helen Kurumada (b.1917) — civil rights activist; first director of the Utah State Office of Asian Affairs (1983)

▶ Brigham Young (b.1801) — early leader of the Mormon faith; led the first group of Mormons from Illinois to Utah; selected the site for Salt Lake City; over the years, he helped to settle more than 350 Mormon towns

▲ The rodeo in Utah has a long and proud tradition.

What kind of things are found inside Hansen, Timpanogos, and Middle caves? Experts think all three caves formed when rainwater seeped underground. The rainwater cut into the soft limestone of the canyon slope. Water filled and then drained the cave areas.

Today, as it has for thousands of years, rainwater slowly drips into the cave. The dripping rainwater builds mineral shapes that look like long icicles (EYE-sih-kuls). These mineral icicles are called **stalactites** (stah-LAK-tyts). Sometimes stalactites meet up with **stalagmites** (stah-LAG-myts) rising from the cave's floor. When this happens, amazing floor-to-ceiling columns (KOL-ums) form.

Also found in these special caves are tiny, fragile shapes designed and built by the workings of water over many years. Underground pools, popcorn shapes made from minerals, sparkling wall coverings called draperies, and tiny cave insects all add to the beauty and mystery of each cave.

What other wonders can be found in Utah? American Fork Canyon cuts into northern Utah. It is found among a line of high mountain ridges called the Wasatch Range. To the west of these mountains, lined with evergreen trees and wildflowers, are Lake City, Ogden, and Provo. These are among Utah's oldest and largest cities.

Southeast of the Wasatch Range lie the state's canyonlands. These marvels of nature are a part of the Colorado Plateau. Rough, flat uplands cut by deep color-lined canyons and valleys offer a view of an amazing land, a land like no other in the country.

Carving this region of red-, gold-, and tan-colored sandstone are the mighty Colorado and Green rivers. Great arches of rock, tall monuments of stone, and jagged rocky spires (SPY-ers) are just some of the many surprises of nature found in Utah's canyonlands.

Covering the western third of Utah is the Great Basin. This area's valleys and low mountain ranges cover some of the driest land in the country. Here are the concrete-hard, dried salt beds of the Great Salk Lake Desert. To the south are the Savier and Escalante deserts.

In the northwest corner of the Great Basin is Salt Lake. This lake is the largest lake west of the Mississippi River. Rivers lead in, but not out, of Salt Lake. Because of this, the water that remains in the lake is four to seven times more salty than ocean water.

What human wonders are found in Utah? Utah is filled with a history of people taking on tasks that seemed hopeless, yet somehow became possible. Early Native Americans found shelter and food in the Great Basin. Other Native Americans settled and by using irrigation, farmed areas of land south of the Colorado River.

The first explorers from Europe to enter the land that was to become Utah were Francisco Atanasio Dominguez and Silvestre Velez de Escalante. Crossing rugged Utah, these Spaniards set out on their 2,000-mile trip from New Mexico to California in July 1776.

The Donner-Reed Wagon Train led the westward journey of white emigrants. This ill-fated group of people chose a shortcut across Utah during their long trip to California. The Donner-Reed wagon train spent many weary and often waterless days trying to find their way across the Wasatch Mountains and the Great Basin. Caught by snow in the mountains west of Utah, only half of the eighty-seven people who began the trip made it to California.

Traveling in the tracks of the Donner-Reed wagon train came the first of what was to become thousands of Mormon pioneers. Starting from Nauvoo, Illinois, they pushed hand-held carts for more than 111 days. The Mormons reached the Salt Lake Valley on July 22, 1847. Quickly, they began to build shelters and to farm the dry land by digging irrigation canals for the fields.

☆ ☆ ☆ ☆ ☆ ☆ ☆ ☆ ☆

Today, most people living in Utah are members of the Mormon faith. Yet, Utah's rich Native American heritage also is honored. Utah is a land where people from all over the world, and of all faiths, share an astonishing land.

Critical Thinking

What kind of problems do you think people traveling for 111 days on foot might have? By wagon? Think of at least three problems for each.

▲ The Sego Lily — Utah's state flower

Did You Know? The Great Basin and the Colorado Plateau get about 5 inches of rain each year. In contrast, the mountains of the Wasatch Range get about 50 inches of rainfall each year, some of which falls as snow. Snow rarely falls in Utah's warm southwest. Yet, in the mountains north of Salt Lake City, up to 400 inches of snow may fall during winter.

★ ★ ★ ★ ★ ★ ★ ★   THINK ABOUT IT!   ★ ★ ★ ★ ★ ★ ★ ★

1. What does the National Park Service warning tell you about the trail leading to Timpanagos Cave?

2. List three land wonders in Utah.

3. Give four reasons why it would be difficult to travel across Utah on foot or by wagon.

Workbook p. 63
Self-Check

NEVADA

★ ★

GEOFACTS
- capital: Carson City
- statehood: 1864 (36th)
- rank in size: 7th
- rank in population: 39th (urban 88%, rural 11%)
- U.S. representatives: 2
- motto: "All for Our Country"

▲ Fishing amidst the splendor of the Ruby Mountains

▲ Ice fishing at Wildhorse, Utah, is a fun-filled family activity.

Critical Thinking
Why would people feel it is important to protect the cui-ui fish?

Places to See! People to Know!

▶ Berlin-Ichthyosaur State Park, Gabbs — site of Ichthyosaur fossils as well as the Berlin silver-mining ghost town

▶ Valley of Fire State Park, Las Vegas — site of fire red sandstone, petrified wood, and Native American stone writings

▶ Sarah Winnemucca Hopkins (b.1844) — Native American author who wrote *Life Among the Paiutes: Their Wrongs and Claims*

▶ Wovoka (b.1856) — created the Ghost Dance religious movement of the late 1800s

On a lone stretch of rocky Nevada soil sits a rain-greedy cactus. Its soft green-and-tan color matches the stiff bushes and dry land bordering it in all directions. Yet, on the tips of this prickly plant are found flowers in rich tones of pink and purple. Nevada, like the flowering cactus that grows in its soil, is a state where beauty and a demanding land blend.

Nevada is a land of rugged, snow-capped mountains bordering grassy valleys and dunes of sand. To some, Nevada is a land rich in nature's many faces: great stretches of desert, lofty mountains, and land shapes that are special to the state. To others, Nevada is a vast wasteland whose land is of little use. To the more than one million people who make their home in Nevada, this daring land is a valued and growing state.

At one time, Nevada was covered by great waters. Melting northern glaciers formed rivers that rushed into the state's valleys. Large glacial lakes formed. The largest of these lakes was Lake Lahontan. Thousands of years ago, this huge lake covered about 8,400 square miles, or about one-tenth of present-day Nevada.

Over time, Lake Lahontan dried up. Today, Pyramid and Walker lakes are all that's left of this once mighty cold-water giant. Pyramid Lake is the only home of a very rare fish called the cui-ui. Experts think the cui-ui got its start some 2 million years ago. Today, this uncommon fish is protected by law.

Where are Nevada's other lakes found? Nevada has few lakes. All of Nevada's lakes are found in the western part of the state. One lake enjoyed by many is Lake Tahoe (TAH-ho). This sparkling blue, cold-water lake sits 6,000 feet above sea level on the California-Nevada border.

Lake Mead is another important lake in Nevada. Found in Nevada's southeast corner, Lake Mead was formed by building a dam on the Colorado River. It took as much concrete to build this mighty dam, called Hoover Dam, as it would take to build a road across the country.

Most of Nevada's rivers flow only during times of rain. Only a handful of them make their way to the ocean. All of its other rivers empty into Nevada's Great Basin. Here, these hapless rivers flow into lakes with no **outlets** or into shallow **sinks**. Most rivers slow to a trickle and then dry to leave behind muddy salt flats.

Nevada gets less rain than any other state in the country. During the July to November dry season, Nevada gets little, if any, rain. Most of Nevada gets about 7 inches of rain each year. Its dry, southern area gets about 4 inches of rain in one year. Yet, in the mountains of the Lake Tahoe area, about 25 inches of rain falls each year, much of which falls as snow.

Is the weather always hot and dry in Nevada? Nevada's climate changes with its land. Long, cold winters and short, hot summers are found in Nevada's northern region. Across Nevada's desert regions are found feverishly hot summer days and mild winters. Here hot, sun-baked desert days quickly turn into cold desert nights.

Much of Nevada's land is owned and managed by the federal government. The United States government uses Nevada's wide-open stretches of land for airplane and atomic testing. In 1951, the United States began testing atomic weapons in Nevada's desert at the Nevada Test site. Over the years this site has drawn protesters (PRO-tes-ters), or people who are against the use of atomic weapons.

What kind of work do most people do in Nevada? There are many different kinds of jobs to be found in Nevada. Farmers in many parts of Nevada raise cattle and sheep. Most ranches cover a wide area of 3,000 acres or more. Across an area of sagebrush, buttes, and rolling dunes of sandy soil, animals roam in search of grass and water.

In Nevada's western valleys and in northern areas where irrigation is possible, farmers raise hay, barley, oats, potatoes, and other crops. Cotton, fruits, and some vegetables can be found growing in some southern valleys.

Some people in Nevada work in printing and publishing, others in the building of homes for Nevada's growing population. Many people work for the federal government. Several people work in Nevada's mines. Nevada is the leading state in the mining of gold, silver and turquoise (TER-kwoiz). Gold, silver, and turquoise are used in the making of fine jewelry.

GeoWords
outlets — a place where a river flows out of a lake
sinks — a low area

Critical Thinking
Why is the desert hot during the day but very cool at night?

▲ Virginia City, Nevada, was a bustling mining town in the Old West.

Did You Know? One of the richest gold strikes was made in Nevada in 1859. The gold strike was soon named the Comstock Lode after Henry Comstock, one of the gold-diggers. All of Comstock Lode's gold had been mined by 1878. Soon, once-thriving Virginia City, the town that gold built, became one of Nevada's many mining ghost towns.

Critical Thinking

Stone markings made by Native Americans thousands of years ago can still be found in Nevada's deserts. Why haven't these stone markings worn away?

Did You Know? From April 3, 1860, until October 24, 1861, the riders of the Pony Express dashed from Missouri to California carrying mail. Changing horses at stations along the route, a Pony Express rider would speed along at 9 miles per hour. Riders as young as thirteen were given two minutes to change from weary to fresh horse and then race off again into unknown dangers. In its eighteen months, the Pony Express lost only one bag of mail.

By far, Nevada's largest industry is tourism. About 30 million people visit Nevada each year. They come to colorful cities that never sleep, such as Reno and Las Vegas. Here, people gamble, watch grand shows, and enjoy the sights and sounds of Nevada's exciting cities. In other parts of the state, tourists can visit ghost towns. These towns grew and died overnight as miners worked and then left Nevada land.

☆ ☆ ☆ ☆ ☆ ☆ ☆ ☆ ☆

From the glitter and noise of Las Vegas to the quiet night of a sheepherder, Nevada is a state of contrasts. Nevada is a spanish word meaning "snow-clad." Nevada's snow-clad mountains rise high above a thirsty land that has tested, and sometimes won against, efforts to settle it.

★ ★ ★ ★ ★ ★ ★ ★ **THINK ABOUT IT!** ★ ★ ★ ★ ★ ★ ★ ★

1. How is there a contrast of climate in Nevada?

2. How does Nevada land contrast?

3. How does Nevada lifestyle contrast?

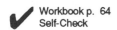

Workbook p. 64
Self-Check

THE PEOPLE'S PUBLISHING GROUP, INC. *Our United States Geography: Our Regions and People*

The Southwest ★ ★ ★ ★ ★ ★ ★ ★ ★ ★ ★ ★ ★ ★

Author Ben Logan wrote, "Once you have lived on the land, been a partner with its moods, secrets, and seasons, you cannot leave." * He wrote about how the land becomes a part of you forever. The land, and the ties people have to it, have been a driving force in the settlement of America. People traveling west found land to their liking and decided to stay. They worked the land, fought for it, and sometimes died for it.

Native Americans, who had lived on land taken over by white emigrants, also had ties to the land. They knew the land's smell, feel, and seasonal change. They, too, fought for the land and sometimes died for it. In the end, they most often lost it. When forced to leave, a part of each Native American tribe stayed with the land: their work, their dead, their homes, but most of all, their love of the land.

Over the years, many people have had ties to land across America's Southwest. The Spanish, in search of the Seven Cities of Gold, used the land and often abused its natives. The fur trappers, traders, and miners of the 1800s also used the land. Some stayed, but most left when the land could give no more. Between 1821 and 1846, the government of Mexico ruled the Southwest. Native Americans, the Mexican government, and white emigrants all claimed the land. Ties to the land soon led to battles over the land.

The Southwest is a full blend of many cultures from around the globe. Mexican Americans, Native Americans, and Americans share the beauty of America's Southwest. After English, Spanish is the language used most often.

The Southwest is a land of flowering deserts, stretches of sand dunes, pine-covered mountains, deep gorges, and wind-carved rock shapes of endless beauty. It is an area where great rock cliffs hold the secret to the lives of early Native American tribes. The Native Americans built their homes among the cliffs and then vanished years before others came.

Look for themes that link the states of America's Southwest. Look for ties people had with the land. Look for reasons why these ties are still important today. Look for new ties people have with the land. In all these will be found the reason why America's Southwest is such a fast-growing area and why people find it so hard to leave.

* excerpt from *The Land Remembers* by Ben Logan, © Northward Press, 1975

ARIZONA

★ ★

GEOFACTS
- capital: Phoenix
- statehood: 1912 (48th)
- rank in size: 6th
- rank in population: 24th (urban 88%, rural 12%)
- U.S. representatives: 6
- motto: "God Enriches"

▲ The Grand Canyon

▲ Colorful Native American Kachina dolls

GeoWords
adobe — a sun-dried block of clay used in building

⚡ Critical Thinking
How do you think Karen Kenyon feels about her childhood home? Explain your answer.

Places to See! People to Know!

▶ Canyon de Chelly National Monument, Chinle — site of many prehistoric Anasazi cliff dwellings

▶ Tubac Presidio State Historic Park, Tubac — site of one of the earliest Spanish settlements in Arizona

▶ Eusebino Kino (b.1660) — missionary from Spain who explored the deserts in southwest Arizona; began several missions in the area; opposed the use of Native Americans as slaves in northern Mexico silver mines

▶ Sandra Day O'Connor (b.1930) — presided on Arizona's court of appeals before being appointed to the United States Supreme Court; first woman to appointed to the U.S. Supreme Court

❝As a child growing up in Arizona, I loved the variety of the land and weather. I could be in the desert one moment, and just a few moments away, be in the quiet of rugged, forested mountains. I remember how I ran in the evenings to watch the splendor of each red sunset. A favorite memory of mine is sliding down Oak Creek where the shallow waters rushed over jagged stone. I would flow with the racing stream until I plunged into a waiting pool of water at the bottom. I tore many a pair of jeans on that fun-filled creek.❞

Karen Kenyon, an Arizona native

Arizona is a land of rushing waters, shifting dunes, pines trees dusted with snow, and rocks of granite painted by the changes of time. It is a land where shy, but wicked-looking, tarantula (tah-RAN-choo-lah) spiders hide among the layers and cracks of mighty stone cliffs. Sharing these stone hideouts are night-loving scorpions (SKOR-pee-ons).

Arizona is a step back into time. Tucked into the shadows of rock cliffs are amazing **adobe** (ah-DOH-bee) homes built long ago by cliff-dwelling Native Americans. Found etched on rocks are thousand-year-old signs and pictures that once meant something special to someone. And then there is the Grand Canyon. Here people can look 1 mile down and see deep into two billion years of Earth history.

Where is the Grand Canyon found in Arizona? The untamed beauty of the Grand Canyon is found in the northwest corner of Arizona. Long ago, the Colorado River began to cut and wear away the stone that lay across this tilted plateau region. Grain by grain, the sometimes rushing, sometimes gentle current of the Colorado River wore away at layers of hard granite.

Today, the Grand Canyon runs for 270 miles. From the air, the Grand Canyon looks like a huge gash in a colorful Earth carved by the forces of wind and water. Close up, the power of the raging Colorado River can still be seen as section after section of river bank crumbles into the muddy river. Reds, yellows, oranges, and browns color layer after layer of hard rock. More than four million tourists come each year to view this Arizona wonder.

What other wonders can be found in Arizona? Found in Arizona's northeast region are several more wonders of nature and human genius. Here, the Hopi Indians live on land that has sheltered Native Americans for many years. Also found here is the Navajo reservation. Homes, pottery, and the writings of Native Americans from centuries (SEN-chur-ees) ago are found across this region.

Both the Painted Desert and Petrified (PEH-trih-fyd) Forest are found in eastern Arizona. Here, stone trees lay cracked and crumbled across an area once covered by lush forests and wide lakes. Today, rainbows of color grace the dry and rocky land.

What is Arizona's climate like? Arizona is a dry state. Most areas get about 13 inches of rain each year. Arizona's desert areas many get as little as 3 inches of rain each year, while the mountain areas may get up to 30 inches. Snow falling in the mountains is enjoyed by downhill skiers. Arizona's many ski resorts add to the state's tourist economy.

Arizona's hot summer days are made easier to bear by its dry air. The state's mild winters attract people from all over the country. Arizona has become one of the fastest-growing states in the country.

Arizona makes great use of its rivers for irrigation (ih-rih-GAY-shun), the machine-method of watering dry land. In 1963, the United States Supreme Court ruled that Arizona has the right to make use of the Colorado River while it flows across the state. This opened the way for grand water projects to aid thirsty cities and farmland.

Arizona is a leading state in the growing of cotton. Lettuce, grapefruit, melons, oranges, and other warm-weather crops grow well in Arizona's waterfed soils. About 75 percent of Arizona's land is used for grazing sheep and cattle.

How did mining affect Arizona? From Arizona's northwest corner to its southeast run several mountain ranges. Gold, silver, and copper finds here in the mid 1800s led to towns that seemed to grow overnight as miners poured into the area. Many of these often lawless towns became long-forgotten ghost towns.

Critical Thinking

Explain three ways Arizona is a step into the past.

▲ The cactus is Arizona's desert flower.

Did You Know? The saguaro cactus is the largest cactus in the world. This slow-growing cactus often does not grow an arm until it is about seventy-five years old. The saguaro's spines help to ward off animals that try to eat the cactus. They also lessen the impact of winds on the cactus.

Mining, the railroads, and western-moving white settlers forced Arizona's first settlers, Native Americans, off land that was useful to whites. Battles were led by great Native American leaders, such as Geronimo, Cochise, and Mangas, to try to keep whites from taking over Native American lands. One by one, the area's Native American tribes were placed on reservations.

Today, Arizona is a leading state in the mining of copper. Sand and gravel used in the paving of roads also are mined in Arizona. Other metals taken from the state's land are zinc, lead, and uranium.

How is Arizona's rich heritage shown? Today, festivals that honor Arizona's Mexican Americans and Native Americans bring splashes of color, joy, and music to all the people of Arizona. Sand painting, basket and blanket weaving, kachina dolls, and finely crafted jewelry are some of the ways Native American talents are shared with people from all walks of life.

Critical Thinking
Why is it important to keep and honor one's heritage?

Arizona is a state where busy cities stand in sharp contrast to **arid** lands that seem to stretch on forever. From the sounds of such cities as Phoenix, Tucson and Mesa to the lonely hush of the Sonoran Desert, Arizona stands as one of America's greatest wonders.

Did You Know? One day Jack Swilling, a Salt River valley miner, found irrigation canals dug many years before by the Hohokam people. He had the canals redug to bring water into the valley. The town that soon grew was named Phoenix. The name "Phoenix" comes from a make-believe bird that died in flames and then rose from the ashes.

★ ★ ★ ★ ★ ★ ★ ★ THINK ABOUT IT! ★ ★ ★ ★ ★ ★ ★ ★

1. Tell three things about Arizona's geography.

2. Tell three things about Arizona's climate.

3. Name three industries that are important to Arizona's economy.

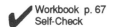
Workbook p. 67
Self-Check

NEW MEXICO

★ ★

GEOFACTS
- capital: Santa Fe
- statehood: 1912 (47th)
- rank in size: 5th

- rank in population: 37th (urban 73%, rural 13%)
- U.S. representatives: 3
- motto: "It Grows As It Goes"

▲ A New Mexico field of flowers

▲ A Mexican-style adobe home

> "Imagine a place where the sun shines more often than not. A place where you can take a walk through tall, cool pines. A place where the cliffs take on a rainbow of colors as they tower against an azure sky. A place to raft the rivers, ski the mountains, and fish the streams."
>
> *New Mexico Vacation Guide,* 1993

Some 20,000 years ago, Native Americans lived among the dry cliffs of present day New Mexico. At first, they lived in homes dug partly into the ground. Later, the Anasazi and other Native American tribes built pueblo apartment buildings. One home, called Pueblo Bonito ("pretty village"), had about 800 rooms.

Spain ruled New Mexico for many years. During the 1500s, Spanish explorers wandered across New Mexico in search of the Seven Cities of Gold. They never found this dream of wealth. Yet, Spanish explorers such as Francisco Vasquez de Coronado claimed that the land they rode upon belonged to Spain.

New Mexico became a Spanish colony in 1598. More than the years, the people of Mexico, as well as Native Americans, battled to be free of Spanish rule. This finally happened in 1821 when Mexico won its freedom from

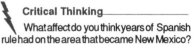

Critical Thinking

What affect do you think years of Spanish rule had on the area that became New Mexico?

Places to See! People to Know!

▶ Pueblos, located in many places in New Mexico — Acoma, thought to be the oldest pueblo, is found on the top of a 365-feet high mesa

▶ Four Corners Monument, near Farmington — only place where the corners of four states meet (Colorado, Arizona, Utah, and New Mexico)

▶ Manuelito (b.1818) — fought to prevent white settlement on Navaho land; helped to secure Navajo homelands

▶ Maria Antonita Martinez (b.1887) — potter; famous for her Pueblo black-on-black pottery

GeoWords
moisture — wetness

Spain. With that, the land that makes up present day New Mexico became part of Mexico.

How did New Mexico become part of the United States? For twenty-five years, there was unrest between the people of New Mexico and the government of Mexico. In 1846, war broke out between Mexico and the United States.

Critical Thinking
Why do you think irrigation is important to New Mexico farmers?

An 1848 treaty between Mexico and the United States government gave New Mexico, as well as a large area to New Mexico's north and west, to the United States. In 1853, Mexico sold more land to the United States. This land purchase helped to set New Mexico's borders.

Today, New Mexico's Mexican American and Native American cultures are honored in the state's many festivals. Lively dancing, colorful costumes, arts and crafts, and folk tales express the ethnic pride people have in their rich heritage. Young faces show a look toward the future; yet, they carry a deep respect for the ways of the past. These values are shared with the festivals' many visitors.

What is New Mexico's land like? New Mexico has four main land regions. To the northwest lies New Mexico's Colorado Plateau. This is a broken country of wide valleys, deep canyons, sharp cliffs, and lonely mesas. The Continental Divide winds its way across the plateau region. To the west of the Continental Divide flow Pacific-bound streams. The Gulf of Mexico swallows waters running east of the Continental Divide.

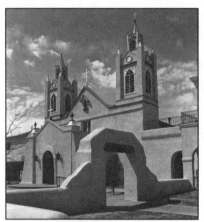

▲ A church in the Spanish mission style

To the state's northwest are tall, eerie rocks that look like soldiers standing watch more than wind-carved lands. Here, the hands of time have slowly worn grand pueblo shelters built by human hands many years ago. These stone-upon-stone villages stand as a reminder of the immense efforts of Native American cultures, long since gone from New Mexico's land.

The southern edge of the Rocky Mountains curves into New Mexico's north central border. Here, winter snows cover more than golden leaves that carpet this mountain region each fall. The Rio Grande Valley cuts between towering mountain ranges. Melting snow brings welcome **moisture** (MOYS-chur) to farmers along the Rio Grande Valley.

The bright city lights of New Mexico's central cities, Albuquerque (AL-bah-ker-kee) and Santa Fe, flicker into the clear sky as if answering the sparkle of the night stars. Zoos — home to polar bears basking in the New Mexico sun, grand museums, music-filled concerts, ballets, folk dance, and humbling churches fill the city spaces. Each evening, a glowing red sunset brings the city day to a close.

What is New Mexico like along the eastern edge of the state? The eastern third of New Mexico is part of the Great Plains. Short prairie grasses in the high plateau of the northeast give way to rippling sand dunes in the southeast. Lying deep under the cactus and dry land are the marvels of the Carlsbad Caverns. The plains area, grazed by sheep and cattle, is a mix of nature's wonders, from its rocky, wildflower-covered mountains to its shifting sands.

Did You Know? The Gila National Forest is the largest national forest in the United States. It stretches across New Mexico for 3.3 million acres. Visitors may enter the Gila Wilderness, deep inside the Gila National Forest, only on horseback. No roads lead into this rugged land.

New Mexico's southwest is a basin area. Beginning in 1840, emigrants, outlaws, railroad workers, and mail carriers followed the Gila River in an attempt to find their way across this often hostile land. California gold rushers trudged their way across the Gila Trail in search of western riches.

Scattered ranges of rugged mountains and desert basins spread across New Mexico's southwest. African American cavalry (KAV-ul-ree) units called the Buffalo Soldiers once patrolled across this region. Several of the soldiers earned medals of honor for acts of bravery.

What is the climate like in New Mexico? New Mexico is a dry, warm state. Most areas get yearly rainfalls of less than 20 inches. The south may get about 2 inches of snow each year. New Mexico's northern mountains, on the other hand, may get as much as 300 inches of snow.

Tourists coming to New Mexico add much to the state's economy. From skiing in the mountains to visiting the wonders of cliff-dwelling's ruins, tourists find New Mexico a fascinating state.

Today, New Mexico is a leading state in mining and in the study of nuclear energy. New Mexico is a state that bridges the old with the new in a way that respects the past while seeking out the ideas of the future. It is a vast and varied land that humbles those who gaze upon it.

⚡ **Critical Thinking**

How can land cause humble feelings in people?

▲ The road-runner is New Mexico's state bird.

Did You Know? The United States entered the age of atomic weapons on July 16, 1945. It was then that the first atomic bomb was dropped at Trinity Site in New Mexico. The bomb was the invention of Robert Oppenheimer. It was made in the science lab of Los Alamos, a town secretly built in the mountains of New Mexico.

★ ★ ★ ★ ★ ★ ★ ★ **THINK ABOUT IT!** ★ ★ ★ ★ ★ ★ ★ ★

1. What was the reason Spanish explorers first traveled across New Mexico?

2. What are New Mexico's four land regions?

3. List five things about New Mexico that tourists might like to see.

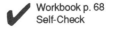 Workbook p. 68
Self-Check

TEXAS

★ ★

GEOFACTS
- capital: Austin
- statehood: 1845 (28th)
- rank in size: 2nd
- rank in population: 3rd (urban 80%, rural 20%)
- U.S. representatives: 30
- motto: "Friendship"

▲ The Alamo

▲ The Dallas-Fort Worth Airport is large and modern — typical of Texas.

⚡ Critical Thinking

Why do you think people such as Davy Crockett and Jim Bowie came from the east to Texas to help the people fight against the Mexican government?

Places to See! People to Know!

▶ Institute of Texan Culture, San Antonio — site of exhibits from twenty-six different ethnic groups who have made their home in Texas

▶ Palmito Hill Battlefield, Brownsville — site of the last battle of the Civil War; Confederate defeat of Union soldiers here came after General Robert E. Lee surrendered to Union General Ulysses S. Grant, signaling the end of the war

▶ George Herbert Walker Bush (b.1924) — 41st president of the United States

▶ Scott Joplin (b.1868) — African American musician; founder of ragtime music; wrote more than 500 music works of music

Texas is the United States's second largest state. Acre per acre, the states of New York, New Jersey, Ohio, Illinois, and Wisconsin all together, could fit inside Texas. Land is not the only thing that makes Texas big. Texas has a great amount of pride, culture, history, and ethnic diversity. It is a state where anyone traveling through can watch city lights and rural nights fold together in their own special Texas way.

At one time, Texas was a country of its own! On March 2, 1836, several men, among them Sam Houston, signed the Texas Declaration of Independence. With this important paper, Texas broke ties with Mexico. The new country called itself the Republic of Texas.

Did Texas and Mexico go to war against each other? Unrest between the people of Texas and the government of Mexico led to war. Fighting began in the small town of Gonzales in 1835. Mexicans who did not agree with the harsh government led by Antonio Lopez de Santa Anna, white emigrants, called "Anglos", and freed African slaves fought against the Mexican army.

One of the more well-known battles of this time happened at a stonewall mission called the Alamo. Inside the walls of the Alamo were 189 defenders. These people had come to Texas from other states and countries to help Texas in its fight for freedom. Among them were Davy Crockett and Jim Bowie. All of the defenders of the Alamo were killed by soldiers of the

Mexican army. Santa Anna led the Mexican forces. Later, Sam Houston led an attack against Santa Anna's forces. With a battle cry of "Remember the Alamo," the Texans overcame the Mexican army and captured Santa Anna.

Sam Houston became the first president of the Republic of Texas. Soon, many white settlers poured into Texas. All along, Native Americans — the Comanche, Apache, Cherokee, and Kiowa — were forced off land that later became the state of Texas. Then, on December 29, 1845, the Republic of Texas joined the Union to become the country's twenty-eighth state.

What is land like in Texas? Texas is made up of four main land regions. From east to west, these land regions are the West Gulf Coastal Plain, the North Central Plains, the Great Plains, and the Basin and Range region.

The West Gulf Coastal Plain lies along the Gulf of Mexico. It varies from 150 miles to 350 miles wide. This hot and humid, wetlands region rises from sea level to about 300 feet above sea level. Shrimp are harvested from the state's coastal waters. Galveston and Corpus Christi are important shipping ports along the Texas coastline.

The Rio Grande valley runs along the southern edge of the West Gulf Coastal Plain. Farmers here grow spinach, green peppers, cabbage, tomatoes, watermelons, and many other fruits and vegetables. A lush, green belt of pine trees called Piney Woods grows along the northern edge of this important region.

To the west and rising from 750 feet to 2,500 feet above the coastal plain of Texas are a group of hills called the Balcones **Escarpment** (es-KARP-ment). This group of southward- and eastward-facing hills marks the line between the West Gulf Coastal Plain and the North Central Plains.

The North Central Plains is a mostly treeless region broken only by streams. Great herds of cattle graze the thick prairie grasses that grow across this region. Texas is a leading state in the raising of beef cattle. The sale of beef cattle is very important to the state's farm economy.

What is the land like in the Texas Panhandle? Cutting across the Texas Panhandle is the Cap Rock Escarpment. Formed by erosion, this rocky area rises from 200 feet to 1,000 feet above the North Central Plains. Farmers here use underground water for crop irrigation. Cattle, sheep, and goats graze on the region's short grasses. This high plateau region has rich underground sources of oil and natural gas.

West of the Pecos River lies the Basin and Range region, also called the Trans-Pecos region. The southern edge of the Rocky Mountains crosses this dry, rocky region. The wind-carved rock and plunging gorges of this area delight both Texans and those just visiting this scenic-packed state.

Do many rivers cross Texas? Texas has several rivers. Most of Texas's vital rivers flow along the state's northwest to southeast land tilt. The longest river in Texas is the Rio Grande. This river forms the border between Mexico and the United States.

GeoWords
escarpment — a steep slope; a cliff

Critical Thinking
The drop in oil prices during the 1980s hurt the Texas economy. How does a change in one part of a state's economy affect many people in the state?

▲ Oil refineries produce gasoline.

Did You Know? The Republic of Texas at times was also called the "Lone Star Republic." This name came from the single star placed on the county's flag and money.

Critical Thinking
Why should people be concerned about pollution taking over the Rio Grande?

In 1993, the 2,000 mile long Rio Grande was named the most endangered river in the United States by American Rivers, a group that watches over the environment. Noted among the concerns for the river were human pollution and toxic chemicals coming from U.S.-owned factories found along the Mexican side of the river.

Weather across Texas can vary from region to region. Snow falling in the Texas Panhandle turns to rain before reaching the south. Rainfall can be as little as 7 inches each year in the Trans-Pecos region and as much as 45 inches each year along the Texas coast. Both hurricanes and tornadoes are a rare, but deadly, threat to Texas.

☆　☆　☆　☆　☆　☆　☆　☆　☆

Texas is a state where people have deep ties to their region, history, and culture. It is a state of festive colors and foods, oil wells, round-the-clock airports, cattle drives, and urban growth. From the crisp beat of Mexican mariachi (mah-ree-AH-chee) music to the mellow tones of a country-western ballad, Texas is a state that shares the richness of many cultures.

▲ A Texas longhorn

Did You Know? The name "Texas" comes from the Caddo word "tashas," which means "friend" or "ally."

 **THINK ABOUT IT!**

1. How was Texas a country before it became a state?

2. List two things about each land region in Texas.

3. How does the climate of Texas affect farming and ranching across the state?

Workbook p. 69
Self-Check

The Emigrants of the 1800s

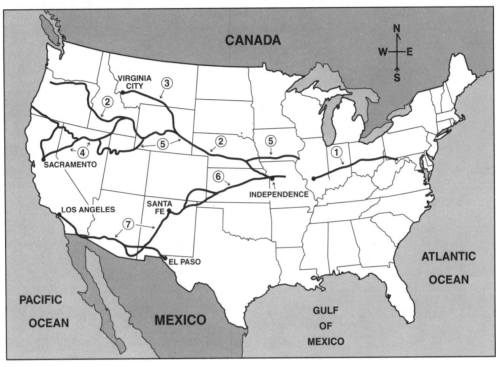

① THE NATIONAL ROAD   ③ THE BOZEMAN TRAIL   ⑤ THE MORMON TRAIL   ⑦ THE GILA TRAIL

② THE OREGON TRAIL   ④ THE CALIFORNIA TRAIL   ⑥ THE SANTA FE TRAIL

In the mid-1800s, newpaperman Horace Greeley wrote this advice to people in New York City who had no job: "Go west, young man!"

From early on, people landing on America's eastern shores looked westward. Immigrants from other countries, and emigrants from every state, looked westward for a job and a piece of land to call their own. First, pathways were cut across the Appalachian Mountains. From there, westward travelers crossed the Great Plains.

Soon new paths were cut across an uncharted land. Emigrants traveled across the deserts of the southwest. They traveled across the Rocky Mountains. Land give-aways, the chance to strike it rich panning for gold, and the need for labor to build the tracks of the westward moving railroads made the west look like a land of promise.

Westward trails, like the ones shown in the map above, were the routes most often taken by westward emigrants. Today, the names of some of those emigrants can still be seen carved into rocks years ago. Wagon ruts, worn deep from years of heavy loads passing up rocky hills, are still clearly seen in some areas of the old Oregon Trail.

Many of the westward trails of the past have become modern roads. Yet, the hardship of those who traveled the trails, the change in the lives of the Native Americans who once lived across the land, and the search for a better life are remembered.

The Pacific Coast ★ ★ ★ ★ ★ ★ ★ ★ ★ ★ ★ ★

Between 1841 and 1866, about 350,000 people traveled the Oregon Trail. Starting in Independence, Missouri, the trail crossed prairie, desert, and the high Rocky Mountains. At its end, it fanned out to Oregon, Washington, and California. People traveling the trail would load all they owned onto wagons drawn by oxen. Along the 2,000-mile trail, they would walk or, if the going got too hard, ride in the wagon. They traveled through days of blistering heat, strong rainstorms, and cold winds.

Yet, on they traveled in search of a better life. Those who made it to the end of their travels tried to buy land. Then came the hard task of putting some order and peace back into their lives. People often kept diaries (DY-ah-rees), or written notes, on their journey. One such diary finished this way:

"A few days later, my eighth child was born. After this we picked up and ferried across the Columbia River. . . . Here, husband traded two yoke of oxen for a half section of land with one-half acre planted to potatoes and a small log cabin and lean-to with no windows. This is the journey's end." *

The states that border the Pacific Ocean are a patchwork of dazzling waterfalls, lonely deserts, and scenic mountains trimming the land with lush forests and, sometimes, snow. Ocean air rising up along the coastal mountains brings rain and warm breezes to exciting coastal cities, untamed lands, and long stretches of beaches graced by quiet, color-rich sunsets.

Today, just as in the past, people come from across the United States to stay in these lands of wonder. Others travel from Mexico, Canada, and several faraway countries. For many, the Pacific Coast states are still a land where dreams can come true, where a job can be gotten, and a free life can be led.

* excerpt from *Women's Diaries of the Westward Journey* by Lillian Schlissel, © Schocken Books, 1982

CALIFORNIA

★ ★

GEOFACTS
- capital: Sacramento
- statehood: 1850 (31st)
- rank in size: 3rd
- rank in population: 1st (urban 93%, rural 7%)
- U.S. representatives: 52
- motto: "Eureka" or "I Have Found It"

▲ The San Francisco Bay boardwalk along the beach

Pan for gold, fish rippling blue-water lakes, ski snow-crested mountains, or just enjoy the quiet of a sunset bursting with color. All are a part of America's Golden State, California.

Over the years, California has been the land of dreams and promise for millions of people. More people live in California than in any other state. Today, ninety-three out of every hundred people living in California live in one of the state's active cities. About half of the people living in California were born outside the state. California is alive with a diversity of languages and cultures.

Earthquakes are a part of California life. Several major **fault lines** crisscross the state. The San Andreas (an-DRA-es) Fault, stretching the length of the state, gives California its greatest earthquake threat.

What are some things California is best known for? California is well known for its Hollywood movie stars and the wonders of Disneyland. Hollywood grew from the 1853 site of an adobe hut to become the center of the country's movie-making industry. In 1910, the city of Hollywood joined with the city of Los Angeles. Soon silent movies, or movies with no sound, amazed moviegoers. The making of movies with sound began in 1920, and the thrill of "going to the movies" captured America.

GeoWords
fault line — a break in the earth's crust; a shift in the Earth's crust along the break causes earthquakes

Critical Thinking
Why do you think so many people live and move to California, knowing that an earthquake could happen at any time?

Places to See! People to Know!

▶ The Cabrillo National Monument, Point Loma—celebrates the travels of Portuguese explorer Juan Rodríguez Cabrillo, whose boat landed where San Diego is now found.

▶ El Pueblo do Los Angeles, Los Angeles — state park within the city that honors California's Spanish and Mexican heritage Muir Woods

▶ Cesar Estrada Chavez (b.1927) — spokesman for California's Mexican-American workers; helped to found the United Farm Workers of America in 1973; led nationwide boycotts against California lettuce and grapes in an effort to win better pay for California's farm workers

▶ Samuel Ichiye Hayakawa (b.1906)—U.S. Senator from California

Critical Thinking

How do you think travelers during the 1800s felt as they walked mile after mile across Death Valley? Give reasons for your answer.

Disneyland began as a dream of artist Walt Disney. His early drawings of a skinny-looking mouse named Mickey became an instant success. Walt Disney made his first Mickey Mouse cartoon in 1928. Today, millions of people visit the exciting make-believe world of Mickey Mouse and friends at Disneyland in Anaheim, California.

The tallest trees in the world are another California wonder. Along a strip of coastal land between San Francisco and the state of Oregon grow California's redwood trees. These towers of wood reach 300 feet into the sky. Also found in California are giant sequoia (see-KWOI-yah) trees. Giant sequoias have trunks as wide as 30 feet and more.

During the 1800s, loggers cut down many of California's redwood and giant sequoia trees. These trees had been growing for more than 2,000 years. Efforts in the late 1800s by John Muir, a man very concerned about the environment, led to protection of California's wonder trees, the redwoods and giant sequoias.

Do forests cover most of California? Forests cover about 40 percent of California. Redwood trees to the north and pine and fir trees to the south and west grace the state in forest beauty. Among the White Mountains of eastern California grow bristlecone (BRIH-sil-kohn) pine trees. One bristlecone tree is believed to be 4,600 years old, making it the oldest living tree in the world.

Logging is still important to California's economy. Only Oregon and Washington sell more lumber than California. Today, logging is better managed than in the past. Most logging companies must replant any area they have cut.

Where are California's deserts? The Mojave (moh-HAV-ee) and Colorado deserts cover California's southeastern region. Little rain falls across this area. Death Valley is named for the many people who died in the 1800s trying to cross this sandswept land.

Death Valley lies 282 feet below sea level. This is the lowest point in the United States. In 1913, the temperature rose to a scorching 134°. This was the hottest day ever recorded in the United States. Death Valley also set the record for the longest time without rain. Between 1912 and 1914, Death Valley went for 760 days before rain once again fell on the desert's lifeless land.

In sharp contrast to California's desert region is the Sierra (see-AIR-ah) Nevada mountain range. This 400-mile wall of forest-covered rock stretches from 40 to 70 miles across. Here, forests soon give way to bare rock as several snow-covered mountain peaks rise to 14,000 feet above sea level.

In the Sierra Nevada mountain range is a wonderland called Yosemite (yoh-SEM-ih-tee) Valley. First cut by streams, this rugged valley was further carved by glaciers thousands of years ago. Within Yosemite National Park are some of the highest waterfalls in North America. The rushing waters of Ribbon Falls plunge an amazing 1,612 feet, crashing on rocks far below its water-worn granite-rock ledge.

▲ Giant California Sequoyah Redwood Trees

Did You Know? An earthquake in 1906 destroyed the city of San Francisco. The earthquake only lasted for a minute and a half. Yet, quickly, fires broke out across the city as gas lines snapped. The fires lasted for three days. About 700 people died and thousands became homeless. Within ten years, the city was totally rebuilt.

Between California's coastal mountains to the west and Sierra Nevada to the east lies California's farm-rich Central valley. The grapes, fresh fruits, vegetables, nuts and other crops grown in California's valley region have made California an important farm state. Few farms in California are family-owned farms. Most farms are owned by large businesses.

Do many of California's farms use irrigation for their crops? Irrigation holds the key to success for many of California's farms. Much water is taken from the Colorado and San Joaquin rivers to water California's thirsty farm regions. Without irrigation, many of California's crops would fail for lack of water.

Large water projects bring water to many of California's cities. California has about 8,000 lakes. Many of these lakes are found in the northern part of the state. Most people in California live in the southern part of the state. Great **aqueducts** (AH-kwah-dukts) bring northern drinking water to Los Angeles and other cities.

☆ ☆ ☆ ☆ ☆ ☆ ☆ ☆ ☆

In 1849, thousands of people set out for California to strike it rich panning for gold. Today, the golden sands of California's coastline, its scenic views, job openings, and ethnic diversity still attract many people to America's Golden State.

GeoWords
aqueduct — a large pipeline used for transporting water

⚡ **Critical Thinking**
Think of at least one reason for arguing against the irrigation of California's crop regions.

▲ Yosemite National Park

Did You Know? Los Angeles is the country's second largest city. More than 3,400,000 people live in Los Angeles. Los Angeles is working hard to deal with such problems as crime, good housing for all, equality in education, and cooperation among different ethnic groups. Los Angeles also must deal with the problem of pollution from the large numbers of cars that travel its highways.

★ ★ ★ ★ ★ ★ ★ ★ **THINK ABOUT IT!** ★ ★ ★ ★ ★ ★ ★ ★

1. Give five reasons why people might like to move to California.

2. List three contrasting land regions found in California.

3. Why is irrigation important to California's farm economy?

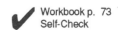 Workbook p. 73
Self-Check

HAWAII

★ ★

GEOFACTS
- capital: Honolulu
- statehood: 1959 (50th)
- rank in size: 47th
- rank in population: 41st (urban 89%, rural 11%)
- U.S. representatives: 2
- motto: "The Life of the Land Is Perpetuated in Righteousness"

▲ The Hawaiian Hula Dance

▲ Hawaii's beaches of sand and surf seem to go on forever.

⚡ **Critical Thinking**
Why does Hawaii get most of its rain on the northeastern part of the islands.

Places to See! People to Know!

▶ Hawaii Volcanoes National Park, island of Hawaii — visitors can view the volcanic activity of two active volcanoes, Mauna Loa and Kilauea

▶ Polynesian Cultural Center, O'ahu — a group of villages that shows the native cultures of people from ancient Samoa, New Zealand, Fiji, Tahiti, Tonga and other places

▶ Daniel Ken Inouye (b. 1924) — first Japanese American elected to Congress (1959)

▶ Lydia Liliou'kalani (b. 1838) — first queen and last ruler of the Kingdom of Hawaii (1891-1893)

❝The loveliest fleet of islands that lies anchored in any ocean.❞

Mark Twain commenting on the islands of Hawaii

Hawaii is a land of bright colors, sweet-smelling flowers, warm ocean breezes, soft white sand, and fire-spitting volcanoes. Hawaii (ha-WY-ee) lies 2500 miles from the shores of California. Hawaii is the country's youngest state. The 132 islands that make up the state of Hawaii stretch for more than 1,500 miles.

Formed by volcanoes, the state of Hawaii is really one long mountain range rising from the ocean floor. This mountain range began to build itself millions of years ago. Seeds brought by air currents gave life to the rocky islands. Over the years, people brought the cattle, horses, and other animals found on Hawaii.

The violent (VY-oh-lent) forces that built Hawaii come from deep in the earth. As the volcanoes erupted along the ocean bed, red-hot **lava** flowed into the cold waters of the Pacific Ocean. The lava cooled and became rock. With each eruption (ee-RUP-shun), more lava flowed and hardened. Over time, the volcanic action built the mountain range until its peaks reached far above the water level of the Pacific Ocean.

Are there still active volcanoes on the islands of Hawaii? Two volcanoes on Hawaii's Big Island (also called the island of Hawaii) are still active. These volcanoes send forth their rivers of fire, burning everything that falls in the path of the moving lava. The lava cools as it flows into the Pacific Ocean.

Other volcanoes found on the islands of Hawaii are not active, for the moment at least. These volcanoes have been quiet for several years. Yet, experts believe three dormant (DOR-mant), or inactive, volcanoes could begin to explode their deadly fireworks at any time.

The island of Hawaii is well known for its black sand beaches. Here, green palm trees rise above a blackened earth. White-capped waves bring the deep blue of the ocean to the island's black shores. The black sand beaches of Hawaii are built, grain by grain and layer by layer, from black volcanic rock. Fierce wave action breaks large blocks of volcanic rock into many smaller blocks and then into grains of sand.

What is the climate of Hawaii like? The climate of Hawaii is a treat for those who enjoy warm, sunny days that seem to never end. Hawaii's temperature stays between 70° and 80° all year long, day and night. The highest temperature ever recorded was 100°. The lowest was a shivering 14°.

The mountains of Hawaii can receive up to 400 inches of rain each year. Because of ocean winds, Hawaii's heaviest rains fall on the northeastern side of Hawaii's mountains. Lowland areas west of the mountains can get as little as 10 inches of rain each year.

What are Hawaii's most important industries? By far, tourism ranks as Hawaii's number-one industry. People from all parts of the world enjoy coming to Hawaii. The islands are known for their friendly welcome.

The ocean waters around Hawaii are warmed by underground volcanic action. One activity many tourists enjoy is scuba (SKOO-bah) diving. Here, people swim among the coral **reefs**. They can enjoy swimming among many kinds of fish that dazzle in color. Hidden among the reefs are fish that match the coral so well they are hard to find.

Another industry that is important to Hawaii is farming. Sugarcane and pineapple are the leading farm products. These crops are grown on large plantations. Bananas, coffee, and tropical flowers, that burst with color are other products grown in Hawaii. Farmers in Hawaii also graze cattle, hogs, and horses on the state's low grassland areas.

How was Hawaii settled? Hawaii's first settlers were from the Pacific Islands called Polynesia (pah-lih-NEE-zha). These settlers came to the islands of Hawaii about 2,000 years ago. Experts think that Spanish, Dutch, and Japanese explorers may have visited the islands during the 1500s.

Many people first learned of the islands of Hawaii from the travels of Captain James Cook. Captain Cook was an explorer from England. Captain Cook landed on the shores of Hawaii on January 18, 1778. Soon, the islands of Hawaii became a stopping point for fur-trading ships traveling from Oregon to China. Illnesses were brought to the islands by men on the trading ships. Many Polynesians died from these illnesses.

Critical Thinking
What effect, beside illness, did the travels of Captain Cook have on the islands of Hawaii?

▲ A statue of Hawaii's last monarch, Queen Liliou'kalani

Did You Know? In the early 1800s the sandlewood forests of Hawaii were nearly wiped out from overcutting. The same happened to the whale population around the islands during the mid 1800s. Whale oil, blubber, and bone were products sought after all over the world. The whales of Hawaii became heavily hunted to fill this world demand.

Critical Thinking

What do you think it would be like to swim among the fish along Hawaii's coral reefs?

How has Hawaii changed since the time Captain Cook landed on the islands? Today, Hawaii has a mix of cultures. People from many countries have come to Hawaii. Asians, or people whose heritage comes from the many countries of Asia, make up about 62 percent of the population. English is the most-commonly spoken language in Hawaii. Yet, more than 25 percent of the people speak a second language in their home.

Many of Hawaii's traditions (trah-DIHJ-shuns), or old beliefs, have been kept and are still used in Hawaii. Native Hawaiian art is honored. Leis (lays), a long necklace made with many flowers, are given as a sign of friendship and welcome. Many people learn to do the hula dance. Others sing or just listen to and enjoy the many special folk songs native to Hawaii.

"Aloha" (ah-LOH-ha) is an Hawaiian word meaning "hello" or "goodbye." It is a word said in friendship and love. The beauty of Hawaii, with its flowers of many colors and scents, warm climate, amazing land and fish, friendly spirit, and ethnic diversity is truly America's Aloha State.

Did You Know? Over 4,000 Japanese Americans, many from Hawaii, joined the United States Army following the Japanese attack on Pearl Harbor. They formed the 100/442 Combat Team. This team became the most decorated military unit of World War II for their heroic acts.

★ ★ ★ ★ ★ ★ ★ ★ **THINK ABOUT IT!** ★ ★ ★ ★ ★ ★ ★ ★

1. How did the islands of Hawaii form?

2. What are three important industries in Hawaii?

3. Give five reasons why people might want to live in Hawaii.

Workbook p. 74
Self-Check

OREGON

★ ★

GEOFACTS
- capital: Salem
- statehood: 1859 (33rd)
- rank in size: 10th
- rank in population: 29th (urban 70%, rural 30%)
- U.S. representatives: 5
- motto: "She Flies With Her Own Wings"

▲ A winery in Forest Grove, Oregon

Logrolling. Great fun and a great sport. This is how it is done. A large log, about 15 inches across and about ten feet long, is placed in the water. Two men wearing boots carefully climb onto the log. As the log bobs in the water, the two men try very hard to balance themselves.

At the sound of "Go," each man tries to turn the log with his feet. The log spins in the water, faster and faster, first one way and then another. Finally, one man just cannot keep his balance any longer and tumbles into the water. Among the laughs and roar of the crowd, the man who is still on the log is named the winner.

The sport of logrolling comes from the days when **logjams** on a river were broken apart by men climbing onto the logs. Ever so carefully, they would try to work the cut trees apart so the many logs could once again float down the river. It was a job filled with danger. Logging, the days of river logjams and the sport of logrolling are all part of life in Oregon.

Is logging a major part of Oregon's economy? Oregon is a leading state in logging. Thousands of people work as loggers, cutting trees in Oregon's thick pine forests. Others work in sawmills where logs are cut and then sold. The wood is used to build homes and business buildings in the United States and other parts of the world. Paper mills and lumber- yards are other businesses that depend on Oregon's logging industry.

GeoWords
logjam — a twisting of many logs that stops all other logs from floating down a river

⚡ **Critical Thinking**
How do you think the men who had to break up log jams felt? Explain your answer.

Places to See! People to Know!

▶ Crater Lake State Park, southwest Oregon — site of Crater Lake, the deepest lake in the country formed 6,600 years ago when a volcano fell into itself

▶ John Day Fossil Beds National Monument, John Day — site of 30-million-year-old fossils of such animals as giant pigs, saber-toothed tigers, and three-toed horses

▶ Abigail Scott Duniway (b.1834) — helped to found the Oregon State Woman Suffrage Association; helped women gain the right to vote in Idaho, Washington, and Oregon

▶ Linus Carl Pauling (b.1901) — received 1954 Nobel Prize in chemistry; received 1962 Novel Peace Prize for leading the protest against the testing of nuclear weapons in the air

Critical Thinking

Is it more important to protect the environment of the northern spotted owl or to protect the jobs that would be lost if old trees cannot be cut? Give at least one reason for your answer.

▲ The Rogue River at Grove Creek Landing, Oregon

Did You Know? Douglas fir trees found in the Klamath Mountains in southwestern Oregon are more than 800 years old.

Today, there is concern that many people who depend on Oregon's logging industry might lose their jobs. Oregon's logging industry is at odds with people who are concerned about the environment and the effect logging has on it.

One of the greatest concerns about Oregon logging is the loss of old trees where a small owl, called the northern spotted owl, lives. The northern spotted owl lives only among these trees. Experts believe that if the old trees are cut down, the owl will lose its environment and die. Loggers say that they themselves are endangered because reducing the amount of logging means the loss of jobs.

How has Oregon dealt with other concerns about the environment? Oregon is well known for its stand on protecting the environment. The state owns about 785,000 acres of protected forestland. It also cares for 223 state parks.

Oregon was the first state in the country to pass a "bottle bill." This law says that all drinks sold in Oregon must be sold in returnable (re-TURN-ah-bl) bottles or cans. This law was passed to keep litter off Oregon's roads. Oregon also has laws protecting its rugged coastline.

Along with its rugged coastline, what else is the land like in Oregon? Oregon is a land where early morning fog lifts and rolls among forests of pine, spruce, and juniper. It is a land of snow-capped mountains and fields of colorful wildflowers. And yet, it also is a land where wild horses gallop across the dry prairie, kicking up clouds of dust as they pass.

Oregon's scenic beauty comes from its two very different land regions. Dividing the state are the majestic Cascade Mountains. Found among the towering peaks of this mountain range are some of the country's tallest mountains. Mount Hood, Oregon's highest mountain, soars an amazing 11,239 feet. To the west of the Cascade Mountain lies a forested area. To its east lie Oregon's dry plateau and basin region.

Most people in Oregon live west of the Cascade Mountains. This region's fertile Willamette Valley became the home of many pioneers traveling the Oregon Trail during the mid-1800s. Today, around such main cities as Portland, Salem, and Eugene are fields of hay, rows of growing vegetables, and flowering fruit orchards.

Crashing against the jagged rocks of Oregon's 400 mile coastline is the rough surf of the Pacific Ocean. Basking in the sun, sea lions and seals find a resting spot on great rocks that line the coast. From the ocean, Oregon's fishers haul about 100 million pounds of fish each year. The sale of salmon, tuna, rockfish, flounder, and other fish are important to the state's economy.

Much of the land east of the Cascade Mountains is part of a region known as "high desert." This area is a dry plateau region that lies between 4,000 feet and 7,500 feet above sea level. Across this region winds the Snake River. The grinding forces of the Snake River have carved out Hells Canyon. This mighty, rock-lined canyon is deeper than Arizona's Grand Canyon.

In what part of the state are found most of Oregon's lakes and rivers? Oregon has more than 6,000 lakes. Most of these lakes are found among the mountains. Rivers crisscross the state. The mightiest of Oregon's rivers is the Columbia River. The Columbia River drains the northern half of Oregon. Because of the Columbia River, the city of Portland has become an inland ocean port.

Hidden by the forests, beavers cut their path and build their dams along Oregon's streams. High in trees, whose leaves turn golden and blaze red in fall, sings Oregon's state bird, the western meadowlark.

☆ ☆ ☆ ☆ ☆ ☆ ☆ ☆ ☆

Oregon's climate, like its land, is filled with change and surprise. Warm coastal breezes are in sharp contrast to the seasonal changes found across Oregon's plateau. With its wealth of natural resources, concern for the environment, and grand beauty, Oregon looks to be a leader among America's states.

Critical Thinking
Why do you think Oregon has taken such care to protect its environment?

▲ An Oregon logjam

Did You Know? Beavers became endangered during the 1800s. Fur trappers caught the beavers and sold their fur. Beaver pelts at this time were sold for $8 to $10 each. New trapping laws passed in the early 1900s helped the beaver population to grow.

★ ★ ★ ★ ★ ★ ★ ★   THINK ABOUT IT!   ★ ★ ★ ★ ★ ★ ★ ★ ★

1. What are two of Oregon's most important industries?

2. List three ways Oregon has protected the state's environment.

3. Tell what is different about Oregon's two major land regions.

Workbook p. 75
Self-Check

WASHINGTON
★ ★

GEOFACTS
- capital: Olympia
- statehood: 1889 (42nd)
- rank in size: 20th
- rank in population: 18th (urban 76%, rural 24%)
- U.S. representatives: 9
- motto: "Alki," a Chinook Indian word meaning "by-and-by"

▲ Crunchy, crisp Washington apples

▲ An icy glacier on Mount Rainier

⚡ **Critical Thinking**

In What do you think caused Spirit Lake to almost double its size after the Mount St. Helens explosion?

Places to See! People to Know!

▶ Tillicum Village, Blake Island — site of early Native American culture; tours given of an Native American longhouse

▶ Grand Coulee Dam, northcentral area — one of world's largest hydroelectric plants

▶ Dixy Lee Ray (b.1914) — first woman governor of Washington (1977-1981); supporter of nuclear energy

▶ Chief Seathl (b.1786) — Native American chief of several tribes; worked with white settlers to bring peace to area; the city of Seattle is named for Chief Seathl

At 8:32 AM on the morning of May 18, 1980, a great explosion (eks-PLOH-shun) happened in the state of Washington. It was at this time that a quiet volcano called Mount St. Helens awoke from its 123-year sleep.

Triggered by an earthquake, first the upper part of the northern side of Mount St. Helens collapsed (kol-LAPSD), or fell, down the side mountain. Rock, snow, and ice raced down the mountain at speeds of more than 200 miles per hour. One part of the mountain crashed into Spirit Lake. When this happened, the level of Spirit Lake rose 200 feet. Wave marks were found as high as 850 feet above the normal water level of the lake.

Moments after the northern edge of Mount St. Helens collapsed, built-up **pressure** (PREH-shur) from deep within the old volcano blasted open the northern side of the mountain. Quickly, the force of the blast overtook the crumbling mountain edge. Carrying rock and hot gases, the 680° blast destroyed everything for up to 23 miles. The booming sound of the blast could be heard as far away as Montana and California.

Where is Mount St. Helens in Washington? Mount St. Helens is found in the Cascade Range. This mighty chain of mountains divides the eastern and western regions of Washington.

Mount St. Helens is only one of several mountain peaks in the Cascade Range. Many of these mountain peaks were made from the action of volcanoes. The highest mountain peak in Washington, and one of the highest in the country, is Mount Rainer (14,410 feet above sea level).

Many of the mountains in the Cascade Range have glaciers. Many of the mountains have year-long snow fields that cap their towering peaks in a shimmering glaze of white. Lining the steep, rocky slopes of the Cascade Range are great forests of Douglas fir trees. Mountain goats, bobcats, and flying squirrels find shelter and food in the shadows of Washington's thick forests.

What is the land like east of the Cascade Range? Northeast of the Cascade Range are the Rocky Mountains. This group of mountains is often called the Columbia Mountains. From here, the rushing waters of the Columbia River twist and turn to flow southward and then to the west. More than half of Washington's waters flow into the Columbia River on their winding journey to the Pacific Ocean.

South of the Columbia Mountains and east of the Cascade Range lies the state's plateau region. This dry yet fertile region rises 500 to 2,000 feet above sea level. Lava oozing out of cracks in the earth's crust formed this region many thousands of years ago.

What kind of land lies west of the Cascade Range? Washington's Olympic (oh-LIM-pik) Mountains are found in the northwestern part of the state. In this region of surprises are found Washington's lush rain forests.

Warm Pacific air currents rising over the Olympic Mountains, along with more than 150 inches of rain each year, form an area where ferns carpet the forest floor. Here yellow-green moss covers a tangle of thick tree limbs. A major industry of this area is logging along the foothills of the Olympic Mountains.

Running from north to south along the western edge of the Cascade Mountains is the Puget Sound Lowland. Three of every four people living in Washington live within this lowland region. Here also are Washington's major cities: Seattle, Tacoma, and Olympic.

Tucked in Washington's southwestern corner lies the rugged beauty of the state's coastal region. Washington's coastal waters hold a bounty of many different kinds of fish. From here Pacific cod, ocean perch, crabs, herring, and tuna are caught and sold. This region's fishing and logging industries are important to the state's economy.

What other industries in Washington add to the state's economy? Heading the state's industries are aircraft and space products. About 100,000 people in Washington work in the airplane industry.

Many people in Washington work in industries that tie directly to the land. Some of the people work in the state's tourist industry. Washington's diversity of land and dazzling beauty draw many tourists to its many parks and festivals. Other people farm, growing bright flowers, crisp

Critical Thinking
Why is irrigation important to farmers east of the Cascade Range?

▲ The Boeing Company designs spacecrafts in Washington

Did You Know? The Native Americans who lived on the coast believed that sharing things was more important than owning them. Early Native American leaders living on Washington's coast would host great parties called "potlatches." The word "potlatch" is a Chinook Indian word that means "to give." The hosting chief offered almost all the food and goods he had to the potlatch guests. Often, he was left with little after the guests left.

Critical Thinking

By what route do you think most emigrants came to Washington during the mid-1800s?

Did You Know? Apple Surprise!

3 crisp Washington apples, peeled, and sliced

1/2 cup brown sugar

1/4 teaspoon cinnamon

Mix apple slices with brown sugar and cinnamon. Chill for 1/2 hour. Have a great snack!

apples, tender asparagus or juicy pears. Dairy farms dot the western part of the state. Cattle and sheep graze among the grassy slopes of the Cascade Range.

Who were Washington's first settlers? Native Americans settled in Washington more than 12,000 years ago. These early dwellers lived in round homes dug about 3 feet into the ground.

By 1500, about seventy different Native American tribes lived across present day Washington. Slowly, explorers from Greece, England, Russia, Spain, and the early American colonies traveled to the area. By the mid-1800s white settlement slowly forced Native Americans off land they had lived on for many years.

In 1855, 6,000 Native Americans from several different tribes met to decide whether they should sign a treaty with the United States government. Signing the treaty meant the Native Americans would agree to move to reservation land. After three weeks, the much disliked treaty was signed. Today, Washington's Native American heritage is shared though festivals, art, song, and dance.

Washington is a state where people can stop and listen to the many voices of nature: the crash of a wave, the rustle of leaves, the scream of a mountain lion. For this, for its mild climate, and for its working industries, Washington is one of America's fastest growing states.

 **THINK ABOUT IT!**

1. Tell five things about the explosion that shook Mount St. Helens.

2. List six land regions found in Washington. Tell two facts about each region.

3. List five of Washington's industries.

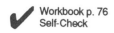
Workbook p. 76
Self-Check

The Territories ★ ★ ★ ★ ★ ★ ★ ★ ★ ★ ★ ★ ★ ★ ★

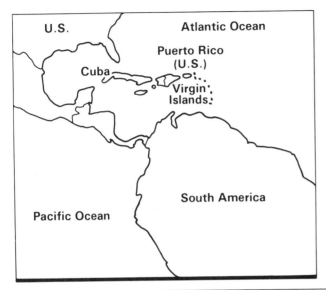

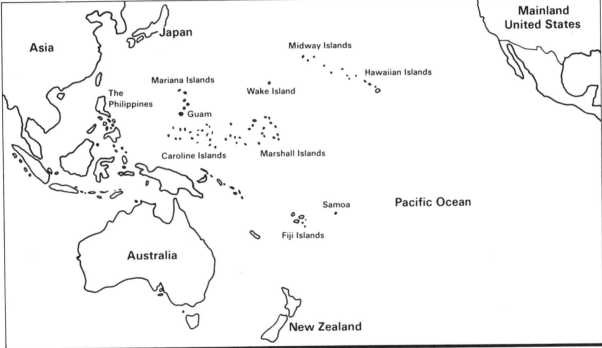

Beyond the shores of the United States lie many ocean islands. Some of these islands are protected by the United States. Some of the islands protected by the United States are very small with very few people living on them. Some islands have no people living on them. These islands are called United States possessions (poh-SEH-shuns).

Other islands protected by the United States have their own government. These are called United States territories (TEH-rih-tor-ees). The people living on these islands use United States money. They are United States citizens. Yet, none can vote in United States elections until the territory becomes a state.

The Island Partners of the United States are important for many reasons. The United States has military (MIL-ih-teh-ree) bases on some of the islands. Many of the islands have strong trade ties with the United States. America's Island Partners add a cultural richness to the country.

UNITED STATES TERRITORIES AND POSSESSIONS

GEOFACTS
Puerto Rico
- capital: San Juan
- total land area: 3,459 square miles
- population: 3,294,997
- government: commonwealth with U.S.

▲ Volcanoes formed the Pacific Islands. Lava rocks and fountains of steam line the coast.

Critical Thinking
Why do you think Island Partners of the United States are popular tourist stops?

Places to See! People to Know!

▶ Luíza's Alda — a town near San Juan, famous for the annual festival called Fiesta Patronal de Santiago Apóstol; this festival mixes African and Spanish traditions

▶ Herman Badillo Rivera (b. 1929) — Puerto Rican American who was named president in 1965 of the borough of the Bronx, a part of New York City

▶ Francisco Gallego — contributed to the development of colonial Puerto Rico; set sail for Puerto Rico from Spain in 1516 and became the first Spanish business person of African origin

THE ATLANTIC ISLANDS

Puerto Rico One thousand miles southeast of Florida and about 500 miles north of South America lie the islands that make up the commonwealth of Puerto Rico. Puerto Rico is made up of several very small islands and one large island. Puerto Rico is a tropical land where colorful birds, masses of sweet smelling flowers, and tumbling waterfalls attract visitors.

Puerto Rico is a blend of coastal lowlands, coastal valleys, foothills, and mountains. Refreshing beaches sheltered by palm trees, lush forests, and rocks shaped by water erosion cover Puerto Rico. Warm breezes grace the land all year round. Sunny days and starry nights are part of Puerto Rico's charm.

Puerto Rico has several industries that are important to its economy. Coffee, fruits, tobacco, coconuts, and sugarcane are some of Puerto Rico's main crops. Factories in Puerto Rico make clothes, chemical products, metal products, and textiles. Most products are traded with the United States. Puerto Rico also gets most of its imports from the United States.

Puerto Rico has a rich ethnic diversity. Spanish is the main language of Puerto Rico. Most people are of Latino heritage. Lively festivals, with colorful costumes and tasty food, give the people of Puerto Rico a chance to share the pride they have in their heritage and their country.

The Virgin Islands Three main islands and fifty very small islands make up the Virgin Islands of the United States. The three main islands are St. Croix, St. Thomas, and St. John. These splendid islands of unending beauty lie about 40 miles east of Puerto Rico. They are about 1,730 miles southeast of Florida.

The Virgin Islands began as volcanoes. Today, lush forests cover hills that rise to a high point of 1,556 feet above sea level. The Virgin Islands are known for their tropical flowers, spirited birds covered by rainbows of color, and dazzling sandy beaches that welcome a joyful tourist. Tourism is the island's leading industry.

Christopher Columbus landed on the Virgin Islands in 1493. He was greeted by Native Americans. Columbus did not treat the islanders very well. Some were enslaved. By the mid-1500s, Spain gave orders to its army to kill all remaining Native Americans on the islands. Those not killed left the islands.

Over the years, the Virgin Islands came under the rule of England, Denmark, and France. Today, the Virgin Islands are a territory of the United States. The islands have their own government. English is the most commonly spoken language in the Virgin Islands. Yet, Spanish and Creole also are spoken by many people of the Virgin Islands.

THE PACIFIC ISLANDS

Guam Rising above the Pacific Ocean is the volcanic island of Guam. Guam has a 78 mile coastline trimmed by the many colors and shapes of coral. Coral is a sea animal that attaches itself to rock. Swaying to the flow of wave action, coral gets its food from the ocean water that passes across it.

Strong storms called **typhoons** (ty-FOONS), at times, cause much damage to the small island of Guam. Typhoons are like the hurricanes that hit Louisiana, Texas, Florida, and other states. Typhoons pack high winds, lots of rain and high waves.

Guam lies across the Pacific Ocean far from America's shores. Guam is 3,700 miles west of Hawaii. Year-round temperatures of between 72°F to 88°F wrapped the island in warm tropical breezes. Some tropical fruits such as bananas are grown. Yet, Guam gets most of its food from other islands or countries.

Samoa The territory of Samoa is made up of six small islands. The islands are found about 2,300 miles west of Hawaii. The largest islands, Tutuila and Aunu'u, cover an area of about 53 square miles. The smallest, Swain Island, has an area of only 2 square miles. Most of Samoa is covered by thick tropical plants.

Colorful coral reefs that shelter bright tropical fish line the rocky edges of the Samoan islands. Samoa, just like other tropical islands, formed from years of volcanic action. Dried coconut is one of Samoa's most important products. Most people living on Samoa are of Polynesian heritage. Most

GeoWords
typhoons — hurricane-like storms found in the Pacific Ocean

Critical Thinking
Why do you think the United States government has chosen to protect islands even though no one may live on the islands?

▲ Puerto Rico imports bauxite and makes aluminum for export.

Did You Know? Roberto Clemente was born in Puerto Rico. He was a successful outfielder for the Pittsburgh Pirates. Clemente won the National League batting championship four times. He died in a plane crash while trying to bring supplies to earthquake victims in Nicaragua.

GeoWords

atoll — an circle of coral reef that goes around a lagoon

Critical Thinking

Why do you think the United States government feels it is important to have strong ties with islands found in the Pacific and Atlantic Oceans?

people speak both Samoan (related to Hawaiian and other Polynesian languages) and English.

THE MIDWAY ISLANDS

The Midway Islands are the western-most islands in the chain of islands that make up Hawaii. Yet, the Midway Islands are not part of the state of Hawaii. These islands are watched over by the United States Navy.

Wake, Wilkes, and Peale islands form an **atoll** (ah-TOHL) about 2,300 miles west of Hawaii. These islands are used as a stopping point for airplanes and ships crossing the Pacific Ocean. These islands are watched over by the United States Air Force.

Between Hawaii and the city of Hong Kong, are a string of islands. Some of these island have no people living on them. All have been shaped by the building up of coral reefs. All of the islands are governed by the United States.

Micronesia The islands of Micronesia (my-kro-NEE-shah) also are called the United States Trust Territory of the Pacific Islands. Micronesia is made up of a three groups of many small islands. The three island groups are called the Caroline, Marshall, and Mariana Islands. People live on about ninety-eight of the 2,141 islands that made up Micronesia. The islands are found about 2,200 miles southwest of Hawaii. These islands are protected by the United States.

▲ San Juan, an interesting blend of old and new, is the capital of Puerto Rico.

GEOFACTS
Virgin Islands
• capital: Charlotte Amalie
• total land area:136 square miles
• population: 99,404
• government: territory of the U.S.

GEOFACTS
Guam
• capital: Agaña
• total land area: 209 square miles
• population: 144,928
• government: territory of the U.S.

GEOFACTS
Samoa
• capital: Pago
• total land area: 76 square miles
• population: 43,052
• government: territory of the U.S.

GEOFACTS
Midway Islands
• capital: none
• total land area: 2 square miles
• population: 453
• government: U.S. possession

GEOFACTS
Micronesia
• capital: Koror
• total land area: 177 square miles
• population:14,411
• government: territory of the U.S.

Did You Know? The islands of the Pacific Ocean enjoy a rich ethnic heritage including people of Filipino, Korean, Japanese, Micronesian, Indonesian, Polynesian, and other backgrounds.

★ ★ ★ ★ ★ ★ ★ ★ **THINK ABOUT IT!** ★ ★ ★ ★ ★ ★ ★ ★

1. List the six groups of United States territories and possessions.

2. List six things that can be said about all the islands.

3. Which of America's Island Partners are territories? Which of America's Island Partners are possessions?

Workbook p. 79
Self-Check

THE PEOPLE'S PUBLISHING GROUP, INC. *Our United States Geography: Our Regions and People*

GLOSSARY

★ ★ ★ ★ ★ ★ ★ ★   ★ ★ ★ ★ ★ ★ ★ ★

A

acre an area of land equal to 43,560 square feet, p.61
adobe a sun-dried block of clay used in building, p.148
aftershocks a smaller shock coming after the main shock of an earthquake, p.46
aqueduct a large pipeline used for transporting water, p.161
arid lacking in moisture, dry, p.150
atoll an circle of coral, p.174

B

ballad a song that tells a story which has been passed on through time, p.17
banks the sides of the river where the water meets the ground, p.21
bay an area of a lake, sea, or ocean extending into the land, p.26
bayou slow-moving river area entering or leaving a lake, p.22
beach a flat shore of sand or small stones that is washed over by water, p.61
bed the bottom of a water area such as a lake or sea, p.35
brackish salty water or marsh water that is near the sea, p.23
brush small bushes and other plants, p.120
buttes steep hills that sometimes have sloping sides, p.110

C

canal a waterway dug across the land so that boats can travel from one body of water to another, p.55
canyon a narrow valley with steep sides, p.133
cape a piece of land that stretches out into the sea or lake, p.76
cash crop crop grown to be sold, p.31
caverns caves, p.92
channels grooves or deep areas where water flows, p.25
cliffs a wall of rock, p.82
colonies area of land whose people live by the laws of some other country, p.64
counties an area in a state, p.65
countryside land in a rural area, p.76
cultures the customs and beliefs of an ethnic group, p.74
current a moving stream of water, p.139
customs the special way of doing things among different cultures, p.127

D

dam a wall built to hold back water, also to hold back water from flowing, p.46
dawn the time of day when the sun rises, p.60
delta a three-sided area at a river's mouth built by the dropping off of soil and sand carried by the river, p.21
deserts a dry, sandy region that has few, if any, plants, p.102
natural formed by nature, p.103
dikes a bank or earth or dam built to prevent flooding, p.15
diversity many different kinds, variety, p.57
drought a long time of little or no rain, p.98

E

earthquake shaking of the Earth's surface caused by the movement of rock below the surface, p.46
endangered to put into danger, p.30
enslave to force one person to become the property of another person; the slave is forced to work for the owner without pay and has no rights, p.10
environment the area around you, p.38
erosion a slow wearing away of the surface by natural forces such as wind or water, p.40
escarpment a steep slope; a cliff, p.155

E (cont.)

ethnic ways and beliefs which are common to one group of people, p.22
ethnic pride a great belief and sense of value in the customs of an ethnic group, p.59

F

fault line a break in the Earth's crust; a shift in the Earth's crust along the break causes earthquakes, p.159
fertile rich in things that promote growth, p.12
festivals special celebrations, p.127
folk tales stories told to others over many years, p.9
foothills a lower hill at the bottom of a mountain, p.50
fossil the remains of something that lived long ago, p.34
frontier the farthest part of settled country, p.55

G

galley a large boat often rowed by slaves, criminals or prisoners of war, p.19
gap an opening in a mountain ridge, p.133
geyser a hot spring that spouts hot water and steam, p.132
glacier a huge mass of ice which can range in thickness from 300 feet to 10,000 feet, p.126
gold rushers people who swelled small towns hoping to get rich by finding gold, p.128
goods things that are made and sold, p.51
government the group of people who pass laws for all to follow, p.31
groundwater water found under the surface of the ground, p.116
gulch a ravine, or deep valley, p.131

H

harbor a place of deep water protected from wind and currents, making it a safe place for boats to dock, p.12
heritage the past culture of a group of people, p.127
homesteading to take on and use as a home, p.64
horizon the line where the sky seems to meet the earth, p.40
humid moist, damp, feel of water vapor, p.22
hurricane a warm climate, violent rain storm with winds of 75 m.p.h. or greater in warm climates, p.15

I

igloos a rounded shelter; Alaskan Eskimos built igloos with sod, whalebone and driftwood, p.126
immigrant a person who settles in a country other than where he or she was born, p.37
industries businesses, p.51
inland away from the coast and toward the land, p.25
integrate to bring together, to end racial segregation, p.14
international of or for people in various nations of the world, p.65
irrigation spreading water over the surface of the ground by using sprinklers or a series of canals, p.116
island an area of land with water on all sides, p.43

L

landlocked shut in, or nearly shut in, by land p.12
lagoons lake or channel that is not very deep, p.73
landmark a point marking a special place, person, or event, p.70
lava hot, liquid rock, p.162
levee a bank built up to keep a river from overflowing, p.22
lode a vein, or area, where a mineral can be found, p.135
logjam a twisting of many logs that stops all other logs from floating down a river, p.165

GLOSSARY

★★★★★★★★ ★★★★★★★★

M

marshes lowlands often covered by water, swamps, p.61
meadows an area of grass and wildflowers, p.70
meandering following a winding course through an area, p.21
mesa a tabletop area of land that rises above a lower plain, p.122
mills a place where grains, such as corn or oats, is ground into flour, p. 67
mineral rock parts found in the ground, p. 86
moisture wetness, p.152
moraines an area of gravel and sand pushed before or along the sides of glaciers, p.96
mounds areas of built-up soil arranged in certain ways, p.10
movement action of large roup of people for a belief or cause, p.13
mushers people who drive dogsleds, p.127

N

natural resources riches of nature, such as coal, timber, oil, land, and water, p.128

O

outlets a place where a river flows out of a lake, p.145

P

palisades a line of steep rock areas, p. 82
panhandle a narrow strip of land shaped like the handle of a pan, p.41
peak the top of the mountain, p.28
peninsula an area of land with water on three sides, p.43
permafrost a layer of soil that is always frozen, p.126
piedmont an area lying along the bottom of a mountain range, p.20
pioneer an early settler, p.101
plain a flat treeless or almost treeless area, p.18
plantation a large, farmed area that makes use of many farmworkers, p.16
plateau a high plain area, p.20
poll tax money charged to a person for voting, p.14
ponds an area of standing water that is smaller than a lake, p.67
population the number of people in an area, p.32
port a place where boats and large ships dock, p.45
prairie a level, treeless grassland, p.86
pressure a strong force made by the build up of gases, p.168

Q

quarries a place where rocks are dug for other use, p. 67

R

ranges a chain of mountains, p.66
ravine a deep valley, p. 79
readmit to admit, or allow in, again, p.11
reef a low, rocky ridge near the water line, p.163
refuge an area of safety, p.65
regionalism beliefs, values, and a way of life of most people in a region, p. 89
relief a design which stands out from the surface from which it was made, p.19
reservation a section of land set aside for Native Americans, p.110
resource something that is a natural part of the Earth, p.34
ridges the top of two rising areas that meet, p.79
routes a way taken to go someplace, p.67
rural part of the countryside, an area not part of a city, p.57
rustic having to do with rural life, p. 68

S

sandbars a sandy area which rises above the water's surface, p.28
sand dunes a large area covered with hills of sand, p.27
scenic an area filled with the beauty of nature, p.34
seasons a time lasting about three months (fall, winter, spring, summer), p.69
shallow not very deep, p.92
sharecroppers a person who farms land for the owner in trade or exchange for a share of the crops harvested, p.17
shoreline the area long the shore of any island, bay, or other coastal area, p.28
sinkholes an area of ground that falls, or sinks, p.31
sinks a low area, p.145
slope a surface area that goes up and down on an angle, p.41
sod the upper layer of grassy land, p.98
sound a narrow area of water, p. 76
spires a rock that, because of wind erosion, is wide at the bottom and narrows as it rises, p.119
springs water rising to the surface of Earth, p.61
stalactites a long form made up of calcium hanging from a cave ceiling, p.142
stalagmites a calcium rising from a cave floor, p.142
streams a small river, p.61
strike to stop working until certain conditions are met, p.38
suburbs a city or town built near or next to a major city, p.78
surf waves that break on a shore, p.76

T

textiles different types of cloth, p.13
ties the rising and lowering of water at certain times during the day, p.44
till soil made up of sand, gravel, and clay, p.96
tornadoes inland storms packing strong winds that can cause much damage, p.28
totem an object that is a symbol of a family, clan, or tribe, p.127
toxic very harmful, filled with poison, p.105
tract a stretch of land or water, p.37
trade to take products for something else, such as money, p.45
trawl a large, strong net dragged along the water's bottom to catch fish and other seafood, p.15
typhoons hurricane-like storms found in the Pacific Ocean, p.173

U

unions a group of workers united together to protect their interests, p.41
uplands high or hilly ground, p.41
urban having to do with a city, p.55

V

valley a long, low area lying between hills or high ground, usually having a river or stream flowing along its bottom, p.9

W

wasteland an area of land where little, if anything, can grow, p.139
wilderness a region with no people living in it, p.37
woods a forest area, p.105